ROUTLEDGE LIBRARY EDITIONS: PHONETICS AND PHONOLOGY

Volume 12

THE PHONETICS AND PHONOLOGY OF KOREAN PROSODY

THE PHONETICS AND PHONOLOGY OF KOREAN PROSODY

Intonational Phonology and Prosodic Structure

SUN-AH JUN

LONDON AND NEW YORK

First published in 1996 by Garland Publishing, Inc.

This edition first published in 2019
by Routledge
2 Park Square, Milton Park, Abingdon, Oxon OX14 4RN

and by Routledge
711 Third Avenue, New York, NY 10017

Routledge is an imprint of the Taylor & Francis Group, an informa business

© 1996 Sun-Ah Jun

All rights reserved. No part of this book may be reprinted or reproduced or utilised in any form or by any electronic, mechanical, or other means, now known or hereafter invented, including photocopying and recording, or in any information storage or retrieval system, without permission in writing from the publishers.

Trademark notice: Product or corporate names may be trademarks or registered trademarks, and are used only for identification and explanation without intent to infringe.

British Library Cataloguing in Publication Data
A catalogue record for this book is available from the British Library

ISBN: 978-1-138-60364-6 (Set)
ISBN: 978-0-429-43708-3 (Set) (ebk)
ISBN: 978-1-138-31779-6 (Volume 12) (hbk)
ISBN: 978-1-138-31780-2 (Volume 12) (pbk)
ISBN: 978-0-429-45494-3 (Volume 12) (ebk)

Publisher's Note
The publisher has gone to great lengths to ensure the quality of this reprint but points out that some imperfections in the original copies may be apparent.

Disclaimer
The publisher has made every effort to trace copyright holders and would welcome correspondence from those they have been unable to trace.

THE PHONETICS AND PHONOLOGY OF KOREAN PROSODY

INTONATIONAL PHONOLOGY AND
PROSODIC STRUCTURE

SUN-AH JUN

GARLAND PUBLISHING, INC.
NEW YORK & LONDON / 1996

Copyright © 1996 Sun-Ah Jun
All rights reserved

Library of Congress Cataloging-in-Publication Data

Jun, Sun-Ah.
    The phonetics and phonology of Korean prosody : intonational phonology and prosodic structure / Sun-Ah Jun.
        p.   cm. — (Outstanding dissertations in linguistics)
    Includes bibliographical references and index.
    ISBN 0-8153-2558-4 (alk. paper)
    1. Korean language—Phonology. 2. Korean language—Accents and accentuation. 3. Korean language—Intonation. I. Title. II. Series.
PL915.J86 1996
495.7'16—dc20   96-9790

Printed on acid-free, 250-year-life paper
Manufactured in the United States of America

To my parents,

Yongjong Jun and Yonghee Kim

and my husband,

Illam Park

Contents

DEDICATION... v
TABLE OF CONTENTS.. vii
LIST OF TABLES... ix
LIST OF FIGURES.. xi
PREFACE... xvii
ACKNOWLEDGMENTS.. xix

CHAPTER I :   INTRODUCTION.. 3

   1.1 Prosodic Phonology and Korean................................. 5
   1.2 Problems with the syntax based phrasing accounts......... 19
   1.3 Theoretical framework of Intonation............................ 28

CHAPTER II :   THE INTONATION AND PROSODIC
                   STRUCTURE OF KOREAN...................... 33

   2.1 Intonational Structure of Seoul dialect......................... 33
   2.2 Intonational Structure of Chonnam dialect................... 42
   2.3 Korean obstruents with laryngeal feature specification..... 52
   2.4 Formalization... 53
   2.5 The intonation and prosodic structure......................... 58

CHAPTER III : THE ACCENTUAL PHRASE........................ 65

   3.1 Experiment 1 : Lenis Stop Voicing............................. 67
   3.2 Other Phonological Rules.. 94
   3.3 Conclusion... 99

CHAPTER IV : THE INTONATIONAL PHRASE................... 101

   4.1 Introduction... 101
   4.2 Experiment 2 : The Domain of Obstruent Nasalization.. 103
   4.3 Experiment 3 : The Prosodic Domain of Spirantization
                     and /s/ Palatalization........................... 131

4.4 Conclusion...	153

CHAPTER V : FACTORS AFFECTING
                PROSODIC PHRASING......................... 155

5.1 Speech Rate Factor...	157
5.2 Phonological Weight Factor......................................	159
5.3 Focus Factor...	162
5.4 Semantic Weight Factor...	172
5.5 Phrasal Compound and Accentual phrasing................	176
5.6 The Syntactic Constraint on the Accentual Phrase..........	181
5.7 Conclusion..	196

CHAPTER VI : INTERFACE BETWEEN THE PROSODY
                 AND THE LEXICON................................. 199

6.1 The Prosodic Word...	199
6.2 Experiment 4 : VOT lenition......................................	200
6.3 The Prosodic Word and the Accentual Phrase................	209
6.4 Conclusion..	212

CHAPTER VII : CONCLUSION...	215
APPENDIX A (Chapter 2)..	217
APPENDIX B (Chapter 3)..	219
BIBLIOGRAPHY	221
INDEX	235

List of Tables

TABLE		PAGE
2.1	Korean Obstruents with Laryngeal Feature Specification.....	52
2.2	Domain of Postlexical Phonological Rules and Prosodic Theories...	61
3.1	Example Sentences or Phrases in the Lenis Stop Voicing Experiment...................................	70
3.2	The Voicing Status of the Word Initial Lenis Stop at the Accentual Phrase Initial and Medial Position for Five Chonnam Speakers..	87
3.3	Voicing Status of the Word Initial Lenis Stop at Fast and Slow Rate Combining Accentual Phrase Initial and Medial Tokens...	87
3.4	The Voicing Status of the Phrase Initial Lenis Stop at Fast and Slow Rate..	89
3.5	Observed Data for Normal Rate....................................	90
3.6	Cho's Expected 2*2 Contingency Table (N=64)...............	90
3.7	My Expected 2*2 Contingency Table (N= 64)..................	90
3.8	Observed Data for Fast Rate...	90
3.9	Cho's Expected 2*2 Contingency Table (N=64)...............	91
3.10	My Expected 2*2 Contingency Table (N= 64)..................	91
3.11	Observed Data for Slow Rate..	91
3.12	Cho's Expected 2*2 Contingency Table (N=64)...............	91
3.13	My Expected 2*2 Contingency Table (N= 64)..................	92

4.1	Background of Each Subject.................................	104
4.2	List of Sentences..	106
4.3	List of Word Internal and Final Stop vs. Nasal..................	111
4.4	The Percentage of Nasalized Obstruents Within the Phonological Phrase and Accentual Phrase. (Nasalized Token/Total Token Numbers) is in the Parenthesis...........	116
4.5	The Percentage of Nasalized Obstruents Across the Phonological Phrases and Accentual Phrases. (Nasalized Ttoken/Total Token Numbers) is in the Parenthesis..........	123
4.6	List of Sentences..	134
4.7	List of Words..	139
4.8	The Number of Tokens of the Stop-Fricative Sequence Occurring in Four Different Prosodic Conditions for Each Speaker...	149
4.9	The Mean Duration and Standard Deviation of Derived and Underlying Frication (in ms) of Word Medial and Across Accentual Phrase Condition................................	150
4.10	The Mean Peak Frequency Value and Standard Deviation of /s/ before /i/ and before Other Vowels in Word Medial and across Accentual Phrase Boundary Position for Each Subject..	152
6.1	Target Words with Initial /p^h/ (top) and with Medial /p^h/ (bottom)..	205
6.2	Eight Types Depending on Prosodic Position of /p^h/.........	205
7.1	Frequency of Voicing (Word-initial & Accentual Phrase-initial)..	219
7.2	Frequency of Voicing (Word-initial and Accentual Phrase-medial)...	220

List of Figures

FIGURE		PAGE
1.1	Pitch Tracks of [tʃaŋnjəne irəbərin mahuraril tʃhadʒat'a.] reflecting two different syntactic structures........................	22
1.2	Pitch tracks and waveforms of three possible actual utterances of the sentence......................................	25
2.1	Pitch track of Seoul showing two Intonational Phrases with each 'I' having more than one Accentual Phrase.........	37
2.2	Pitch tracks of (1) showing the initial high tone depending on the number of syllables of the Accentual Phrase...........	38
2.3	The large initial rising pattern of Seoul Accentual Phrase when the first word and the third word are contrastively emphasized. {əlluŋmal aranni}{tʃoraŋmal aranni}?...........	41
2.4	Pitch tracks of the same sentence used in Fig.2.1, produced by a Chonnam speaker.....................................	44
2.5	Pitch tracks of a triple pair of onomatopoeia "tallaŋtallaŋ -tʰallaŋtʰallaŋ - t'allŋt'allaŋ", meaning 'jingling' with different connotations.................	45
2.6	Pitch tracks of sentences in Chonnam dialect with each Accentual Phrase having the LHL pattern. The number of moras in the first noun phrase increased from three to seven..	47
2.7	Pitch tracks of sentences in Chonnam dialect with the first two Accentual Phrases having the HHL pattern.........	49
2.8	Kagaya's (1974) glottal width over time. One frame in the X-axis corresponds to 20 ms and the Y-axis gives the apparent glottal width in an arbitrary scale.................	54

2.9	Pitch tracks of the English sentence 'Marianna wants some milk.' with different pitch accent placements............	62
2.10	Pitch tracks of Korean sentence 'jəŋaga ujurɨl tʃoahandejo' in two different accentual phrasings uttered by a Chonnam speaker...	63
3.1	Audio & EGG waveforms...	77
3.2	Audio and EGG waveforms of 'jəŋsunɨn heɡjəŋirɨl tʃoahe' The first and the second windows are audio waveforms and the third and fourth window are EGG waveforms. The first window in Audio and EGG shows the whole sentence and the second window of each waveform shows the expanded waveforms around underlined part of the sentence...............	78
3.3	Pitch tracks of {kəmɨn kojaɲie palmok} 'a black cat's ankle' uttered in one Accentual Phrase by C2. Audio & EGG waveforms show a voiced /k/ of *koyaɲie* at the Accentual Phrase medial position......................................	80
3.4	Pitch tracks of {kəmɨn}{kojaɲie}{palmok} 'a black cat's ankle' uttered in three Accentual Phrases. Audio & EGG waveforms show a voiceless /k/ of *kojaɲie* at the Accentual Phrase initial position......................................	81
3.5	Pitch track of (a) #1 by C3 and (b) # 28 by S1 (c) # 24 by S2 and (d) # 35 by S1...................................	84
3.6	The number of Accentual Phrases against three self-selected speech rates for five subjects........................	86
3.7	Pitch tracks and spectrograms of /mijəkkuk puəra/ 'Pour the seaweed soup.' uttered in two different accentual phrasings...	96
3.8	Pitch tracks and spectrograms of (6d).............................	97
4.1	Two measurements from the audio waveform (duration of vowel and duration of coda plus onset nasal) and three measurements from oral /nasal air flow waveform. Three places of nasal airflow were marked........................	114

4.2	Mean duration of vowel and of the nasal measured from audiowaveforms and averaged over the tokens for each subject..	117
4.3	Mean durations of the nasalized portion of the preceding vowel from airflow waveforms. (N=20, A Standard Error is shown on top of each bar.)..	118
4.4	Nasal flow transducer signal (Volts) at three different places (base line arbitrary)...	119
4.5	A pitch track of a sentence, Subj.NP *nə* +Obj. NP *nuɾinbap* +V *məgəbwanni*, meaning 'Have you tried scorched rice?', uttered (a) by S3 and (b) by C1. The waveform below the pitch track shows a part of a sentence spanning the boundary between the Obj. NP and the verb, and the spectrogram shows the stop is nasalized.............	120
4.6	Pitch tracks of sentences (a){tʃagɨnbaŋ}{kudʒo-ga} {isaŋhandɛ} (Poss. N. *tʃagɨnbaŋ*, a head N-NOM *kudʒo-ga*, VP *isaŋhandɛ*) and (b) {tʃagɨnbak}{nɛmsega} {isaŋhandɛ} (Poss. N. *tʃagɨnbak*, a head N.-NOM *nɛmsega*, VP*isaŋhandɛ*), both uttered by S2...................	126
4.7	An audio waveform spanning the boundary between (a) the subj. NP i *hobak* and the VP *maʃinnɨndɛ*. and (b) the subject NP *sujəŋbok* and the verbal adverb *nəmu*. For each example, the second window is the expanded waveform around [ŋ] on the first window.........................	127
4.8	Pitch tracks of a sentence in two different intonational phrasings uttered by a Seoul speaker (S2).......................	128
4.9	Pitch tracks of the same sentence in two different intonational phrasings as in Figure 4.8, but uttered by a Chonnam speaker (C1)...	129
4.10	Spectrograms of [kɨ kwaŋtʃut'ɛk, maɨms'ika nəmu tʃoa] in (a) the Intonational Phrase boundary after [kwaŋtʃut'ɛk] without a pause but only with the stop release. (b) produced in one Intonational Phrase...........................	130

4.11   A sample spectrogram and a power spectrum showing measurements. (a) the duration of frication, (b) the initial 20 ms of the frication and (c) the lowest peak frequency during the 20 ms of the frication. Both the vertical line on the spectrum and the horizontal line on the spectrogram refer to the same frequency value.................... 142

4.12   Spectrograms for (a) /miso/ 'a smile' and (b) /mitso/ 'believe' without stop closure and (c) /mitso/ with stop closure.. 143

4.13   Spectrograms of palatalized /s/ in /kasi/ 'a thorn' vs. non-palatalized /s/ in /kasa/ 'house work'........................ 144

4.14   Pitch tracks and spectrogram of /tʃaŋmik'otʃʰ sirənwassni/? [tʃaŋmik'oʃ ʃirənwanni] 'Have you loaded a rose?', uttered by the Seoul speaker (S1) in two accentual phrasings........ 145

4.15   Pitch tracks and spectrograms of /kɨ tʃʰəmamitʰ siwənhatɨra? in two different Intonational phrasings produced by the Chonnam speaker, C1. (a) in one Intonational Phrase, ({kɨ tʃʰəmamiʃ ʃiwənhadɨra}), meaning 'It is cool under the eaves'. (b) in two Intonational Phrases, ({kɨ tʃʰəmamit}) ({ʃiwənhadɨra}), meaning 'Under the eaves, it is cool'........ 147

5.1   Rate effect on the Accentual Phrase (a) a sentence uttered at normal rate as in {igən}{adʒu}{tʃoɨn}{kɨrimija} and (b) at fast rate as in {igən} {adʒu dʒoɨn gɨrimija} 'This is a very good picture'.. 158

5.2   Weight effect on the Accentual Phrase. (a) a pitch track of a sentence with three-syllable head nouns..................... 161

5.3   Pitch tracks of sentences in (4a-e) produced by a Chonnam speaker... 165

5.4   Pitch tracks of 'Marianna wants some milk' with focus on (a) milk, (b) Marianna and (c) both 170

5.5   Pitch tracks of an utterance produced (a) with neutral focus. 171

5.6   Pitch tracks of (7a) {na}{pam məgɨllejo} (7b) {na}{pap} {pərɨllejo}, and (7c) {na}{tol məgɨllejo}........ 175

6.1 Pitch tracks of [igəsɨn koɡumahago kamdʒagɨman]. 'These are a sweet potato and a potato', showing different phrasings by (a) neutral focus (b) focusing the first conjunct 204

6.2 Bar graphs showing 3 different groupings of the mean duration of VOT in ms... 208

7.1 Pitch tracks of same sentences as in (4) uttered by the Seoul speaker (S2).. 217

Preface

Except for the formalization of the Accentual Phrase in both Seoul and Chonnam dialects of Korean (p.55-58), this book is almost the same as my doctoral dissertation submitted to the Department of Linguistics at the Ohio State University in 1993. This revision reflects the modification of the assumptions made about the tonal pattern of the Accentual Phrase by later work. Jun (1995, 1996) experimentally proves that the Accentual Phrase initial tone is influenced by the laryngeal feature of the phrase initial segment in Seoul as well as in the Chonnam dialect of Korean. The possibility of segmental influence on the tonal pattern in Seoul dialect was mentioned in my thesis, but only one figure was shown in the Appendix. Comparing data from English and French, Jun (1996) further argues that the Accentual Phrase initial High tone in Korean is not due to phonetic undershoot originated from the universal phenomenon of consonantal perturbation on tone, but exists as an underlying tone. Thus both phrase initial Low and High tone were assumed to be underlying in this book.

Based on further experiments, I argue that the second L tone of the LHLH Seoul tonal pattern is associated with the penultimate syllable of an Accentual Phrase, and not to the third syllable of the Phrase as was originally claimed in the thesis. This revision is based on the consistent slope of the final rise as well as the perceptual salience of phrase boundary demarcation due to the final rise. This revision is also reflected in Jun and Oh (1996) where we showed that the Accentual Phrase boundary is an important perceptual cue in distinguishing three types of wh-phrases: wh-question, yes/no-question, and incredulity question. This paper also illustrates the tonal patterns of four boundary tones (H%, LH%, HL%, HLH%) and the frequency of each boundary tone related to the question type. Furthermore, Jun (1995) suggests the possibility that the second tone (i.e. L*H*LH) is a pitch accent, based on the production and perception of stress in Korean. This shows a good contrast with French: French has the same tonal pattern for the Accentual Phrase as Seoul Korean, LHLH, but the final H tone functions as a pitch accent (Jun & Fougeron 1995).

The Lenis Stop Voicing rule has also been further investigated in Jun (1993). In my thesis, this rule was shown to apply anywhere within an Accentual Phrase. But, Jun (1993) shows that a coda lenis stop is still voiced at the end of an Accentual Phrase when followed by a vowel initial Accentual Phrase. In addition, based on the duration of the lenis stop and the adjacent vowels, this rule was claimed to be a phonetic rule. This claim was made in my thesis but with less direct phonetic evidence. The other two rules, Obstruent Tensing and Vowel Shortening in Chapter 3, which were claimed to apply within an Accentual Phrase have been confirmed in an on-going research based on more extensive data (Jun in preparation). The intonation model developed in this thesis and the factors affecting accentual phrasing (proposed in Chapter 5) were tested in Kang (1995) based on the narrative speech of dialogues and short story. He shows that accentual phrasing is part of the cues distinguishing different informational status of entities in discourse (new vs given information; current vs. displaced given information). He also proves that the accentual phrase formation is influenced by speech rate and phonological weight.

Finally, the idea that prosodic units serve as the hierarchical domain of phonetic feature strengthening (Chapter 6) has been applied to other languages. For example, Fougeron (1996 for French), Gordon (1996 for Estonian), Fougeron & Keating (1995, 1996 for English), and Hsu & Jun (1996 for Taiwanese) all show that the phonetic realization of the segment is stronger at the initial position of a higher prosodic level than at the initial position of a lower prosodic level, and similarly it is stronger at the prosodic level initial position than at the prosodic level medial position.

Sun-Ah Jun

May 27, 1996

Acknowledgments

I want to thank UCLA Phonetics Laboratory members and especially Pat Keating, Bruce Hayes, Abigail Cohn and Mary Beckman for their encouragements in the publication of my dissertation. I also want to acknowledge Academic Press Limited and Ryohei Kagaya to allow me to reproduce a figure from Kagaya's 1974 article in *Journal of Phonetics*. Original acknowledgments from my dissertation follow.

During the course of my graduate studies here and in Korea, I received intellectual, emotional, and financial support from many sources, all of whom I would like to thank. First of all, I thank my advisor Mary Beckman for so many things: for her encouragement and good advice concerning both my studies and my future career; for helping me to develop and sharpen my world-view of phonetics; and for giving me such detailed comments on many rough drafts. I also like to thank my other committee members for this thesis or other requirements, Beth Hume, Michel Jackson and Rob Fox, for their valuable comments and interests in my paper.

I owe thanks to several people for their guidance of my studies from the beginning: to Professor Hwan-Mook Lee, who first introduced me to linguistics and made me major in it; to Professor Young-Nam Pae who shared the ideas of GB syntax with me and encouraged me to study in the United States; and to David Odden, who first introduced me to the world of Phonology and made me realize that my own dialect has tonal properties.

I would also like to thank Bruce Hayes, Julia Hirshberg, Pat Keating, Janet Pierrehumbert, and Donca Steriade, who broaden my knowledge of Phonetics, Phonology, and Pragmatics, and their interfaces. I also want to acknowledge those who motivated me to pursue my interest in Prosodic Phonology of Korean: Young-mee Yu Cho, Ongmi Kang, and David James Silva.

I would also like to take this chance to thank my wonderful friends in our Phonetics Lab, the Labbies or Lab Rats — always near me but rarely acknowledged — Gayle Ayers, Keven Cohen, Stefanie Jannedy, Sook-hyang Lee, Shu-Hui Peng, and Jennifer Venditti. Stefanie Jannedy deserves special thanks for her company through many sleepless nights in the lab and for her help in putting my figures in the right places.

Other members of my department also made my stay at OSU a happy and enjoyable one for this; I thank Benjamin Ao, Hee-Rahk Chae, Young-Hee Chung, Islay Cowie, John Dai, Eliza Segura-Holland, Hyeree Kim, No-Ju Kim, Gina Lee, Betina Migge, Mutonyi Nasiombe, Yongkyun No, Mira Oh, Frederick Parkinson, Marlene Payha, Robert Poletto, A. Hoobie Schott, and Jae-Hak Yoon. I especially thank Chan Chung, Heonseok Kang, Ki-Suk Lee, and Eun Jung Yoo, for spending hours in the sound booth for me as subjects of my experiments, as well as for their friendship during my time at OSU. Also, I would like to thank my other consultants — Guedae Cho, Yoon-Suk Chung, Chung-Hwa Kim, Jin-Sook Kim, Hyo-Seung Lee, Kyunghi Lee, Kyung-Hee Lee, Deok-Ryong Park, In-Woo Park, Ji-Young Seo, and Jean Suh.

Last but not least, I would like to thank my family in Korea — my mother and father, my sister and brothers, and my in-laws for their support and encouragement for all these years. I especially feel so grateful for having my husband, Illam, for his endless support, care, and encouragement. Without his help, I would never have made it this far. Finally, to my daughter, Yujin, my apologies for being away from you for so many nights. Thank you for bringing me such a joy in my life.

I would also like to acknowledge the financial support of the OSU Linguistics department, the College of Humanities, and the Graduate School. The work reported in this dissertation was also supported by the National Science Foundation under grant number IRI-8858109 to Mary E. Beckman.

The Phonetics and Phonology of Korean Prosody

I
Introduction

This book is about the phonetics and phonology of Korean prosody. Based on phonetic experiments, it proposes intonationally marked prosodic constituents above the word which condition various connected speech phenomena. The function of Prosody in speech production and perception has long been noticed (e.g., Lehiste 1973a,b, Cooper and Sorensen 1977 and Price et al. 1991). Tones and rhythm play an important role in grouping informational units of an utterance. Lehiste (1973a) found that intonational differences can disambiguate a sentence with ambiguous "surface syntactic structures" (e.g. old man and woman); Lehiste et al. (1976) and Scott (1982) found that durational difference can disambiguate a syntactically ambiguous sentences. Even when there is no ambiguity involved, prosody aids greatly in comprehension (Silverman 1993).

In addition to these studies that relate phonetics and acoustic aspects of prosody to syntax, we can also find studies that relate phonological aspects of prosody to syntax (Selkirk 1984, 1986; Nespor and Vogel 1986; Hayes 1989; etc.) or phonetic aspects of prosody to phonology (Pierrehumbert 1980; Beckman and Pierrehumbert 1986; etc.). The former defines the phonological constituents based on the syntactic structure of a sentence and known as Prosodic Phonology. The latter defines a prosodic constituent based on the intonation of an utterance, thus, I will refer to the latter as Intonational Phonology. In this book, I will focus on relating the phonetic aspect of prosody to phonology and syntax, a combination of the two approaches. That is, I will define the boundaries of prosodic constituents above the word level based on the intonational pattern of an utterance and show that these prosodic constituents also serve as the domain of several phonological rules. Furthermore, I will discuss factors affecting the prosodic phrasing; these include a syntactic constraint as well as non-syntactic factors such as focus, speech rate, weight of a phrase.

The intonation contour in Korean demarcates a prosodic constituent which is larger than a word and smaller than the Intonational Phrase, as well as the Intonational Phrase proper. I call the former prosodic constituent the *Accentual Phrase* to distinguish it from the latter. The Accentual Phrase is similar to the Phonological Phrase proposed by the Prosodic Phonologists in that both are larger than the prosodic word and smaller than the Intonational Phrase but the two differ in that the Phonological Phrase is defined strictly by the syntactic structure of the phrase whereas the Accentual Phrase is defined by the surface tonal pattern whose domain is determined by all the syntactic and non-syntactic factors that are recognized or yet to be discovered to influence intonational units. To emphasize its connection to the tonal pattern, I will use the term "Accentual Phrase" in my model of prosodic structure. As the phonetic representation of intonation, I will use the fundamental frequency (F0) contour. My reason for this choice is the same as that in Pierrehumbert (1980); F0 contours are the most accessible data which are relevant to a quantitative description of intonation.

This essential connection between prosodic structure and the intonation pattern was also recognized in Beckman and Pierrehumbert (1986) and Pierrehumbert and Beckman (1988). That is, as in English and Japanese, some types of prominence relationship or certain prosodic constituents are defined phonologically by such intonational phenomena as pitch accents and boundary tones. Intonation contours have also been related to Prosodic phonology by defining the Intonational Phrase (Selkirk 1980, 1984, 1986; Nespor and Vogel 1986, Kanerva 1990). Furthermore, adopting the formal theory of intonation developed in work by Liberman (1975), Pierrehumbert (1980) and Beckman and Pierrehumbert (1986), Hayes and Lahiri (1990) found that the constituency relevant to the insertion of a boundary tone of intonation contour or to the boundary tone docking site is the phrase edge provided under the theory of the Prosodic Hierarchy (Selkirk 1980) (see Section 1.1).

However, Prosodic phonologists typically neglected relating the domains defined by tonal properties, especially the domain smaller than the Intonational Phrase, to the domain of a segmental phonological rule. Based on several phonetic experiments, I will show that the tonally marked prosodic phrases in Korean — i.e. the Accentual Phrase and the Intonational Phrase — serve as the domain of several segmental phonological rules such as Lenis Stop Voicing and Obstruent Nasalization. Furthermore I will show that these tonally based prosodic domains can account for the variable domains of phonological rules which depend on non-syntactic or non-linguistic factors better than the syntax based prosodic domains proposed by the Prosodic Phonologists can account for these phenomena. Therefore, I propose that prosodic constituents in Korean should not be defined based on the syntactic information as proposed elsewhere (Cho 1989, 1990; Silva 1989, 1990; and O. Kang 1992, etc.). Rather, they should be defined based on the intonational pattern of an utterance.

The organization of this book is as follows. In the rest of Chapter 1, I give an overview of work in prosodic phonology and intonational phonology. In Chapter 2, I first describe the intonational structure of two dialects of Korean, the Seoul and Chonnam dialects. Then, based on this intonational structure, I propose an analysis of the prosodic structure of Korean. In Chapter 3, I introduce a phonetic experiment which shows that positing the Accentual Phrase as the domain of several postlexical phonological rules can account for the observed patterns better than the Phonological Phrase proposed under previous accounts. In Chapter 4, I describe two experiments showing that the Intonational Phrase is a prosodic level higher than the Accentual Phrase and that it also serves as the domain of several postlexical phonological rules. In Chapter 5, I will discuss factors affecting accentual phrasing and propose a syntactic constraint on accentual phrasing by examining all the possible phrasings of a sentence with the same syntactic structure. In Chapter 6, I will discuss the interface between the prosody and the lexicon by examining the Prosodic Word defined in two ways: in terms of the intonation and the in terms of segmental phonological rules. I also describe an experiment showing a phonetic effect at the boundaries of prosodic words. Finally, in Chapter 7, I provide a conclusion and make suggestions for future research.

Throughout this book, the symbols { } are used to indicate the accentual phrasing where relevant, and utterances within { }, [ ] and // are transcribed in IPA symbols rather than the standard romanization.

1.1 PROSODIC PHONOLOGY AND KOREAN

Prosodic Phonology is a theory of prosodic structure and of the relation between syntactic or morphological structure and prosodic structure. The theory assumes that an utterance is divided into prosodic constituents at different levels and these constituents are hierarchically organized. These prosodic constituents form the domains of application of phonological rules. Thus, Prosodic Phonology is often called a theory of phonological domains. There are two different positions within the prosodic phonology concerning the relationship between prosodic structure and syntactic structure. These positions differ in the degree to which phrasing is assumed to depend on syntax. (The syntactic theory assumed is usually some variety of the X-bar theory of syntax, Jackendoff 1977). One main position posits that prosodic phrasing refers to syntactic information only indirectly and that prosodic constituent structure exists separately from syntactic constituent structure. Thus, prosodic structure is not isomorphic to syntactic structure although it is defined in terms of the syntactic structure. The other position posits that the application of phonological rules directly refers to the labeled surface syntactic structure and that a separate phonological representation of prosodic constituents is not needed. This latter position has been called the Direct Syntax Approach (Kaisse 1985; Odden 1987, 1990) and the former has been called the Prosodic Hierarchy theory or Prosodic Phonology or the Indirect Syntax Approach (Selkirk 1979, 1984, 1986, 1990; Nespor and Vogel, 1982, 1986; Hyman et al. 1987; Hayes 1989; Selkirk and Shen, 1990).

In this book, I will discuss and compare my model of prosodic structure with the application of the Prosodic Hierarchy theory to Korean, but not with the Direct Syntax theory for two reasons. First, most work on the Prosodic Phonology of Korean has assumed the algorithms of the Prosodic Hierarchy theory. Also, a comparison with the Direct Syntax theory would be redundant if I show that even the Indirect Syntax theory depends on syntactic information more directly than seems warranted in defining the domain of phonological rules.

A common thread in many accounts of the Prosodic Hierarchy is Selkirk's (1984, 1986) Strict Layer Hypothesis, which is stated in (1).

(1) Strict Layer Hypothesis (Selkirk 1984, 1986)

(a) A given nonterminal unit of the prosodic hierarchy, X^{p}, is composed of one or more units of the immediately lower category, X^{p-1}.

(b) A unit of a given level of the hierarchy is exhaustively contained in the superordinate unit of which it is a part.

This hypothesis is also known as the Prosodic Structure Wellformedness Constraint as formulated in Selkirk and Shen (1990): The prosodic structure of a sentence must conform to the rule schema, $C^n \longrightarrow C^{(n-1)*}$.

Prosodic Hierarchy theory defines the domain of phonological rules, i.e. prosodic constituents, by referring to the syntactic structure indirectly in algorithms that build independent prosodic constituents on the basis of the edge of a lexical or phrasal category or the relation between a head and its complements. The main idea of this theory is that utterances are phrased in prosodic constituents projected from syntactic structures, conforming to the properties of prosodic structure

Introduction

(i.e. the Strict Layer Hypothesis, Selkirk 1981, 1984, 1986; Nespor and Vogel 1986; Hayes 1989). The properties of prosodic structure given in Selkirk (1986) are as follows.

(2) Properties of prosodic structure (Selkirk, 1986)

(a) It consists of prosodic (phonological) categories of different types, e.g. syllable(Syl: σ), foot(Ft), prosodic word (PWd: ω), Phonological Phrase(PPh: φ), Intonational Phrase (I), utterance(U).

(b) For any prosodic category, the sentence is exhaustively parsed into a sequence of such categories.

(c) The prosodic categories are ordered in a hierarchy (in the order given above), and in phonological representation they are strictly organized into layers according to that hierarchy. i.e. prosodic constituents of a same category are not nested.

Thus, the hierarchical prosodic structure proposed in Selkirk (1979, 1984, 1986, etc.) can be illustrated as in (3). And illformed structures under the theory of Prosodic Hierarchy are illustrated in (4). Symbols are used for each prosodic unit in (4) for the sake of simplicity: ω for a prosodic word, φ for a Phonological Phrase, and I for an Intonational Phrase.

(4a) is illformed because a prosodic constituent must belong to the immediately higher prosodic constituent (by Selkirk's algorithm, the edge of a higher constituent must coincide with the edge of the immediately lower constituent). (4b) is illformed because prosodic constituents of a same category are nested (the Strict Layer Hypothesis forbids recursion). (4c) is illformed because a constituent of the type X^p is contained within a constituent of type X^q, $q<p$. (4d) is illformed because a prosodic constituent at a lower level belongs to more than one prosodic constituent at a higher level.

(3) The Prosodic Hierarchy

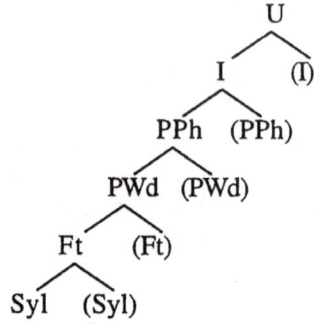

(4) Illformed prosodic structures

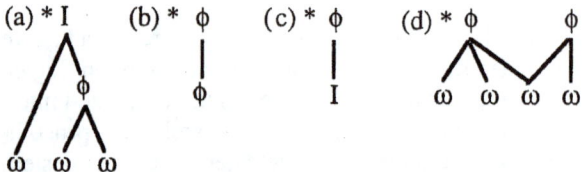

Most theories of the prosodic hierarchy observe these wellformedness conditions but several exceptions to this conditions have been suggested. For example, Ito and Mester (1992) argue that a morphological clipping process of Japanese is best explained by relaxing the Strict Layer Hypothesis somewhat to allow some lower level nodes to be not included in any constituent at the next higher level (see also Pierrehumbert and Beckman, 1988). A stronger objection to this condition was proposed by Ladd (1988, 1992) who argued that the depth of prosodic structure is indeterminate based on the phonetic characteristics of boundary strength; i.e. phrases can be recursive or in his term 'compound'. Hyman et al. (1987) also claim that the Strict Layer Hypothesis must be either rejected or weakened to account for Luganda: they showed a case of overlapping postlexical domains based on Luganda Low Tone Deletion rule and Final Vowel Shortening rule.

Setting aside these exceptions, there are still differences among Prosodic Phonologies; the inventory of types of the prosodic constituent is not the same across different algorithms which follow the Strict Layer Hypothesis. Inkelas (1989) and Zec (1988) assume the same types of prosodic constituents as those proposed in Selkirk (1984, 1986). But, in other variants, (the Relation-based theory proposed by Nespor and Vogel (1986) and by Hayes (1989), and p-command theory of McHugh (1990)), it has been proposed that there is a constituent called the Clitic Group between the Phonological Word and the Phonological Phrase. However, the status of the Clitic Group is controversial: Inkelas (1989) and Zec and Inkelas (1991) claim that the phonological dependence of clitics may be expressed directly in their lexical representation, in the form of a subcategorization frame. Providing cross-linguistic data showing that clitics attach not only to the word but also to the Phonological Phrase and the Intonational Phrase, they argue that adding a new Clitic Group level to the universal Prosodic Hierarchy would weaken the theory in a fundamental way. For the apparent evidence for Clitic Groups, such as languages showing two word-sized rule domains: one that excludes clitics, and one that contains clitics, they propose a lexical/postlexical distinction at the Phonological Word level.

On the other hand, Selkirk (1979, 1986) has argued that the prosodic constituents below the Phonological/Prosodic Word (namely the Foot and Syllable[1]) do not belong to the prosodic hierarchy and require a separate subtheory of the syntax-phonology relation. Inkelas (1989) also argues that a natural account for the mismatches between metrical structure (the mora, syllable, and foot) and phonological rule domain can be obtained only by separating prosodic and metrical constituents into two independent hierarchies. In this book, only levels above the Word level will be discussed as part of the theory of Prosodic Hierarchy.

Another dimension of difference among the proponents of the Prosodic Hierarchy theory is the algorithm for building prosodic structure from syntax. They are the end-based theory and the relation-based theory, and both of these algorithms have been applied to Korean.

1.1.1 *The End-Based Theory and Korean Prosody*

The End based theory was proposed by Selkirk (1986). Her proposal is that the relation between syntactic structure and prosodic structure above the foot and below the Intonational Phrase is defined in terms of the *ends* or *edges* of syntactic constituents of designated types. The idea is that a unit of phonological structure, a derived domain, will have as its terminal string the stretch of the surface syntactic structure that is demarcated by the right or left ends of selected constituents. This is formalized as the Syntax-Phonology Mapping in Selkirk and Shen (1990) as in (5).

(5) The Syntax-Phonology Mapping

For each category C^n of the prosodic structure of a
language there is a two-part parameter of the form
C^n: {Right/Left; X^m}
where X^m is a category type in the X-bar hierarchy.

A syntactic structure-prosodic structure pair satisfies
the set of syntax-phonology parameters for a language
iff the Right (or Left) end of each constituent of
type X^m in syntactic structure coincides with the edge
of constituent(s) of type C^n in prosodic structure.

A prosodic constituent is defined by the left or right edge of a lexical or syntactic category. For example, the prosodic word is defined by the left or right edge of the lexical category and the Phonological Phrase is defined by the left or right edge of the maximal projection of a lexical category. Example (6) shows how the end rules of the mapping creates the derived domain. Assume a language with end setting for two derived domains: $]_{word}$ and $]_{xmax}$. The tree in (6a) from Selkirk (1986:21) has the edges shown in (6b). (Line b is not to be construed as a part of any representation: it only indicates the location of the ends of (6a) which play a role in the mapping into (6c).)

Here, 'fw' means 'function word'. Function words are not identified as 'real' words, and are instead included in other larger derived domains. Only the right end of a 'real' word can mark the boundary of the Prosodic Word level and only the right end of the phrasal category, XP, can mark the boundary of the Phonological Phrase level. Selkirk notes that the domain-formation operates in a bottom-up fashion, operating on the full labeled bracketing, or tree, of the sentence.

The choice of right or left end is a parameter for each language: a language can use either the right end or the left end of the relevant syntactic constituent to trigger the matching prosodic constituent. The choice of right or left end parameters usually corresponds to the language's direction of headedness. That is, in general, the position of a head relative its complement determines the end parameter; a head final language is likely to have the left end setting for the parameter while a head initial language is likely to have the right end setting. However, as in the case of two dialects of Chinese described by Chen (1987) and Selkirk and Shen (1990), it is not always predictable; Xiamen uses the right end setting while Shanghai takes the left end setting, even though they have the same syntactic structure. Korean follows the more general

Introduction

pattern. That is, as a head final language, it takes the left end parameter setting in end-based accounts.

(6) a.
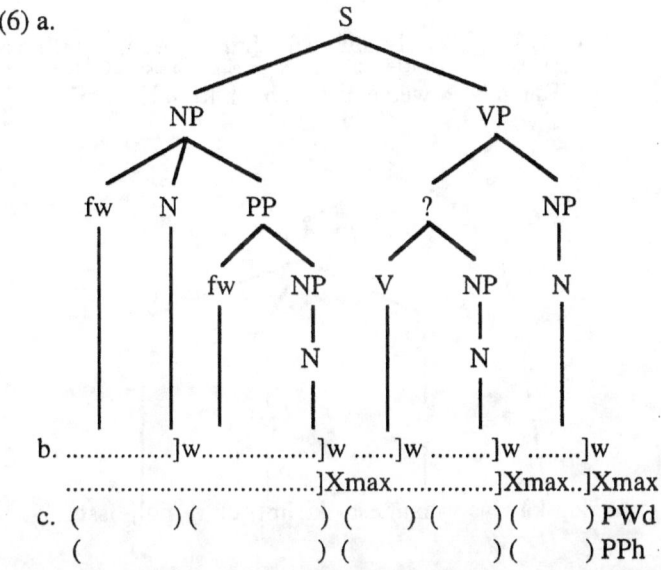

b. ....]w.................]w ......]w ....]w ....]w
   ....]Xmax...............]Xmax..]Xmax
c. (   )(   )(   )(   )(   ) PWd
   (   )(   )(   ) PPh

The end-based algorithm has been applied to Korean prosodic phonology by Cho (1987), Silva (1989, 1990), O. Kang (1992) and Y. Kang (1992), etc. (Henceforth, Kang (1992) refers to O. Kang (1992) unless mentioned otherwise.) These phonologists propose to define the Phonological Phrases by the *left* end of the maximal projection, NP, VP, AP, AVDP, {left, X^{max}}, and the Phonological Word (or Prosodic Word) by the *left* end of a lexical item, N, V, Det, A, and Adv, {left, X^{lex}}(Kang, 1992). An example sentence with Phonological Phrases is shown in (7). The relevant phonological rule used to support the posited phrasing in this case is the Intervocalic Obstruent Voicing rule. That is, these accounts claim that Korean obstruents are voiced intervocalically within Phonological Phrases but not across Phonological Phrase boundaries, as shown in the proposed phonetic transcription in bold within { }.

There are three places in the string of segments corresponding to the left edge of XP categories, thus the sentence has three Phonological Phrases. All Phonological Phrase medial lenis stops are voiced intervocalically including the verb initial lenis stop /p/, but the intervocalic lenis stops at the beginnings of the two NPs within the VP remain voiceless because they are in Phonological Phrase initial position. Thus, the Intervocalic Obstruent Voicing is blocked because the V-Lenis stop-V environment crosses the Phonological Phrase boundary.

(7) $_{NP}$[kaŋi-ka] $_{VP}$[$_{NP}$[kjəŋi-hantʰesə] $_{NP}$[kɨrimtʃʰek-ɨl] $_{V}$[pillj-əssta]]
'Kangi-NOM'   'Kyungi-from'   'a picture book-ACC' 'to borrow-past'
=> 'Kangi borrowed a picture book from Kyungi'

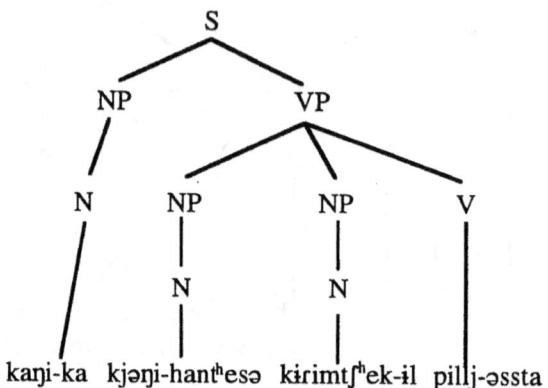

1.1.2 The Relation-Based Theory and Korean Prosody

Other phonologists have proposed to form the Phonological Phrase based on the relation between a head and its complement, therefore referring to the syntactic structure indirectly. Nespor and Vogel (1986) define a Phonological Phrase Formation rule as in (8).

(8) Phonological Phrase Formation
(Nespor and Vogel 1986:168)

The domain of Phonological Phrase consists of a Clitic Group which contains a lexical head (X) and all Clitic Groups on its nonrecursive side up to the Clitic Group that contains another head outside of the maximal projection of X.

A representative example is shown by a phonological rule found in central and southern varieties of Italian, "syntactic doubling" (*raddoppiamento sintattico* or RS), which applies in a sequence of two ωs ($ω_1$ and $ω_2$) to lengthen the initial consonant of $ω_2$ if a) the

Introduction

consonant to be lengthened is followed by a sonorant, specifically a vowel or other nonnasal sonorant, and b) if ω ends in a vowel which is the main stressed syllable of ω. Since Italian is syntactically right branching, the recursive side with respect to the head is the right side. The following tree (9) (Nespor and Vogel 1986:171 (10)) shows how the Phonological Phrase is formed based on the syntactic structure, thus showing the mismatch between these two structures. In (9), each head, V, N, and A, forms a Phonological Phrase together with the complement in its left side, the non-recursive side, thus resulting in three Phonological Phrases.

(9) an example of Phonological Phrasing based on Italian RS rule domain.

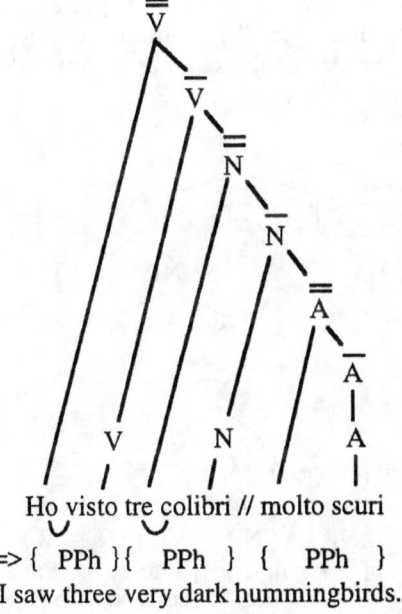

'I saw three very dark hummingbirds.'

There are three possible places where RS could apply: between *Ho* and *visto*, between *tre* and *colibri* and between *colibri* and *molto*. Among these, RS applies to only the first two cases (the application of RS is indicated by the linking arc underneath the segment string). The application of RS in the first two cases can be explained either by the syntactic structure or by the prosodic structure since *Ho* is grouped into a V-double bar with the following V-single bar, and *tre* is grouped into an N-double bar with the following N-single bar, and so on. However, the blocking of RS between the N and the following adjective phrase cannot be explained by the syntactic constituency directly because both of these words are within the same syntactic constituent, the N-single bar. Thus, the application of RS depends on the prosodic constituency and not on the syntactic constituency. This prosodic constituent — the Phonological Phrase — posited in Italian to account for RS is further supported by two other phonological rules, Stress Retraction and Final Lengthening, which also apply within this domain. Nespor and Vogel (1986) also describe a variety of other languages where the Phonological Phrase as defined above appears to be the domain of application of a number of phonological rules.

However, if we apply Nespor and Vogel's Phonological Phrase formation rule to Korean, the rule cannot explain all the Korean data, especially phrasings of the complex NPs such as NP containing a relative clause. For example, the relation based algorithm would yield the Phonological Phrase in (b) from the syntactic tree in (10). Furthermore, this phrasing is the same as what would be predicted by the end based algorithm shown in (a).

(10)

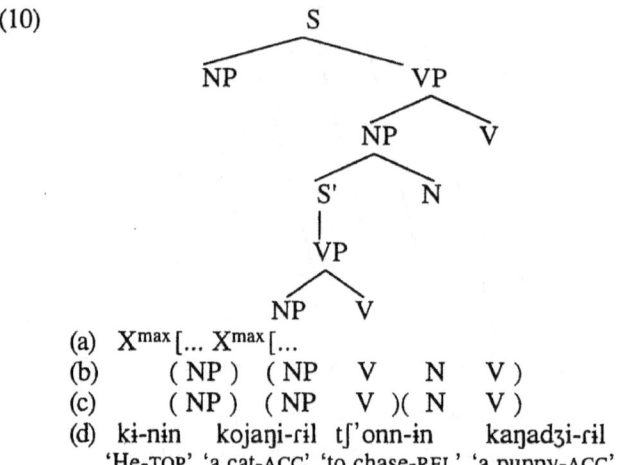

(a) X^{max} [... X^{max} [...
(b)   (NP) (NP   V   N   V)
(c)   (NP) (NP   V)(N   V)
(d) kɨ-nɨn   kojaɲi-ɾɨl tʃ'onn-ɨn   kaŋadʒi-ɾɨl   t'ɛrjət'e
  'He-TOP' 'a cat-ACC' 'to chase-REL' 'a puppy-ACC' 'beat'
  => He beat the puppy that was chasing the cat.

This structure can have only two Phonological Phrases in both theories: according to the end-based theory, there are two left ends of the maximal projection in this structure; according to the relation-based theory, the subject NP forms one Phonological Phrase and the predicate VP as a whole forms one Phonological Phrase because V is the head and the preceding NP, which is a complex noun containing a relative clause, is its complement. I.e., {kɨ-nɨn}{kojaɲi-ɾɨl tʃ'onn-ɨn gaŋadʒiɾil t'eɾjət'a}. However, according to Cho (1990) and the intuitions of several native speakers whom I have consulted, the most common phrasing is the phrasing in (10c), (i.e., {kɨ-nɨn}{kojaɲi-ɾil tʃ'onn-in}{kaŋadʒi-ɾil t'eɾjət'a}), which is different from the phrasings predicted by both algorithms.

To explain this common phrasing in Korean, Cho (1990) revised Nespor and Vogel's (1986) Phonological Phrase Formation rule as shown in (11).

(11) Apply the following rules cyclically to all maximal projections, proceeding from the bottom up. At any given stage, (a) applies before (b). Let the maximal projection under consideration on a given cycle be M.
 (a) If M branches, combine the head of M into a Phonological Phrase with all adjacent unphrased material, up to and including the closest XP, or if no such phrase is present, the left edge of M.
 (b) Phrase any focused word with the next word, unless that word is already phrased.
 After (a) and (b) have applied in all possible environments, (c) applies.
 (c) Unphrased words form Phonological Phrases of their own.

In applying this rule to (10), the lowest maximal projection, VP, forms one Phonological Phrase. In the next maximal projection, NP, there is no unphrased complement of N, thus mark the left edge of NP as a phrase boundary and go up to the higher maximal projection, VP. Here, the head V and its complement NP, whose only unphrased material being N, forms another Phonological Phrase. Finally, at the highest maximal projection, S, the NP forms its own Phonological Phrase, thus three Phonological Phrases, {NP} {NP V} {N V}.

Silva (1989), on the other hand, claims that a revised end-based theory can better explain the complex noun cases than the relation-based theory. Observing a tendency towards limiting the number of phonological words in the complex noun phrase to two, he proposed, in addition to the left-edge parameter, a constraint on the formation of phrases that limits them to be binary branching structures working from left to right. He called the smaller units 'the minor phrase' following Selkirk and Tateishi (1988) and proposed the Korean Phrase formation rule in (12). (13) shows the derivation of the phrasing using the example (10).

(12) Korean Phrase Formation
Major Phrase : {Left, Xmax},
Minor Phrase : binary branching, l-to-r

(13) ₛ[ₙₚ[ki-nin] ᵥₚ[ₙₚ[ₛ[ᵥₚ[ₙₚ[kojaɲi-ril] ᵥ[tʃ'onn-in]]]
     'He-TOP'   'a cat-ACC'   'to chase-REL'

    ₙ'[kaŋadʒi-ril]] ᵥ[t'erj-ət'e]]]
    'a puppy-ACC' 'beat-PAST'

⇒ 'He beat the puppy that was chasing the cat.'
(a) Major Phrasing:
    {ki-nin} {kojaɲi-ril tʃ'onn-in kaŋadʒi-ril t'erj-ət'e}
(b) Minor Phrasing:
    {ki-nin} {kojaɲi-ril tʃ'onn-in} {kaŋadʒi-ril t'erj-ət'e}

Under Nespor and Vogel's relation-based algorithm, we can predict the whole verb phrase in (13) to be one Phonological Phrase since the NP containing the relative clause is the complement of the head V. On the other hand, under the Selkirk's end-based algorithm, the sentence would form two Phonological Phrases, as in the Major Phrasing in (13) {ki-nin}{kojaɲi-ril tʃ'onn-in kaŋadʒi-ril t'erjət'e}. i.e., there are two left ends of the maximal projections, beginning of subject NP [ki-nin] and beginning of subordinate NP [kojaɲi-]. If we apply Silva's Korean Phrase Formation rule, (13b) will be predicted since the second Major Phrase having four words will break into two minor phrases, which is the same as the phrasing predicted by Cho's rule (11).

1.1.3 Patterns of Phrasing in Korean accounted for by Both Theories

As shown so far, even though the ways of deriving phonological domains are not the same in all accounts, the resulting phrases are very similar, except for a few cases. However, since, the different ways of deriving phrasing are not really relevant in the current work, I will illustrate patterns of phrasing which are generally agreed upon by these two different syntax based approaches. The patterns in (15) are some of them. A specific sentence is given to illustrate each pattern. The names of categories in (15) are syntactic categories, so IP is a sentence containing a tense marker, INFL, (i.e. 'S' in the traditional literature of syntax). CP has an IP and a topic or a topicalized or moved constituent, thus a mother node of an IP. XP means a maximal projection category of any type: NP, VP, AP, etc.

Introduction

'Shared φ' means a prosodic phrase where a postlexical phonological rule such as the Lenis Stop Voicing (also known as Intervocalic Obstruent Voicing) rule applies within the syntactic phrase. This is sometimes represented by an equal sign, '=' between lexical categories. Thus, all syntactic phrases written under 'Shared φ' in (15) will form one Phonological Phrase, φ. On the other hand, 'Split φ' means a sequence within which there is a Phonological Phrase boundary, thus, a postlexical phonological rule is blocked between its constituent phrases. Here, the blocking place is marked by a slash. For example, if we use as our metric for phrasing the Lenis Stop Voicing rule by which a lenis stop becomes voiced between voiced segments, a noun initial /k/ is predicted to be voiced in the structure of NP[Det N] as in <ki = ke> ('that'='dog') => [ki **ge**] but *not* voiced in the structure of IP[NP /VP] as in <kike/ke-ja> ('that'/'a dog-be') => [kige **ke**ja]. The word initial lenis obstruent is in bold and underlined to show the application or the blocking of the voicing rule depending on the structure. Schematic tree representations of a shared and of a split phrase are shown in (14).

(14) Schematic representation of Shared and Split phrases
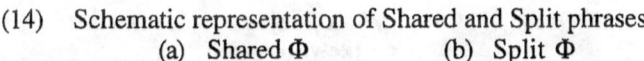
(a) Shared Φ   (b) Split Φ

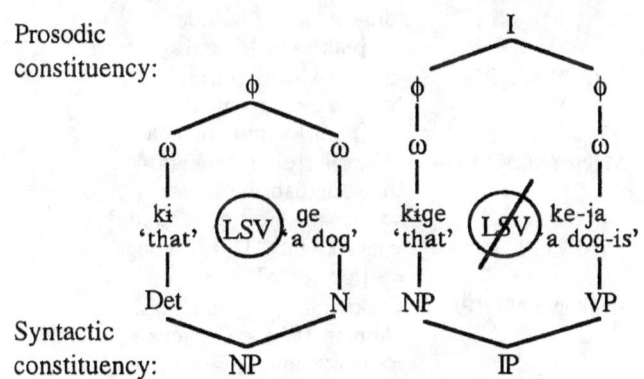

These patterns showing possible Phonological Phrases (=Shared φ) and impossible Phonological Phrases (=Split φ) are all defined based on the syntactic information, end of maximal projection or head complement relation. Based on the phrasings in (15), it seems that we can make the generalization that a lexical head and its complement will form a single phrase together but there will be no grouping between the maximal categories. Next, I will show cases when a phonological phrasing seems to reflect the different syntactic structures of a sentence and discuss problems of this approach based on actual data.

(15) Shared and Split Phonological Phrases (Φ) common in Cho, Kang and Silva.

Shared Φ

NP[Det N]　　　　　　<i = ke> 'this dog' => [i **g**e]
NP[AP N]　　　　　　<hən = tʃatʃənkə> 'old bicycle'
　　　　　　　　　　=> [hən **dʒ**adʒəngə]
NP[NP N]　　　　　　<jəŋine = tʃip> 'Youngi's house'
　　　　　　　　　　=> [jəŋine **dʒ**ip]
VP[ADVP V]　　　　　<tʃal = kassta> 'went well' => [tʃal **g**at'a]
VP[NP V]　　　　　　<sakwaril = tʃunta> 'give an apple'
　　　　　　　　　　=>[sagwaril **dʒ**unda]
AP[ADVP A]　　　　　<atʃu = tʃoin> 'very good'
　　　　　　　　　　=> [adʒu **dʒ**oin]
ADVP[ADVP Adv]　　　<atʃu = tʃal> 'very well' => [adʒu **dʒ**al]

Split Φ

XP[XP conj /XP]　　　<kewa / kojaŋi> 'a dog and a cat'
　　　　　　　　　　=> [kewa **k**ojaŋi]
VP[PP /NP V]　　　　<pak'esə / kirimil kirinta>
　　　　　　　　　　'draw a picture outside'
　　　　　　　　　　=> [pak'esə / **k**irimil **g**irinda]
VP[ADVP/ NP V]　　　<p'ali / kirimil kirinta>
　　　　　　　　　　'draw a picture quickly'
　　　　　　　　　　=> [p'ali **k**irimil **g**irinda]
VP[NP /ADVP V]　　　<jəŋəril tʃeil tʃoahanta>
　　　　　　　　　　'like English the most'
　　　　　　　　　　=> [jəŋəril **tʃ**eil **dʒ**oahanda]
IP[NP /VP]　　　　　<ike / ke-ta> 'This is a dog.'
　　　　　　　　　　=> [ige **k**eda]
CP[Topic NP /IP]　　　<sakwanin / kjəule masissta>
　　　　　　　　　　'Apples, they are delicious in winter'
　　　　　　　　　　=> [sakwanin **k**jəure maʃit'a]
IP[Sentential ADVP /NP /VP]
　　　　　　　　　　</taheŋito / kaŋatʃika tolawassta>
　　　　　　　　　　'Luckily, a puppy came back'
　　　　　　　　　　=> [taheŋhido / **k**aŋadʒiga **d**o/awas'ta]
IP[NP /VP external ADVP /ADVP V]
　　　　　　　　　　<kaŋatʃika / kimpaŋ / tʃal tomaŋkas'ta>
　　　　　　　　　　'Soon, a puppy ran away well'
　　　　　　　　　　=> [kaŋadʒiga / **k**imbaŋ / **tʃ**al
　　　　　　　　　　　　domaŋgas'ta]

1.2 PROBLEMS WITH THE SYNTAX BASED PHRASING ACCOUNTS

As mentioned in the introduction, prosodic structure can be used to disambiguate syntactically ambiguous structures (Lehiste, 1973, Price et al., 1991). Even though it was suggested that there are several ways to cue such syntactic distinctions (for example, the placement of pauses or phrase-final lengthening), phrasing at higher levels of the prosodic hierarchy perhaps seems to be the most salient cue. Thus, a different syntactic structure is realized in a different phonological phrasing. For example, the string of segments in (16) 'Ayoungi pap məgille?' could have either of two syntactic structures, (16a) and (16b), and these different syntactic structures are necessarily realized by different phonological phrasings as shown by the phrasings given for each syntactic structure.

(16)　　　　　Ayoungi　　　pap　　məgille
   (a)　IP[NP[subj.NP] VP[[obj.NP]　　[V]]]
     => 'Ayoung, do you want to eat rice?'
     : phrasing => {ajəŋi}{pam məgille}

   (b)　VP[NP[Poss. N　　head N]　　[V]]
     => '(Do you) want to eat Ayoung's rice?'.
     : phrasing => {ajəŋi bam}{məgille} or
     　　　　　　　{ajəŋi bam məgille}

These different phrasings in (16a) and (16b) are also predicted by algorithms proposed by Cho (1990), Kang (1992) and Silva (1989): for (16a), they all predict the sentence to have one Phonological Phrase for the subject noun NP and another Phonological Phrase for the object noun and the verb, VP, thus the object NP initial /p/ would remain voiceless. For (16b), by Cho's Phonological Phrase formation rule (11) and Silva's Korean Phrase Formation (12), the sentence is phrased by forming a Phonological Phrase for the first two nouns and another Phonological Phrase for the verb, thus /p/ at the beginning the head N would be phrase-medial and thus voiced. By Kang's end-based approach, the whole sentence, as a VP, would form one Phonological Phrase. Regardless of this difference, however, the phonological phrasing seems to reflect the syntactic relation between words in this case: The subject noun is separated from the object noun but the genitive case noun is combined with its head noun.

However, a different syntactic structure is not always predicted to have different phonological phrasings. For example, according to Cho and Silva's rules, the NP in (17-1a) is supposed to have two Phonological Phrases, one for AP and the other for the head noun. Kang (1992) would have the same phonological phrasing because she assumes the AP in this case is the relative clause and the head noun having a NP category, thus triggering a phonological phrase boundary between the relative clause and the head noun. However, the most common phrasing is what is shown in (17b): a Phonological Phrase boundary between the adverb and the adjective and one Phonological Phrase for the adjective and the head noun.

(17) 1. (a) NP[AP[atʃu tʃoin] N[kirim]]
            very good   a picture
         = 'a very good picture'
      (b) (adʒu) (tʃoin girim)
   2. tʃaŋnjən-e   irəbəri-n   mahura-ril   tʃʰadʒ-at-ta.
      'last year-in' 'to lost-REL' 'muffler-ACC' 'to find-Past-DEC'

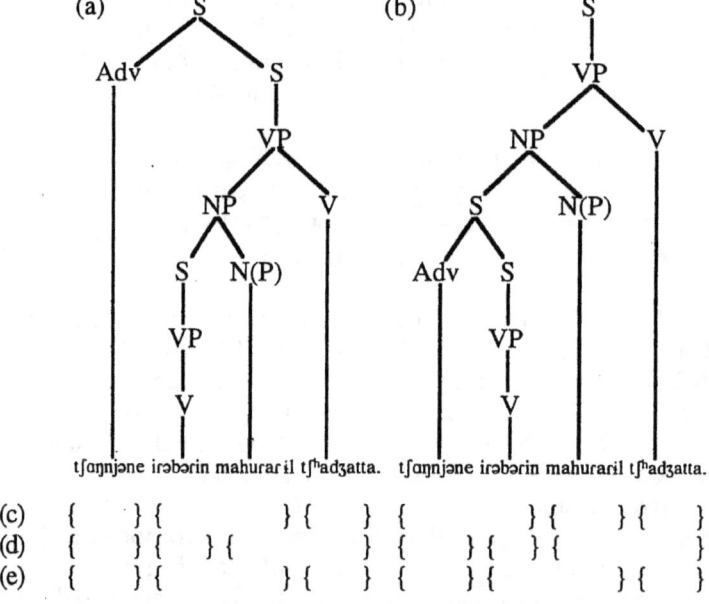

=> 'Last year, I found the muffler I lost.' => 'I found the muffler that I lost last year.'

Another example can be shown from a case in which a time adverb modifies a verb of the main clause as in (17-2a) or a verb in the subordinate clause as in (17-2b). The syntactic category of a head noun is given as N(P) since Kang (1992) proposed an NP while others an N category. The phrasings in 'c' are what we can often find in native speakers' productions, reflecting the modifying scope of the adverb: a phrase boundary right after the adverb when it modifies the verb in the main clause; and no phrase boundary after the adverb when modifying the following verb within the subordinate clause. These different phrasings are realized as different pitch heights as shown in the pitch tracks in Figure 1.1. (Figure from Venditti, Jun and Beckman 1996). Y-axis refers to a fundamental frequency (F0) in Hz and X-axis refers to time. This format is used for all the pitch tracks in this thesis.

Fig.1.1(a) is when the adverb modifies the main verb and (b) is when the adverb modifies the subordinate verb (a verb within a relative clause). In other words, in (a), the head noun is modified by the preceding verb only but, in (b), the head noun is modified by the preceding adverb and the verb, as shown by the arrow in the figure. In (a) the F0 of the subordinate verb initial is higher than the preceding phrase, cueing a separation from the preceding adverb which itself also shows the end of a phrase by the HL boundary tone, HL%, an apparent mark of the Intonational Phrase boundary, (which will be discussed in Chapter 2). On the other hand, in (b), the initial F0 of the subordinate verb, *irəbəɾin*, is very low and continuously falling from the preceding adverb. Also the preceding adverb does not have any boundary tone, indicating these two words are in the same group. In the same way, in (a), the F0 contour of the head noun, *mahuɾaɾil*, is lower than that of the preceding verb and continuously falling, but, in (b), the F0 starts rising in the middle of *mahuɾaɾil* and its peak is higher than that of the preceding verb, *irəbəɾin*, showing the head noun *mahuɾaɾil* is separated from the preceding group and initiates a new phrase. These phrasings are shown in (17c). Thus, it is very clear that the different syntactic structures are reflected in different prosodic groupings which are realized in different intonational contours.

However, these groupings in Fig. 1.1. cannot be predicted by the end-based approach: Kang would predict the phrasings in (17d) assuming the head noun as an NP category, while Silva would predict phrasings in (17e) after applying the Minor phrase rule. Cho's Phonological Phrase formation rule (11) also would predict the same phrasings as Silva's, i.e. (17e), thus it can predict the groupings in Fig.1.1 (a) but not the groupings in Fig.1.1 (b). That is, for the 'a' structure, starting from the lowest maximal category, the non-branching

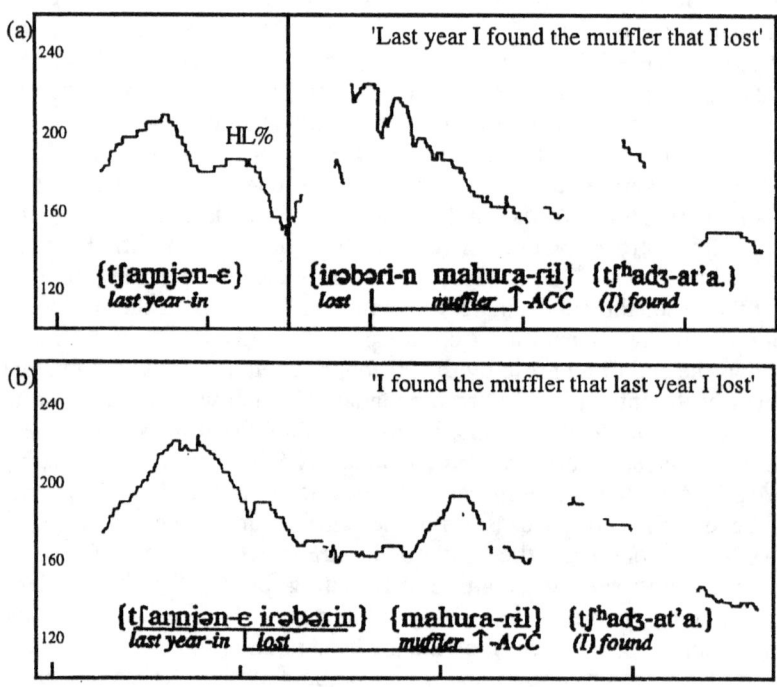

Figure 1.1. Pitch tracks of [tʃaŋnjəne irəbərin mahuɾaɾil tʃʰadʒat'a.] reflecting two different syntactic structures: (a) {tʃaŋnjəne}{irəbərin mahuɾaɾil} {tʃʰadʒat'a.} - Last year, I found the muffler I lost.' and (b) {tʃaŋnjəne irəbərin} {mahuɾaɾil} {tʃʰadʒat'a.}- I found the muffler lost last year.' Y-axis is the fundamental frequency in Hz and X-axis is the time.

VP would mark the left edge of Phonological Phrase and would form a Phonological Phrase together with the following N in the higher Maximal projection, NP, while for the 'b' structure, starting from the lowest maximal category, VP, since it has only a V node, its left edge will be M, thus, there will be phrase boundary between the adverb and the subordinate verb. In the next higher maximal category, NP, the head N will form a Phonological Phrase combining the left maximal projection whose unphrased item is now only the VP, resulting in the same Phonological Phrasing as that of 'a' structure. Thus, the Phonological Phrase formation rules based on the syntactic information can not always predict the possible phrasing of an utterance.

We can also notice another problem in the syntax-based prosodic theories in the predicted phrasings in (17). Since the prosodic phrasing depends on the syntactic structure assumed, different assumptions derive different predictions about the prosodic phrasing. Therefore, the syntax-based prosodic theories do not provide a consistent prediction of phrasing with each other, not only because their ways of defining the prosodic level are different, but also because their assumptions about syntactic structures and the categorical status of certain lexical items are different. For example, three different syntactic categories were proposed for a head noun within a complex noun phrase: NP[CP, NP] (Kang, 1992), vs. [S', N] (Cho, 1987a, 1987b), vs. [S, N'] (Silva, 1989). All these have the same syntactic structure but the syntactic category of the head noun is not the same, resulting in different phonological phrasings as shown in (18).

(18) Three different proposals of the syntactic category of a relative clause and a head noun and their predicted phonological phrasings.

(Kang, 1992) vs. (Silva, 1989) vs. (Cho, 1987)

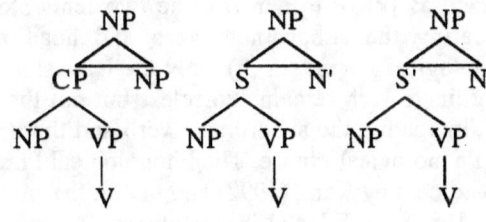

syntactic category posited =>

phonological phrasing predicted   =>{NP}{V}{NP} =>{NP}{V N'} =>{NP}{V N}

These different syntactic categories are what makes them predict different phonological phrasings because these three proposals are all based on Selkirk's end based algorithm (Note Cho's early proposal was end-based model). When the relative clause, here represented as CP, S, and S'(S-single bar), has a subject NP and a predicate VP, the predicate VP always starts a Phonological Phrase by being the left end of the maximal category, VP. Thus, when the head noun is assumed as an N-bar as in Silva (1989) or as an N as in Cho (1987a, 1987b), the head noun does not form its own Phonological Phrase but rather belongs to the preceding VP because N-bar is still not a maximal projection. On the other hand, when the head noun is assumed as an NP as in Kang (1992), the head noun forms its own Phonological Phrase, predicting a different phrasing from Silva and Cho. Kang (1992) proposed the NP status of the head noun to explain the case when she believes the head noun forms a Phonological Phrase separately from the preceding relative clause. This is circular. But, at the same time, the fact that the same or similar data described in each proposal have different phonological phrasings also indicates that the actual phrasing of an utterance is not fixed.

When we observe the actual phrasings of a sentence, it is clear that there are many possible phrasings for the same sentence, more than can be predicted by the different proposals mentioned above. I will show the actual phrasings of one example phrase, a structure consisting of a relative clause and a head noun as in [jəŋmaniəmmaga kɨrjənon kɨrim], 'a picture which Youngman's mom drew'. The lenis stops at the beginnings of the subordinate verb, *kɨrjənon*, and the head noun, *kɨrim*, allow us to see if the word comes at the beginning or in the middle of a Phonological Phrase: The lenis stop will be voiced if in the middle of a Phonological Phrase and will be voiceless if it is at the beginning of a Phonological Phrase. Figure 1.2 shows waveforms and pitch tracks of three possible utterances of the sentence.

The waveforms and pitch track show where the lenis stop /k/ is realized as [k] or [g]. In (a), the two lenis stops are both voiceless, indicating the subordinate verb and head noun each forms one Phonological Phrase. In (b), only the lenis stop at the beginning of the subordinate verb remains voiceless but not the head noun initial lenis stop, indicating the subordinate verb and the head noun together form one Phonological Phrase. The Phonological Phrasing in (a) is what can be predicted by Kang (1992) and that in (b) is what can be predicted by Cho (1987) and Silva (1989). However, as we can see in Fig. 1.2 (c), it is also possible for the head noun initial lenis stop to remain voiceless and the subordinate verb initial lenis stop to become voiced, thus indicating the subordinate verb does not form one Phonological

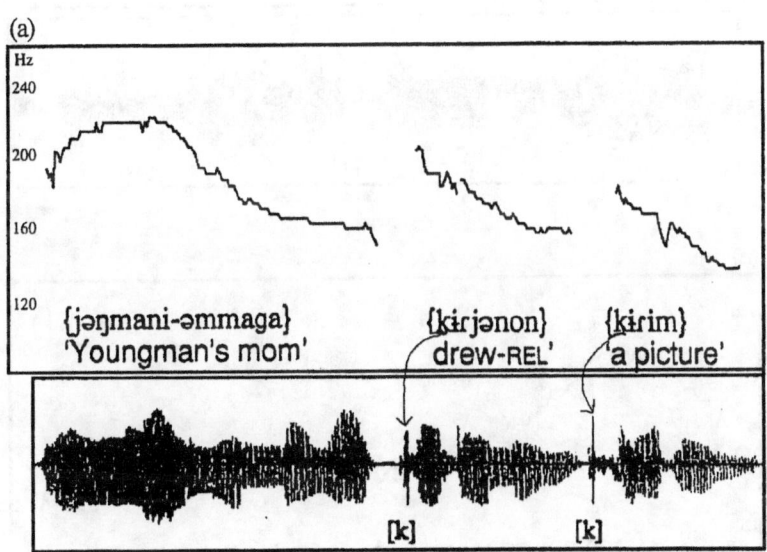

Figure 1.2. Pitch tracks and waveforms of three possible actual utterances of the sentence : [jəŋmaniəmmaga kɨrjənon kɨɾim] 'The picture Youngman's mom drew.' (a) NP{jəŋmaniəmmaga} V{kɨrjənon} N{kɨɾim}

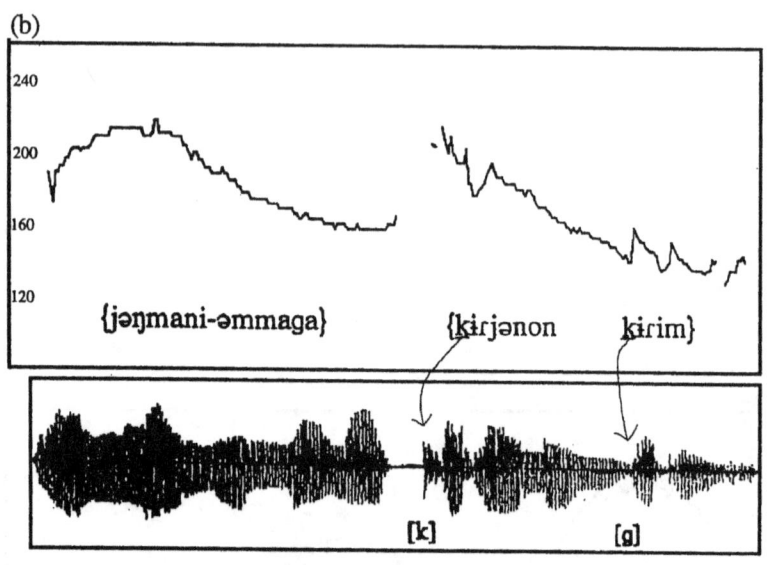

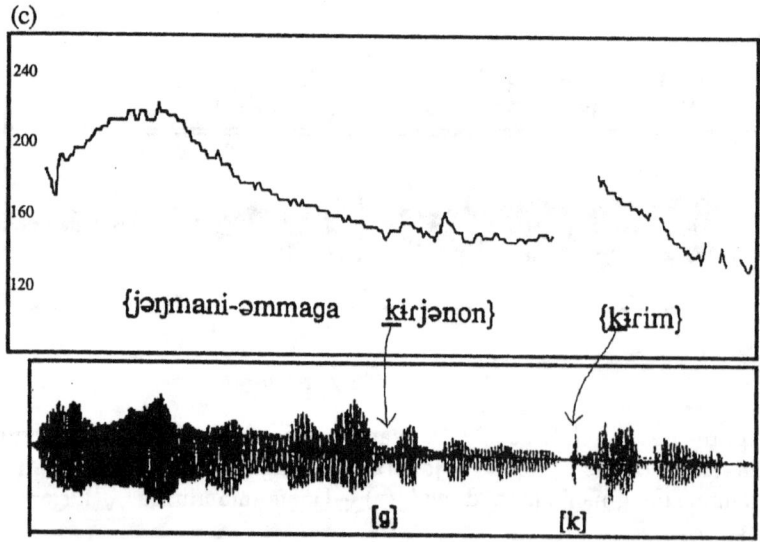

Figure 1.2. (continued)
(b) NP{jəŋmaniəmmaga} V-N{kirjənon girim}
(c) NP-V{jəŋmaniəmmaga girjənon} N{kirim}

Phrase, but the head noun forms one Phonological Phrase. These different phrasings are given in (19).

(19) jəŋman-i-əmma-ga   kɨrj-ə-non   kɨɾim
    'Youngman-Poss.-mom-NOM' 'to draw-past-REL' 'a picture'
=> 'A picture which Youngman's mom drew'.
  (a) {jəŋmaniəmmaga} {kɨrjənon} {kɨɾim}
     - predicted by Kang (1992)
  (b) {jəŋmaniəmmaga} {kɨrjənon gɨɾim}
     -predicted by Silva (1989) and Cho (1987)
  (c) {jəŋmaniəmmaga gɨrjənon} {kɨɾim}
     -not predicted by any of them

Then, how can we predict what forms the Phonological Phrase, i.e., the domain of Lenis Stop Voicing? If we look at the pitch tracks of each utterance, we see that each phrase (i.e., each string with an initial voiceless stop) begins with an F0 rise to about 200-220 Hz so that the peak F0 value of the word beginning with a voiceless lenis stop is higher than the F0 values of preceding syllables, while the F0 value of the word beginning with a voiced lenis stop is lower than the preceding F0 values. In other words, the F0 peaks at about 200 Hz occur at the same places as the phonetic realization of [k], namely, at the left edge of phrases. Thus, it seems that the F0 contour is correlated with the domain of Lenis Stop Voicing in such a way that the rising F0 marks the beginning of each such domain and the end of a subsequent F0 fall marks the end of the domain. This relationship between F0 pattern relative to the lenis stop voicing is true for all three utterances. These data indicate that syntax based Phonological Phrases do not account for all the actual data. Rather, the domain of Lenis Stop Voicing is better predicted by the intonational pattern of the utterance. We can see that there is a consistent pattern in the intonational contour (the rising and falling contour) but the domain covered by this intonation contour varies, indicating that the consequent domain of phonological rule application is more variable than is allowed for in the theories proposed by Cho, Kang, and Silva. (The specific contour here defines a level of tonally marked phrasing which I will call the *Accentual Phrase* (α) - see below.)

So, it seems that the domain of phonological rule is determined not solely by the syntactic structure of a sentence but more by whatever factors affecting the realization of the intonational pattern of an utterance. And this intonation related phrasing can easily explain why phrasing varies depending on speech rate, focus or the size of the phrase, etc. The syntax-based approaches can not explain these variable phrasings since syntactic structure is the same regardless of speech rate or weight of the phrase, etc. To account for these non-syntactic effects on phrasing, syntax based approaches may need many *ad hoc* phrase restructuring rules, optional or obligatory. These factors affecting prosody will be discussed in detail in Chapter 5. Before discussing the intonational structure of Korean, a background of intonation theory which is related to Korean intonation is discussed in the next section.

1.3 THEORETICAL FRAMEWORK OF INTONATION

The intonational framework I assume in this book is based on the descriptive framework developed by Pierrehumbert (1980), Liberman and Pierrehumbert (1984), Beckman and Pierrehumbert (1986) and Pierrehumbert and Beckman (1988). Pierrehumbert's (1980) theory of the phonology of English intonational contours assumes that the intonational contour consists of a sequence of discrete tonal entities as in autosegmental theories of Bantu tonal systems (Goldsmith 1976, 1992). There are only two tonal levels, High and Low. These tonal entities have different compositions in terms of tones and different distributions within the Intonational Phrase: A pitch accent in English may consist of either one or two tones. One of these tones is phonologically linked to the "primary-stressed" syllable of the accented word and is marked by an asterisk (or star). There are six types of pitch accent in English: H*, L*, L*+H, L+H*, H+L*, H*+L. Choosing different types of pitch accent does not change the lexical meaning of the word but only the pragmatic meaning of an utterance.

It is also proposed that there are two distinct types of tonal entity making up the intonational contour of every Intonational Phrase. They are the pitch accent and the phrase tones. In English the pitch accent is a pitch event phonologically linked to a particular stressed syllable and phonetically realized at or around that designated syllable in an utterance. There are two kinds of phrase tones: phrase accents and boundary tones. The phrase accents occur after the rightmost pitch accent, and a boundary tone occurs at the right edge and (optionally) at the left edge of the Intonational Phrase. These two phrasal tones mark different levels of phrasing; The boundary tone marks the Intonational Phrase and the phrase accent marks the intermediate phrase. The phrase accent is either H or L (sometimes written as H⁻ and L⁻) and is realized not on any particular syllable, but within a certain time period after the last pitch accent (= nuclear accent or sentence stress). The boundary tone is also a single tone, H% or L%, a percent sign (%) to distinguish it notationally from tonal entities of other types. Thus, the minimal intonational contour of an Intonational Phrase consists of a pitch accent, a phrase accent and a final boundary tone. In other words, the intonational pattern is hierarchically organized in that an Intonational Phrase can have one or more intermediate phrases and an intermediate phrase can have one or more pitch accents. But there is no phonological constituent of which the pitch accent marks the beginning or ending.

The intonational pattern of Japanese also has been described under Pierrehumbert's framework. Japanese is similar to English in that it also has an Intonational Phrase and an intermediate phrase but differs in that Japanese does not have a prosodic category definable based on stress as in English and rather has one more phrasal level, an Accentual Phrase, the lowest level of phrasing that is well defined by the intonation pattern. In these regards, Korean is similar to Japanese but distinct from English. Both Korean and Japanese have been claimed to have an Accentual Phrase (Beckman and Pierrehumbert 1986, Jun 1989, S. Lee 1989, and de Jong 1989). The tonal properties of the Japanese Accentual Phrase is described and compared with Korean Accentual Phrase in the next section.

1.3.1 The Accentual Phrase

An Accentual Phrase in Japanese is tonally defined (Beckman and Pierrehumbert 1986, Pierrehumbert and Beckman 1988). The Accentual Phrase has at most one High tone and is delimited by a Low boundary tone, thus sometimes called the domain of initial rising tone. The Accentual Phrase has a phrasal High tone which is phonologically associated with the second sonorant mora of the Accentual Phrase unless this conflicts with the lexical association of an accent H to the first mora. The low boundary tone marks the end of the Accentual Phrase and the beginning of an utterance. Thus, in general, the tonal pattern of an Accentual Phrase is an initial rising pattern. However, for Tokyo (Standard) Japanese, the tonal pattern of the Accentual Phrase is somewhat more complicated when at least one word in the Accentual Phrase is lexically accented. That is, an Accentual Phrase containing an accented word has a lexically marked HL fall associated with a certain mora of the accented word (or the first accented word) in addition to the phrasal tones of the Accentual Phrase. But the Accentual Phrase of an unaccented word shows the phrasal tone pattern, an initial rising.

The Korean Accentual Phrase is similar to an Accentual Phrase containing only unaccented words in Tokyo Japanese, in that the tonal pattern of an Accentual Phrase in Korean is not specific to a lexical item but is a property of the phrase. The Accentual Phrase in Korean can have more than one word, just as in Japanese. In Japanese, all accents after the first word within the Accentual Phrase, if there is any, are deleted. The tonal pattern of the Accentual Phrase in Korean differs for different dialects: Seoul has a final rising pattern and Chonnam has an initial rising pattern. The North Kyungsang dialect, which has lexically distinct pitch accents would have more complicated tonal pattern for the Accentual Phrase, like the Accentual Phrase in Tokyo Japanese. The tonal patterns of Seoul and Chonnam dialects will be described in detail in Chapter 2.

Thus, Korean, Japanese and English all have tonal phenomena which can be described in terms of the notion "accent". In English, this "accent" is associated with the stressed syllable of a word, and the pitch shape for the accent is not specific to the accented lexical item. The pitch shape only contrasts different intonational meanings. The only aspect of pitch accent that is lexically specified is the accent docking place, the stressed syllable in a word. In Japanese and Korean, the 'accent' is distributed among the Accentual Phrases in an utterance. But in Tokyo Japanese, the location of a pitch accent is lexically distinct and the pitch accent marks the tonally prominent mora, even though there are no different melodies at the same accented mora to contrast lexical items. In Korean, the tonal events which can be described as 'pitch accent' does not function to mark prominent syllables, but to delimit a prosodic grouping of words. This tonally marked grouping is functionally similar to that of the phrasal tones of Japanese.

1.3.2 Tone Underspecification and Interpolation

In addition to proposing the different types of tonal entity and tonal patterns of intonational contour, Pierrehumbert (1980) developed a system of underlying representation of intonation and rules which map the underlying representation into phonetic realization in the F0 contour. Pierrehumbert (1980) and Pierrehumbert and Beckman (1988) argue that in English as well as in Japanese there are fewer tones than possible tone bearing units. Pierrehumbert and Beckman (1988) claim this based on the slope of the tone between the phrasal H and the L boundary tone in unaccented phrases in Japanese; the F0 falls gradually from the H to the L% and the slope of this fall is negatively correlated with the number of moras of the Accentual Phrase. The F0 values of tone bearing units that do not carry tones phonologically are supplied by phonetic processes of interpolation, which determine transitions between one tone and the next.

The data of F0 contour of the Accentual Phrase in Korean also suggest that there seems to be an undershoot of the phonetic value of tones when the tones are sufficiently crowded compared to the number of tone bearing units, as assumed in Pierrehumbert (1980). The actual F0 slope with respect to the number of syllables or moras within the Accentual Phrase is shown in the next chapter.

NOTES

1. Zec (1988) and Ito (1987) include the mora as the level lower than the syllable. For more arguments, see Hyman (1985) and Hayes (1988).

II

The Intonation and Prosodic Structure of Korean

In this chapter, I will describe the intonational structure of two dialects of Korean, Seoul and Chonnam, and propose a prosodic hierarchy for both dialects based on the groupings evident in intonation patterns. Even though the intonational patterns of other dialects such as Kyungsang or Chungchung have not been described, I assume they would share similar patterns of prosodic groupings despite their tonal differences. The Seoul dialect is also known as the Standard dialect of Korean, defined as a language spoken by middle class people living in the Seoul area. However, due to the expansion of Seoul into surrounding areas and also due to the increasing movement of people into Seoul from other dialect areas, we cannot use this definition any more, and, it is getting hard to find a native speaker of pure Seoul dialect. The Chonnam dialect is spoken in the Chonnam (South of Cholla) province located in the Southwestern part of South Korea. This dialect is spoken by at least five million people (as of Dec. 1992). The Chonnam data I examine here are from speakers from several different major cities in the Chonnam province, including Kwangju, Mokpo, Naju, Hwasoon and Henam.

2.1. INTONATIONAL STRUCTURE OF SEOUL DIALECT

2.1.1 The structure and tonal pattern of Seoul Intonational Phrase

The structure of Seoul intonation assumed in this thesis is based on previous work by De Jong (1989), S. Lee (1989) and Jun (1990). The intonational structure in Seoul is hierarchically organized in such a way that an Intonational Phrase can have more than one Accentual Phrase, which in turn can have more than one word. As in many other prosodic hierarchy models, the Intonational Phrase is exhaustively parsed into a sequence of Accentual Phrases conforming to the Strict Layer Hypothesis (Selkirk 1981, 1984; Nespor and Vogel 1986; Hayes 1989). So, the Intonational Phrase contour includes tonal patterns of one or more Accentual Phrases and the Intonational Phrase boundary tone. The last syllable of the Intonational Phrase is lengthened and optionally followed by pause. The Accentual Phrase has a tonal pattern demarcating the beginning and the end of the phrase. The first segment of the Accentual phrase is lengthened (Jun 1990a, 1993) but the last syllable of the Accentual Phrase is not noticeably lengthened (Koo 1986, Jun 1993).

The Accentual Phrase has a phrase final rising pattern, a LH, and the Intonational Phrase has several boundary tones such as L, H, LH, HL, LHL and HLH. However, when the syllable is final to the Accentual Phrase and at the same time is final to the Intonational Phrase, the final rising tone of the Accentual Phrase is preempted by the tones of the higher level, the Intonational Phrase boundary tone. For example, the last syllable of the last Accentual Phrase can be realized with a low tone when the sentence is uttered as a declarative or with a super-high tone when the sentence is uttered as an interrogative regardless of the tonal pattern of the Accentual Phrase.

Figure 2.1 is a pitch track of a sentence *nəmuna məsinnɨn jəŋinɨn miun jəŋmiɾil miwəhe.* ('Too handsome Youngi hates ugly Youngmi.') showing the tone patterns for the two levels. There are two Intonational Phrases with the HL Intonational Phrase boundary tones (HL%) after the subject noun phrase, *jəŋinɨn*, and after the main verb, *miwəhe*. Here, each Intonational Phrase consists of two Accentual Phrases, {nəmuna} and {məsinnɨn jəŋinɨn}, marked by the F0 rising with a sharp fall contour corresponding to the last syllable of the phrase. The latter Accentual Phrase {məsinnɨn jəŋinɨn} has two lexical words, an adjective, /məsinnɨn/, and a head noun, /jəŋinɨn/. This is also true for the first Accentual Phrase in the second Intonational Phrase, {miun jəŋmiɾil}= /miun/ ('ugly') and /jəŋmilɨl/ ('Youngmi-ACC'). But there is no tonal marking for word boundaries as there is for the Accentual Phrase boundaries. H.Y. Lee (1990), even though he didn't show any experimental results, also proposed a hierarchical structure of Seoul intonation but his analysis is not entirely comparable with ours because he adopts the British intonation model developed by O'connor and Arnold (1973).

As noted in many earlier studies of Seoul intonation (e.g., Martin (1954), W. Huh (1963), H.B.Lee (1964), S.B. Cho (1967) and H.Y.

Lee (1990)), the pattern of the Intonational Phrase final boundary tone is very important because an utterance can have different meanings (speech act, style, and speaker's attitude) depending on the tonal pattern of the boundary tone such as rise, fall, rise-fall, rise-fall-rise, or level tone, etc.. For example, the low boundary tone of [pap məgəs'ə] (pap 'rice' + məgəs'ə 'ate') can make the utterance a declarative sentence, meaning 'I ate rice', while the high boundary tone can make an interrogative sentence, meaning 'Did you eat rice?'. The boundary tone also conveys contrastive attitudinal meanings: the low tone sounds 'definitive' and the high tone sounds 'surprised or interested', etc. Those early studies relied exclusively on auditory observations, they were not based on any instrumental work and do not agree completely with each other. Martin (1954) proposed 7 intonation morphs such as Period intonation, Comma intonation, and Question-mark intonation, etc., while H.B. Lee (1964) proposed 3 static (a perceptually level pitch) tones and 17 kinetic (a gliding pitch) tones (9 uni-directional tones and 4 bi-directional tones and 4 tri-directional tones). S.B. Cho (1967) proposed 12 directional intonational forms (4 unidirectional, 4 bidirectional and 4 tridirectional forms) with three levels of voice range.

Koo (1986) is the first acoustic study of Seoul intonation based on pitch track analysis. He identifies 5 different patterns : (1) rise (2) rise-fall-rise (3) rise-fall (4) level and (5) fall from monosyllabic utterances, and three terminal tonal variations : (1) rise-fall (2) large rise-large fall (3) rise from various sentences. However, since what is relevant in this thesis is the grouping into Intonational Phrases, not the paradigmatic contrasts among different tonal patterns at the boundaries, I will not go into the details of inventory of the different tonal patterns.

Koo also identifies the basic pattern of a phrase final rising for what he called 'a minor phrase'. His minor phrase seems to correspond to the Accentual Phrase in my model. As will be shown later in this chapter, the Accentual Phrase is the lowest prosodic level that can be redefined in terms of the intonation pattern of an utterance. Its position within the prosodic hierarchy is lower than the Intonational Phrase; thus it occupies the same place as the Phonological Phrase proposed in the theory of Prosodic Hierarchy. However, since this prosodic unit in my model is defined based on its tonal pattern, I will call this prosodic unit an *"Accentual Phrase"*. In the next section, I will discuss the tonal pattern of the Accentual Phrase in Seoul dialect.

2.1.2 The tonal pattern of Seoul Accentual Phrase[1]

The surface tonal pattern of the Seoul Accentual Phrase (= Koo's minor phrase) differs depending on the number of syllables within the Accentual Phrase. In Accentual Phrases with one or two syllables, the observed melody is LH or rise (Koo's pattern 1); in Accentual Phrases with three or more syllables, the observed melody is LHLH (= rise-fall-rise; Koo's pattern 2). Figure 2.2 shows pitch tracks of five sentences in (1) where the first phrase has a different number of syllables.

(1) a. {na-nin}   {jəŋa-ril}   {miwəh-e} => 'I hate Younga'
       'I-TOP'   'Younga-ACC' 'to hate-DEC'
    b. {jəŋmi-nin}   {jəŋa-ril}   {miwəh-e}
       'Youngmi-TOP' 'Younga-ACC' 'to hate-DEC'
       => 'Youngmi hates Younga'
    c. {jəŋman-inin}   {jəŋa-ril}   {miwəh-e}
       'Youngman-TOP' 'Younga-ACC' 'to hate-DEC'
       =>'Youngman hates Younga'
    d. {jəŋman-ine-nin}   {jəŋa-ril}   {miwəh-e}
       'Youngman-family-TOP' 'Younga-ACC' 'to hate-DEC'
       => 'Youngman's family hates Younga'
    e. {jəŋman-i+əmma-nin}   {jəŋa-ril}   {miwəh-e}
       'Youngman-GEN+mom-TOP' 'Younga-ACC' 'to hate-DEC'
       => 'Youngman's mom hates Younga'

The five sentences were digitized and saved with the same duration as the longest sentence, i.e. (a,b,c,d) has the same length as (e) to see the tonal pattern of Accentual Phrase with different number of moras. That is, the X-axis covers the same time range for all five pitch tracks. A long-dashed vertical line marks right after the second syllable and a short-dashed vertical line marks the end of each Accentual Phrase. As we can see, the first Accentual Phrase in (a) and (b) shows only the final LH rising pattern, whereas the first Accentual Phrase in (c) has a small initial peak in addition to the final rise and this peak is bigger in (d) and even bigger in (e).

Thus it seems that the tonal pattern of the Accentual Phrase is realized only as a rising contour when the phrase is short as in (a) and (b), but realized as a rise-fall-rise contour (=LHLH) when the phrase is longer than three or four syllables[2]. In this case, the initial High is not as high as the final High tone. When uttered fast, five-syllable-accentual phrase may not have the initial high tone. But, the initial high still appears in fast speech when the accentual phrase gets heavier in terms of the number of syllables. Since all the Accentual Phrase

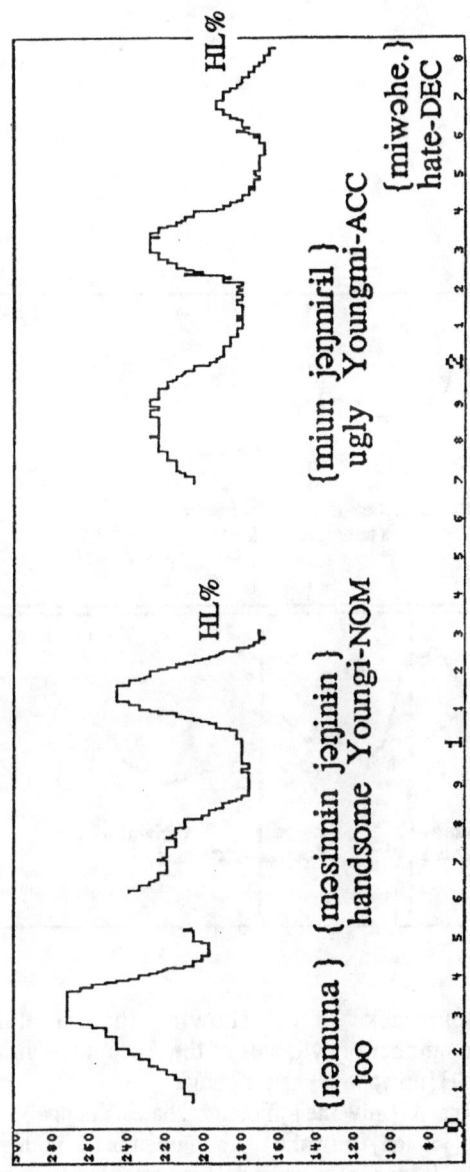

Figure 2.1. Pitch track of Seoul showing two Intonational Phrases with each 'I' having more than one Accentual Phrase: {nəmuna} {məsinnɨn jəŋinɨn} HL% {miun jəŋmiɾɨl} {miwəhe.}HL% - 'Too handsome Youngi hates ugly Youngmi.'

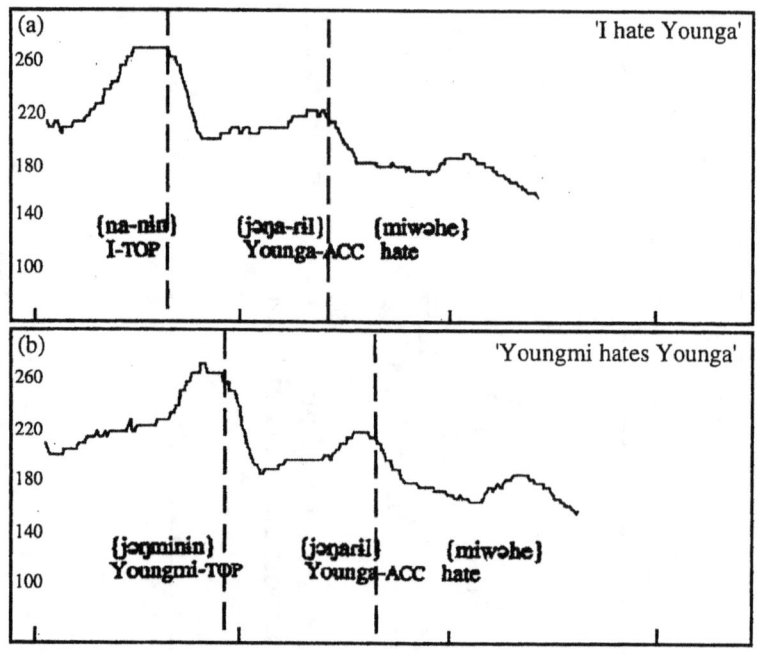

Figure 2.2. Pitch tracks of (1) showing the initial high tone depending on the number of syllables of the Accentual Phrase.
(a) {nanɨn}{jəŋaɾil}{miwəhe} 'I hate Younga'
(b) {jəŋminɨn}{jəŋaɾil}{miwəhe} 'Youngmi hates Younga'
(c) {jəŋmaninɨn} {jəŋaɾil}{miwəhe} 'Youngman hates Younga'
(d) {jəŋmaninenɨn}{jəŋaɾil}{miwəhe} 'Youngman's family hates Younga'
(e) {jəŋmaniəmmanɨn}{jəŋaɾil}{miwəhe} 'Youngman's mom hates Younga'

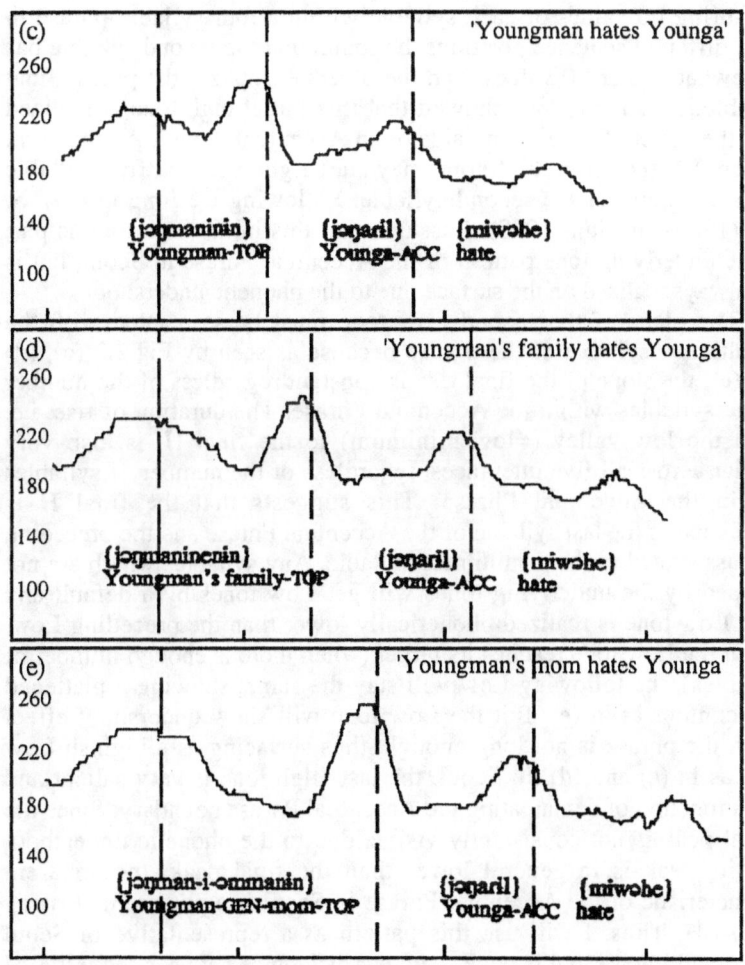

Figure 2.2. (continued)

starts with a L tone, the first Low tone would be associated with the first syllable of the phrase but the next High tone seems to be loosely associated with the second syllable of the phrase, thus being realized when there is enough time to reach the target but not when the phrase is short. As can be shown by the long-dashed vertical line in Figure 2.2 (c, d, e), the initial hump reaches its peak and starts falling right after the second syllable. Koo (1986) also noticed a similar fact: by measuring F0 values of each syllable within a four-syllable-phrase in three different sentence positions, he found that the second syllable has somewhat higher F0 values than the others except for the phrase final syllable. De Jong (1989) showed that this initial high tone is realized near the offset of the first syllable of an Accentual Phrase. As shown in Figure 2.2, the initial high tone may start right after the first syllable and stays high for the second syllable. Following De Jong (1989), S. Lee (1989) and Jun (1990), I assume that this initial high tone is part of the underlying tone pattern of the Accentual Phrase in Seoul, but is not always realized on the surface due to the phonetic undershoot.

The place of the second Low tone must be associated with the penultimate syllable of the phrase because as seen by Fig.2.2 (c), (d) and (e), the slope of the final rise is constant regardless of the number of the syllables within the Accentual Phrase. The duration of rise, i.e. from the low valley (=low minimum) to the final H, is also very similar across all five utterances, regardless of the number of syllables within the Accentual Phrase. This suggests that the final H is associated to the last syllable of the Accentual Phrase and the preceding L is associated to the penultimate syllable. Any syllables which are not mapped by the underlying tones will get Low tones by a default and each Low tone is realized phonetically lower than the preceding Low. When the Low tone reaches its target (when there is enough number of syllables), the following Low will stay the same, showing a plattened low contour as in (e). But the Low tone will show undershoot effect when the phrase is not long enough, thus surfacing as a highish Low tone as in (c) and (d). In Seoul, the last High tone is very salient and has a function of demarcating the Accentual Phrase boundary. Since the initial peak is not consistently visible due to the phonetic undershoot and its peak is in general lower than the final peak, the apparent characteristic of the Accentual Phrase in Seoul is a phrase final rising tone, LH. Thus, I will use this pattern as a representative of Seoul Accentual Phrase in this book. Another difference between the initial H and the final H lies on their slope of falling toward the following L tone. The falling slope of the first H to the following L is shallower as the number of syllables between the initial H and the final H increases,

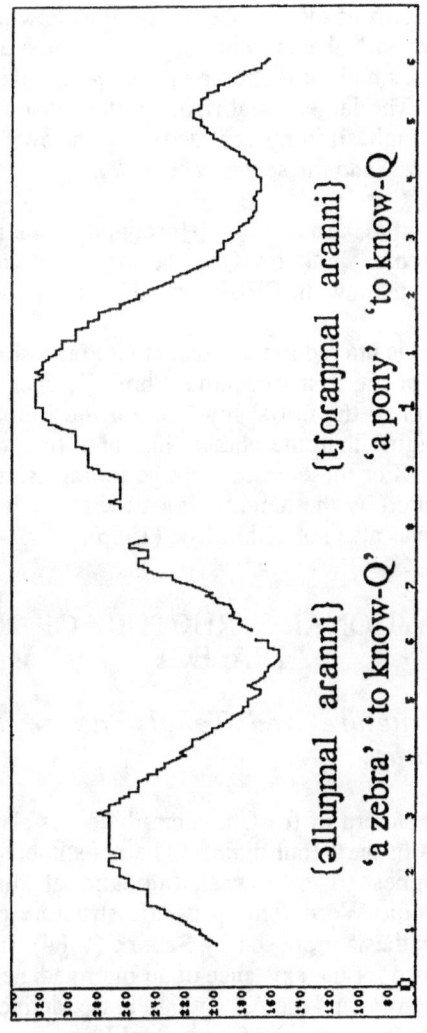

Figure 2.3. The large initial rising pattern of Seoul Accentual Phrase when the first word and the third word are contrastively emphasized. {əlluŋmal aɾanni} {tʃoɾaŋmal aɾanni}?

but the falling slope of the final H to the following L is constant since this L is the beginning of the following Accentual Phrase.

The tonal pattern of the last Accentual Phrase whose last syllable is also associated with the Intonational Phrase boundary tone shows two types: either a small initial hump or a large initial rise followed by a boundary tone. The large initial rising pattern can also be seen in a phrase which is emphasized by contrastive or narrow focus, and this is shown in Figure 2.3, and the sentence is in (2).

(2) {əlluŋmal aɾanni}   {tʃoɾaŋmal aɾanni}
     'a zebra' 'to know-Q'   'a pony' 'to know-Q'
= 'Did you know the ZEBRA or (did you) know the PONY?'

This sentence is uttered in two Accentual Phrases in this figure; the initial high tone of the first Accentual Phrase is even higher than the phrase final high and the initial low tone of the following Accentual Phrase is even higher than the phrase final high tone of the preceding Accentual Phrase. For these cases of large initial rising, the first High tone is not obscured by the neighboring Low tones. This tone pattern for an emphasis was also noticed in Koo (1986).

2.2 INTONATIONAL STRUCTURE OF CHONNAM DIALECT

2.2.1 *The Structure and Tonal Pattern of Chonnam Intonational Phrase*

The intonational pattern of the Chonnam dialect is also hierarchically organized just as in the Seoul dialect. The constituent prosodic levels are, from the highest to the lowest, Intonational Phrase, Accentual Phrase and Prosodic Word. This prosodic structure conforms to the Strict Layer Hypothesis proposed by Selkirk (1984). In previous work (Jun 1989), I argued for the existence of an Intermediate phrase between the Intonational Phrase and the Accentual Phrase, defined as the domain of downstep of the pitch range of Accentual Phrases. However, for the following reasons, I will not include this level as one of the constituents in the intonational structure of Korean; in Japanese and English, certain tonal sequences can trigger downstep within the Intermediate Phrase (Beckman and Pierrehumbert 1986, Pierrehumbert and Beckman 1988). That is, in Japanese, the presence of HL accent of an Accentual Phrase triggers downstep of the following phrase, while in

The Intonation and Prosodic Structure

English, the presence of the bitonal accent such as H*+L triggers downstep of the following pitch accent. However, in Chonnam, it is not by itself sufficient to determine whether or not a downstep will occur triggered by a tonal event. Furthermore, an Intermediate Phrase has never been found to serve as a domain of any segmental phonological rule, different from the other prosodic levels.

The Accentual Phrase in this dialect is similar to that in Seoul in that it is a prosodic level higher than the Prosodic Word and lower than the Intonational Phrase. But, the Chonnam Accentual Phrase differs from the Seoul Accentual Phrase in its tonal pattern which I will describe in the next section. Figure 2.4 is a pitch track showing the tonal patterns for the Accentual phrases within the Intonational Phrase, which are the same as those in the Seoul utterance in Fig. 2.1, {nəmuna}{mədinnɨn jəŋinɨn}HL% {miun jəŋmiɾil} {miwəhe}L%, but produced by a Chonnam speaker. (Both *mədinnɨn* and *məsinnɨn* are found in both dialects in free variation and the choice is speaker dependent.)

2.2.2 The Tonal Patterns of Chonnam Accentual Phrase

The tonal pattern of the Chonnam Accentual Phrase has two alternate forms: one is LHL and the other is HHL. This pattern is determined by the laryngeal feature of the phrase initial segment. If the segment has a [+constricted glottis], i.e. tense obstruents, or [+spread glottis], i.e. aspirated obstruents, the phrase has a HHL pattern, otherwise the phrase has a LHL pattern. Figure 2.5 illustrates this effect of segment on the tonal pattern of the Accentual Phrase.

Fig.2.5. shows fundamental frequency contours of three words uttered by a Chonnam speaker, *tallangtallang* -t^h*allangt^{h}allang* - *t'allangt'allang*. These three reduplicated onomatopoeic words have exactly the same segmental string except for the first segment of the base stem. Thus, any difference in their tonal pattern would be due to their different initial segment. These words have basically the same meaning with different connotations[3]. Generally, a tense consonant is associated with heaviness or tenseness of the sound/motion while an aspirated consonant with lightness of the sound/motion. Here, for example, 't^hallangt^{h}allang' is a lighter jingling sound, while 't'allangt'allang' is a heavier jingling sound. As we can see in this figure, the F0 contour is high at the beginning of t^h*allangt^{h}allang* which begins with an aspirated stop and *t'allangt'allang* , which begins

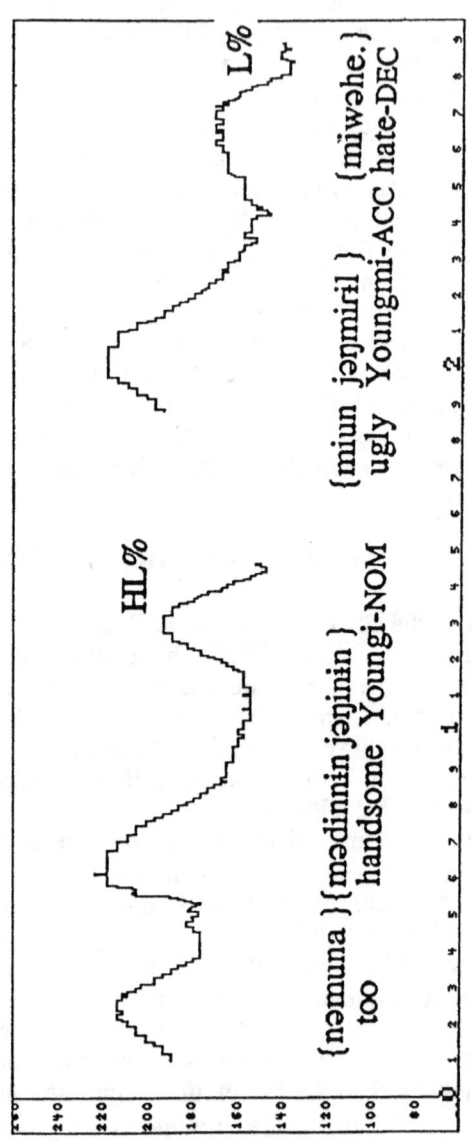

Figure 2.4. Pitch tracks of the same sentence used in Fig.2.1, produced by a Chonnam speaker. {nəmuna} {mədinnɨn jəŋinɨn} L% {miun jəŋmiril} {miwəhe.}L% - 'Too handsome Youngi hates ugly Youngmi.'

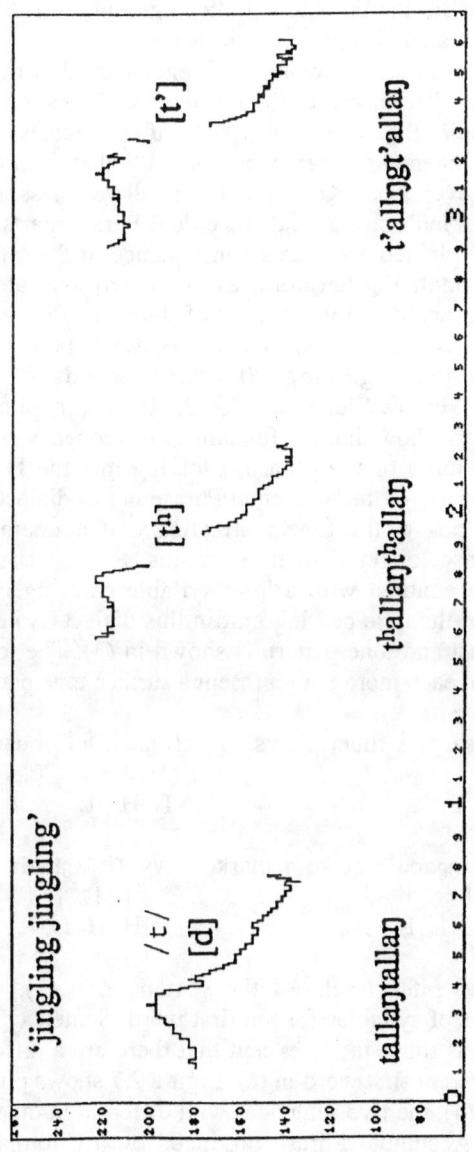

Figure 2.5. Pitch tracks of a triple pair of onomatopoeia "tallaŋtallaŋ -tʰallaŋtʰallaŋ - t'allŋt'allaŋ", meaning 'jingling' with different connotations.

with a tense stop. But the F0 is low at the beginning of *tallangtallang*, which begins with a lenis stop.

It is well known that consonants influence the F0 of the following vowel (House & Fairbanks, 1953, Lehiste & Peterson, 1961, Han 1963). For example, the vowel onset right after voiceless consonants has a higher fundamental frequency compared to that right after voiced consonants. However, since Korean stops are all voiceless, the fact that only the voiceless lenis stop initial Accentual Phrase starts with a low tone cannot be explained away as a consequence of the influence of a preceding consonant. Furthermore, even though aspirated or tense obstruents are observed to raise the F0 of the following vowel onset, this effect of a consonant on the following vowel's F0 is shown to be limited only to the beginning 20-40milliseconds of the vowel (Hombert, 1978, Han & Weitzman, 1970). However, pitch tracks of words by Chonnam show that the fundamental frequency remains high until the second mora of the phrase, showing that the H tone is the phonological property of the Accentual Phrase in this dialect.

Next, let's look at the tone realization of Chonnam Accentual Phrase in a phrase longer than three moras. Since Chonnam has a phonemic length contrast with a long syllable carrying two tones, I assume a mora as the tone bearing unit in this dialect. An example for the length contrast and tone pattern is shown in (3). The tones are not lexically linked to each mora but represent a surface tone pattern.

(3) a. tʃaaŋsa   'a funeral'   vs.   tʃaŋsak'un 'business man
     | | | | | | (derogatory)'
     LH L   L H   L

   b. ʃi itʃaŋgada 'go to a market' vs. ʃitʃaŋhada 'hungry'
     | | | | | | | | |
     HH L L L   H   H   L L

Figure 2.6 shows pitch tracks of the sentences in (1), which have different numbers of syllables for the first word. Sentences (a) through (e) are the same as those in (1) except that there are a different verbal ending and a different first word in (a). Figure 2.7 shows pitch tracks of the sentences in (4), the five sentences with different numbers of moras within the first Accentual Phrase produced by a Chonnam speaker. Sentences (a) through (e) have topic nouns beginning with /h/ so that the Accentual phrase has the HHL pattern instead of the LHL pattern.

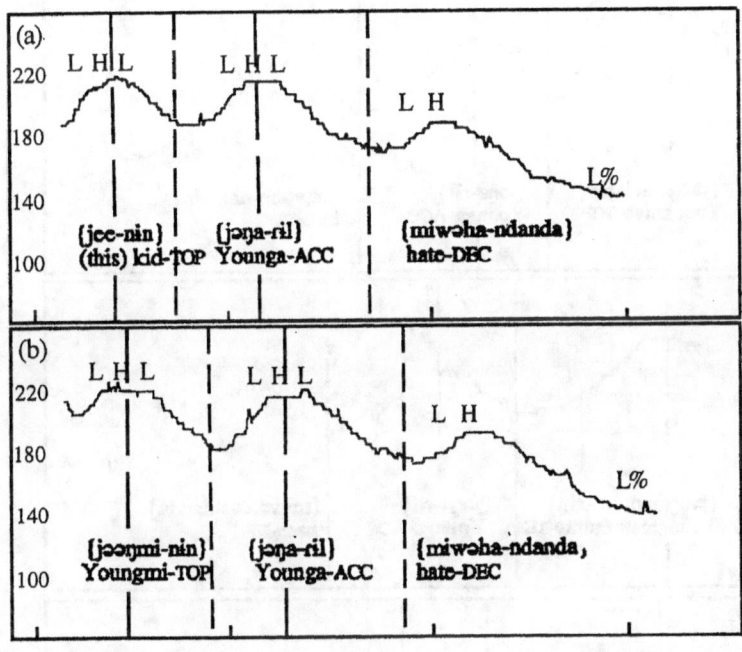

Figure 2.6. Pitch tracks of sentences with each Accentual Phrase having the LHL pattern.
(a) {jeenin}{jəŋaɾil}{miwəhandanda} - 3 moras
(b) {jəəŋminin}{jəŋaɾil}{miwəhandanda} - 4 moras
(c) {jəəŋmaninin} {jəŋaɾil} {miwəhandanda} - 5 moras
(d) {jəəŋmaninenin}{jəŋaɾil}{miwəhandanda} - 6 moras
(e) {jəəŋmaniəmmanin}{jəŋaɾil}{miwəhandanda} - 7 moras

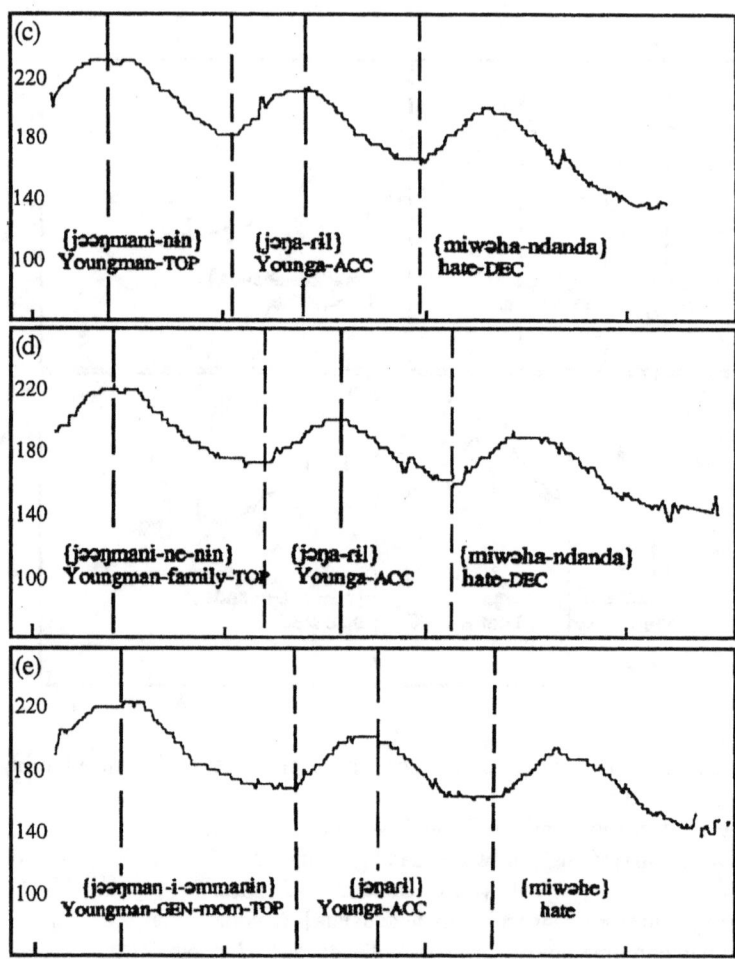

Figure 2.6. (continued)

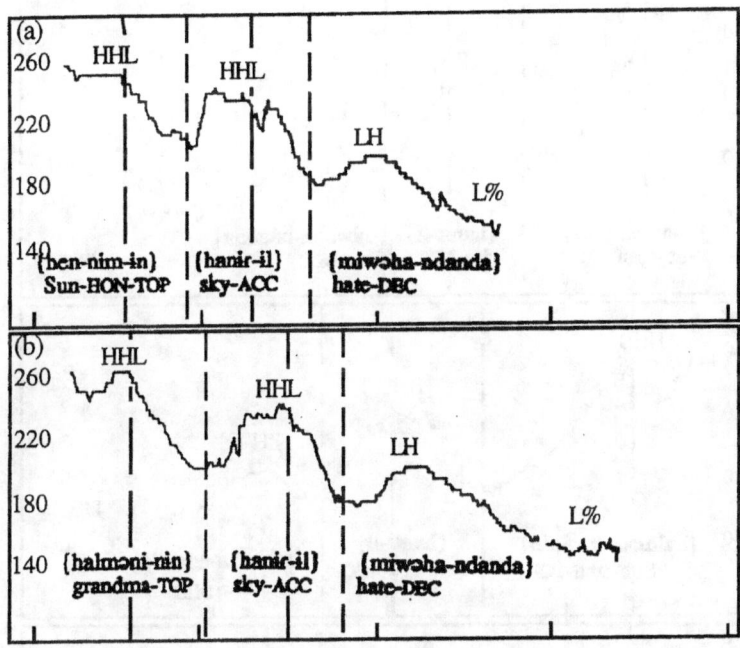

Figure 2.7. Pitch tracks of sentences with the first two Accentual Phrases having the HHL pattern.
(a) {hennimin}{haniɾil}{miwəhandanda} 'Sun hates the sky.'
(b) {halmərinin}{haniɾil}{miwəhandanda} 'Grandma hates the sky.'
(c) {halməniboda}{haniɾil}{miwəhandanda} '(He) hates the sky more than Grandma.'
(d) {halməniimonin}{haniɾil}{miwəhandanda} 'Grandma's aunt hates the sky.'
(e) {halməniimobunin}{haniɾil}{miwəhandanda} 'Grandma's uncle hates the sky.'

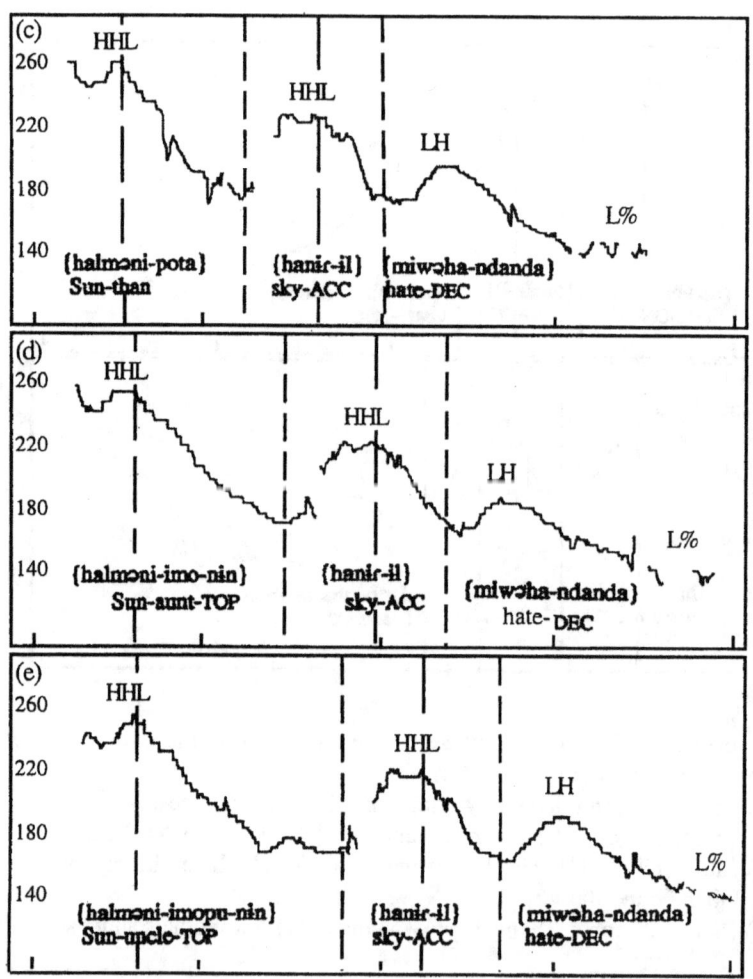

Figure 2.7. (continued)

As in the case of the Seoul Accentual Phrases in Fig. 2.5, all sentences were digitized and saved with the same duration as the longest sentence. That is, in both Fig.2.6 and Fig.2.7, the X-axis covers the same time range for (a) to (e).

(4) a. {hennim-in}{hanɨr-ɨl} {miwəh-andanda}
    'sun-TOP' 'sky-ACC' 'to hate-DEC'
    => 'Sun (honor.) hates sky'
b. {halməni-nɨn} {hanɨr-ɨl} {miwəhandanda}
    'grandma-TOP' 'sky-ACC' 'to hate-DEC'
    => 'Grandma hates sky'
c. {halməni-boda} {hanɨr-ɨl} {miwəh-andanda}
    'grandma-than' 'sky-ACC' 'to hate-DEC'
    => '(X) hates sky more than grandma'
d. {halməni+imo-nɨn} {hanɨr-ɨl} {miwəha-ndanda}
    'grandma+aunt-TOP' 'sky-ACC' 'to hate-DEC'
    => 'Grandma's aunt hates sky'
e. {halməni+imobu-nɨn} {hanɨr-ɨl} {miwəha-ndanda}
    'grandma+uncle-TOP' 'sky-ACC' 'to hate-DEC'
    =>'Grandma's uncle hates sky'.

In both Figures 2.6 and 2.7, each utterance has three Accentual Phrases and each Accentual Phrase has an initial rising pattern, either LHL or HHL, differing from the Seoul accentual pattern which is marked by a consistent final rising pattern. The rise-fall pattern of the first Accentual Phrase (the phrase with different number of syllables) looks roughly similar across the five utterances in Fig. 2.6., and differs primarily in how low the F0 gets flattens out in the longest ones. The HHL pattern of the first Accentual Phrases in Fig. 2.7. also looks similar in the same way as in the LHL pattern in that the rising and initial falling part is the same for all sentences. This phenomenon is different from the tonal pattern of Japanese utterances with unaccented Accentual Phrases (Pierrehumbert and Beckman 1988). In Japanese, the slope of the F0 fall from the Accentual Phrase initial peak to the low boundary tone on the last mora of the Accentual Phrase is negatively correlated to the number of the moras between the high peak and low boundary tone. But in Chonnam, the slope from the initial peak to the lowest F0 at the boundary is very similar across Accentual Phrases with a different number of moras except for the portion where it flattens out at the ends of the two longer cases. Thus, I assume that the second L is associated with the third mora of the Accentual Phrase and all the following moras within the Accentual Phrase get a Low tone by a default. But these low tones may not reach their target if there is not enough space, resulting in phonetic undershoot. This assumption is supported if we look at the F0 contour of the longest Accentual Phrase, i.e. the first Accentual Phrase in (e) in both figures. The F0 shows a low plateau for a while before the rise for the following Accentual Phrase.

2.3 KOREAN OBSTRUENTS WITH LARYNGEAL FEATURE SPECIFICATION

In order to state formally the choice of LHL versus HHL, I will describe the laryngeal characteristics of Korean obstruents. Korean obstruents have a three way phonological distinction in terms of laryngeal features, as shown in the table 2.1. I assume that both values of the laryngeal features are underlyingly specified.

Table 2.1. Korean obstruents with laryngeal feature specification

Type of obstruent	Laryngeal feature
tense or fortis obstruents [p', t', k', tʃ', s']	[+constricted glottis]
aspirated obstruents [p^h, t^h, k^h, tʃ^h, h, s]	[+spread glottis]
lax or lenis obstruents [p, t, k, tʃ]	[-constricted glottis], [-spread glottis]

Among the sounds categorized as the aspirated obstruents, [s] needs more attention because it has dual characteristics, classing with other lenis obstruents in some ways and with other aspirated obstruents in other ways. It behaves like the other lenis obstruents in that it becomes tensed after a lenis stop, by the Post-Obstruent Tensing rule, as can be seen in (5).

(5) /hakte/ => [hakt'e]   'abuse'
    /haktʃa/ => [haktʃ'a]   'scholar'
    /paktʃ^{h}a/ => [paktʃ^{h}a] 'a spur'
    /paksu/ => [paks'u].   'a clap'

On the other hand, it behaves like other aspirated obstruents in that it does not become voiced intervocalically by the Lenis Obstruent Voicing rule, as can be seen in (6).

(6) /kepaŋ/ => [kɛbaŋ] 'to open'
 /kjepʰi/ => [kjɛpʰi] 'cinnamon'.
 /kjesan/ => [kjɛsɑn] 'calculation'

Therefore, the status of /s/ is ambiguous in terms of its behavior with respect to the phonological rules. Even though Korean orthography, having only the tense counterpart of fricative but not the aspirated counterpart, assumes /s/ as a lenis obstruent, the fiberscopic data of glottal width over time suggest that the glottal gesture of /s/ is similar to that of other aspirated obstruents rather than that of the lenis stop, thus belonging to the aspirated obstruent with [+spread glottis] feature. Therefore, Kagaya (1974) claims, based on the laryngeal configuration of Korean obstruents, that Korean /s/ belongs with the aspirated consonants. Figure 2.8 is from Kagaya (1974). As can be seen in this figure, even though the timing of the glottal opening relative to the vowel onset (=fricative offset for /s/ or oral release for stops) is not the same, the size and duration of the glottal opening during /s/ is similar to those observed during aspirated stops. Also the glottis is not approximated during /s/ between voiced segments within a word while it is approximated (closed) during lenis stops between voiced segments, producing a voiced allophone. This laryngeal patterning of the /s/ with aspirated obstruents supports the claim that /s/ belongs to the aspirated obstruent category. Furthermore, the fact that the Chonnam Accentual Phrase beginning with /s/ has the HHL pattern as in the case of aspirated obstruent initial Accentual Phrase also supports /s/ being an aspirated obstruent.

2.4 FORMALIZATION

2.4.1. The Chonnam Dialect

For the Chonnam Accentual Phrase, when there are more than three moras in an Accentual Phrase, the tones are realized as LHL or HHL, where each tone is mapped to each mora of the Accentual Phrase from left to right and the fourth and the following moras are all realized as low tones. When there are two moras, the second mora has a falling tone (HL) and the first mora has either L or H depending on the

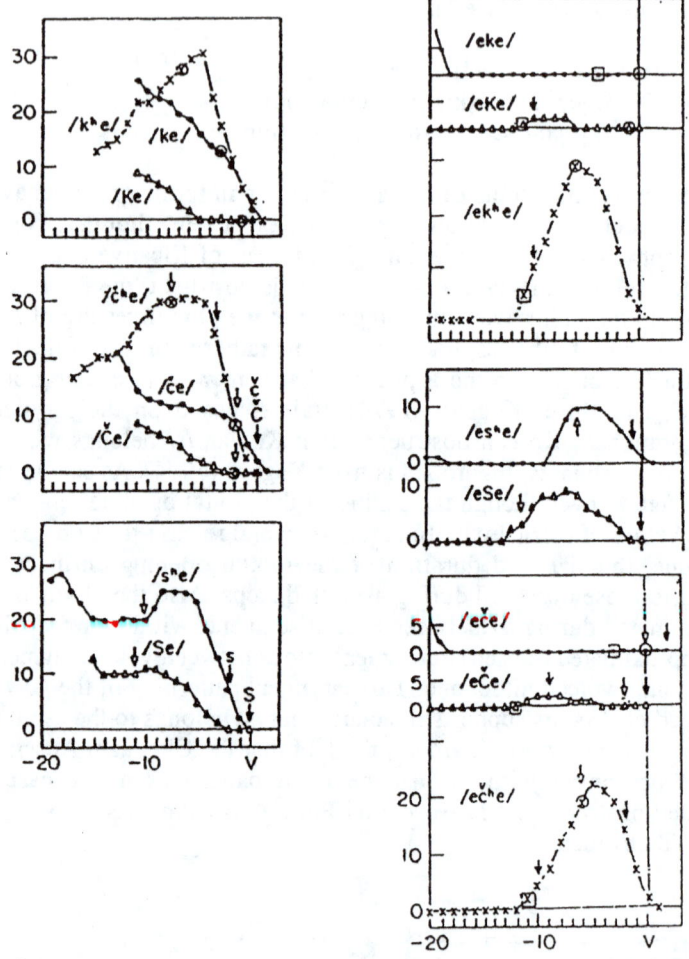

Figure 2.8. Glottal width over time (reproduced selectively from Kagaya's (1974) Figure 2 and 3). One frame on the X-axis corresponds to 20 ms and the Y-axis gives the apparent glottal width in an arbitrary scale. Empty circle : oral release; empty rectangular : oral implosion; empty triangle : frication onset; filled triangle : frication offset; and arrow : voice offset of the preceding vowel. In each case, the capital letter represents the tense obstruent and /č/ is equal to /tʃ/.

54

laryngeal features of the initial consonant. When there is only one mora, the single mora is realized as LHL, or as HL when the phrase has the relavant laryngeal feature.

Since the surface tonal pattern of an Accentual Phrase is always an initial rise (either by LHL or HHL) regardless of the number of moras, I assume the underlying tone melody is LHL or HHL, choise of which depends on the laryngeal feature of the phrase initial segment. The surface tone is realized following the Universal Association Convention (Goldsmith 1976). That is, one tone is mapped to one mora from left to right. When there are more number of tones than the number of moras, the extra tone(s) is mapped to the last mora, creating a contour tone. When there are more number of moras than the number of tones, the extra mora(s) is mapped to the last tone. (7) below shows the derivation of the surface tone for four mora Accentual Phrase and (8) shows the derivation of surface tone for two mora Accentual Phrase. The left column is for the LHL pattern and the right column is for the HHL pattern. The laryngeal feature of the first segment of the Accentual Phrase is not shown in the derivation. (α for an Accentual Phrase.)

(7) Tone Derivation

	{LHL}	{HHL}
UR	L H L	H H L
	$\alpha\{\mu\,\mu\,\mu\,\mu\}$	$\alpha\{\mu\,\mu\,\mu\,\mu\}$
mapping (l-to-r)	L H L | | |\\ $\alpha\{\mu\,\mu\,\mu\,\mu\}$	H H L | | |\\ $\alpha\{\mu\,\mu\,\mu\,\mu\}$

(8) Tone Derivation

	{LHL}	{HHL}
UR	L H L	H H L
	$\alpha\{\mu\,\mu\}$	$\alpha\{\mu\,\mu\}$
mapping (l-to-r)	L H L | |/ $\alpha\{\mu\,\mu\}$	H H L | |/ $\alpha\{\mu\,\mu\}$

When there is one mora, three tones are mapped to the single mora, thus having a surface tone of LHL or HL. In this case, the mora is often lengthened. When an Accentual Phrase is long with seven or eight moras, all moras after the third one are mapped to a L tone. In this case, the surface tones are not a flat low tone from fourth mora to the last mora, but gradually falling from the third mora towards the last mora by a constant degree. Detailed phonetic implementation rules, which are not within the scope of this book, will be needed for the application of this intonation model in speech synthesis.

2.4.2. The Seoul Dialect

For the Seoul Accentual Phrase, since long Accentual Phrases show a rise-fall-rise pattern, I will assume the underlying tone melody is LHLH. Since Seoul speakers do not have the length contrast phonologically, I assumed a syllable as the tone bearing unit in this dialect. As we have seen in Figure 2.2, two and three syllable Accentual Phrases both have a rising pattern, LH. By applying two rules in order, we can get the correct surface form. First, for all Accentual Phrases, we need a Final Two tone Mapping (9): the final two toens, LH, are mapped to the final two syllables of an Accentaul Phrase from right to left. Second, the Initial two tone Mapping (10) applies: the first two tones, LH, are mapped to the first two syllables of the Accentual Phrase from left-to-right.

When there is only one syllable, the phrase is realized with a rising tone, LH, as a result of (9). In this case, the syllable is very often lengthened. In the same way, two syllable Accentual Phrase has a rising tone pattern, LH; the initial syllable with a L tone and the final syllable with a H tone. When there are three syllables, we have two types of surface tone of an Accentual Phrase. One type is LLH and the other is LMH. The LLH surface tonal pattern is derived by mapping the final LH into the penultimate and fanal syllables (i.e. (9)) and by mapping the initial L into the initial syllable of an Accentual Phrase (i.e. (10)). That is, the second tone, H, is not realized because it is not mapped to any syllable. The LMH surface tonal pattern is derived by mapping the initial tone into the initial syllable and the second tone, H, into the second syllable which is already associated with the L tone as a result of (9). However, in this case, the second syllable is not realized with a contour tone but with a mid tone between the initial L and the final H tone due to phonetic undershoot. Thus, when the three syllable phrase is lengthened either due to by focus or speech rate, all four underlying

The Intonation and Prosodic Structure

tones are realized. In general, however, the initial hump (High tone) is realized on the surface when there are at least four syllables within the Accentual Phrase, reflecting its realization depends on the phonetic factors like undershoot. Finally, when the prhase is longer than four syllables, the syllable from the third until the antepenult will get the default Low tone; any toneless syllable is linked to a Low tone. The tones of syllables between the fourth and the penultimate, if there is any, will be realized by a default Low tone. Tonal derivations for three and five syllable Accentual Phrase are given in (11).

(9) Final Two tone Mapping (right-to-left) (FTM)
$$\begin{array}{c} L\ H\ L\ H \\ |\ \ | \\ ...\ \sigma\ \sigma\}a \end{array}$$
(σ: syllable, }a : right boundary of the Accentual Phrase)

(10) Initial Two tone Mapping (left-to-right) (ITM)
$$\begin{array}{c} L\ H\ L\ H \\ |\ \ | \\ a\{\sigma\ \sigma\ ... \end{array}$$

(11) Tone Derivation

	a. three syllable phrase	b. five syllable phrase
UR	{LHLH}	{LHLH}

FTM (9)	LHLH
	  | |
	α{ σ σ σ}
		LHLH
		    | |
		α{σ σ σ σ σ}

ITM (10)	L H L H | (\\) α{σ <u>σ σ</u>} (<u>σ</u> has a tone)	LHLH | | α{σσσ <u>σ σ</u>}
Default L	not applicable	L | α{<u>σ σ σ σ σ</u>}
Output	L LH or LHLH | | | | \\/| α{σ σ σ} α{σ σ σ}	L H L L H | | | | | α{σ σ σ σ σ}

Phonetically, the initial high tone is in general lower than the final high tone for a non-emphatic Accentual Phrase. The height of the initial tone is also dependent on the number of syllables within the Accentual Phrase and the F0 value of the phrase final High tone. Furthermore, the default L tones in the middle of the Accentual Phrase are getting lower towards the end of the phrase. To account for these phonetic difference, detailed phonetic implementation rules are needed.

2.5 THE INTONATION AND PROSODIC STRUCTURE

Since one Accentual Phrase can have more than one lexical item, a prosodic level corresponding to the Accentual Phrase is the Phonological Phrase proposed in Selkirk (1986) or Nespor and Vogel (1986), or Hayes (1989), etc. A prosodic level corresponding to the Intonational Phrase in this model is the same as the Intonational Phrase proposed by the Prosodic Phonologists, in that it is higher than the Accentual Phrase and lower than the utterance level. The domain of utterance is not defined in this model but I will use an utterance level meaning a string of segments which can contain one or more Intonational Phrases. Thus, the maximal utterance is not known. Furthermore, since I couldn't find so far any phonological rule in Korean applying across the Intonational Phrases, I will not include the utterance level in the prosodic hierarchy in Korean.

These prosodic levels in my model are similar to those proposed by the Prosodic Phonologists in that these levels conform to the Strict Layer Hypothesis. Thus the Intonational Phrase exhaustively dominates one or more Accentual Phrases. But this dominance relationship is not the result of bottom up prosodic structure building rules as assumed by other prosodic phonologists in their prosodic unit formation rules, but rather is due to the characteristics of the intonational phrasing. This is possible because the prosodic constituents in my model are not generated by a phrase building mechanism but is defined based on the output tonal pattern of an utterance. That is, when we produce an Intonational Phrase, the intonational contour includes the tonal pattern of the Accentual Phrase, even though the tonal pattern of the Accentual Phrase falls out from the phrasing. Thus, when the domain of the Intonational Phrase varies, small or large, due to focus or speech rate and so on (see Chapter 5), the different place of the Intonational Phrase boundary may affect the position of the Accentual Phrase relative to the Intonational Phrase. That is, the Accentual Phrase, once in the middle of the Intonational Phrase, may come at the beginning or the end of the

Intonational Phrase, or the other way around. And this variability in the intonational phrasing may affect the phonetic realization of the segment or syllable belonging to the right end boundary of the Accentual Phrase: a segment may be lengthened or shortened, and a syllable may carry a boundary tone, etc. An example is illustrated in (13). A sentence can be uttered in various intonational phrasings. We can produce each word as one Intonational Phrase as in (13a), or two words as one Intonational Phrase but with a different phrase boundary (%) as in (13b) and (13c).

(13) jəŋa-ga   uju-lɨl   tʃoahandejo
    'Younga-NOM'   'milk-ACC'   'to like-she says'
    = '(Younga says) she likes milk.'
    a. {jəŋaga}%{ujuɾil}%{tʃoahandejo}
    b. {jəŋaga}%{ujuɾil}{tʃoahandejo}
    c. {jəŋaga}{ujuɾil}%{tʃoahandejo}

Thus, {ujuɾil} can be at the beginning of the Intonational Phrase as in (13a,b) but at the end of the Intonational Phrase as in (13c). At the same time, the last syllable of {ujuɾil} will be lengthened and carry a boundary tone in (13a,c) but not in (13b).

Furthermore, since the Accentual Phrasing of a sentence also varies within the same Intonational Phrase, due to many factors as in the intonational phrasing, the intonational contour can be various for the same sentence leaving aside the various boundary tones. Thus, what is affected by varying the accentual phrasing is the intonational contour. In other words, the accentual phrasing is like pitch accent placement in English: The intonational contour is determined depending on where the pitch accent is associated within the Intonational Phrase. Example English sentence 'Marianna wants some milk.' with different pitch accent placement is shown in Figure 2.9 (Figure from Venditti et al. 1996) and Korean sentence, same as in (13), with different accentual phrasing within one Intonational Phrase is shown in Figure 2.10. Figure 2.9(a) has a nuclear accent on *milk* and (b) on *Marianna*, and (c) on both *Marianna* and *milk* with an intermediate phrase Low boundary tone after *Mariannna* marked by a vertical line in the picture.

Each of the three utterances in Figure 2.9 has a different Intonational Phrase contour with a different pitch accent type and different place of nuclear pitch accent. In Figure 2.10, each case has a different intonational contour not because each Accentual Phrase changed its tonal pattern but because the Accentual Phrase boundary changed. Therefore, the variability in a lower prosodic unit does not affect the structure of the higher prosodic unit, but the variability in a higher prosodic unit may change the organization of the lower prosodic units.

Finally, this model does not provide any tonal pattern specific to the prosodic word level. However, we can define the prosodic word as a minimum sequence of segments which can form the Accentual Phrase by itself. Most of time, the smallest unit which can form the Accentual Phrase is a lexical content word (N,V,A,Adv) plus any following suffix, case markers, postpositions, or clitics. (However, this definition does not work when we consider an utterance with a contrastive focusing on a part of a word. The Accentual Phrase relative to the narrow focus will be discussed in Chapter 6.) Thus, a prosodic level corresponding to the prosodic word in this model would be the same as the phonological word (and the clitic group proposed by Nespor and Vogel (1986) and Hayes (1989)) proposed by the prosodic phonologists.

The positing of this intonation-based prosodic structure is further supported by the fact that they serve as domains of several postlexical phonological rules and I will show in the following chapters that the accentual phase and the Intonational Phrase are domains of several phonological rules, and these domains defined based on the intonational structure can better account for the actual data than the syntax based domains proposed by other prosodic phonologists. The following table compares both positions in terms of the domains of each postlexical phonological rule I discuss in this dissertation.

The domain of Lenis Stop Voicing has been proposed by prosodic phonologists as the Phonological Phrase (=P-phrase) (i.e. Cho, 1987; Kang, 1990, 1992), defined based on the syntactic structure of a sentence, the left end of maximal projection. The domain of Post Obstruent Tensing was claimed to apply within the Phonological Word by Cho (1987) but within the Phonological Phrase by Kang (1992). However, as I will show in Chapter 4, the domain of these rules is found to be the Accentual Phrase defined based on the intonational structure of an utterance.

Table 2.2. Domain of postlexical phonological rules and prosodic theories: prosodic phonologists (syntax-based) vs. intonation-based model. (AP=Accentual Phrase, IP=Intonational Phrase, PP=Phonological Phrase, PW=Phonological Word)

Postlexical phonological rule	Domains of the rule	
	syntax-based	intonation-based
Lenis Stop Voicing	PP	AP
Post Obstruent Tensing	PW/PP	AP
V-Shortening (non-standard)	?	AP
Obstruent Nasalization	PP/IP	IP
Spirantization	?	IP
/s/-palatalization	?	IP

The domain of Obstruent Nasalization has been proposed by prosodic phonologists either as the Phonological Phrase (Cho, 1987; Kang, 1992) or as the Intonational Phrase (Kang, 1990). As will be shown in Chapter 4, however, it is found that the domain of Obstruent Nasalization is the Intonational Phrase larger than the Accentual Phrase. Finally, the domain of Vowel Shortening (for non Seoul dialects), Spirantization and /s/-palatalization has not been claimed by any prosodic phonologists; the domain of Vowel Shortening will be shown as the Accentual Phrase in Chapter 3, and the domain of Spirantization and /s/-palatalization will be shown as the Intonational Phrase in Chapter 4. In the next chapter, I discuss the Accentual Phrase level in my model and show that this prosodic constituent serves as the domain of at least three postlexical phonological rules.

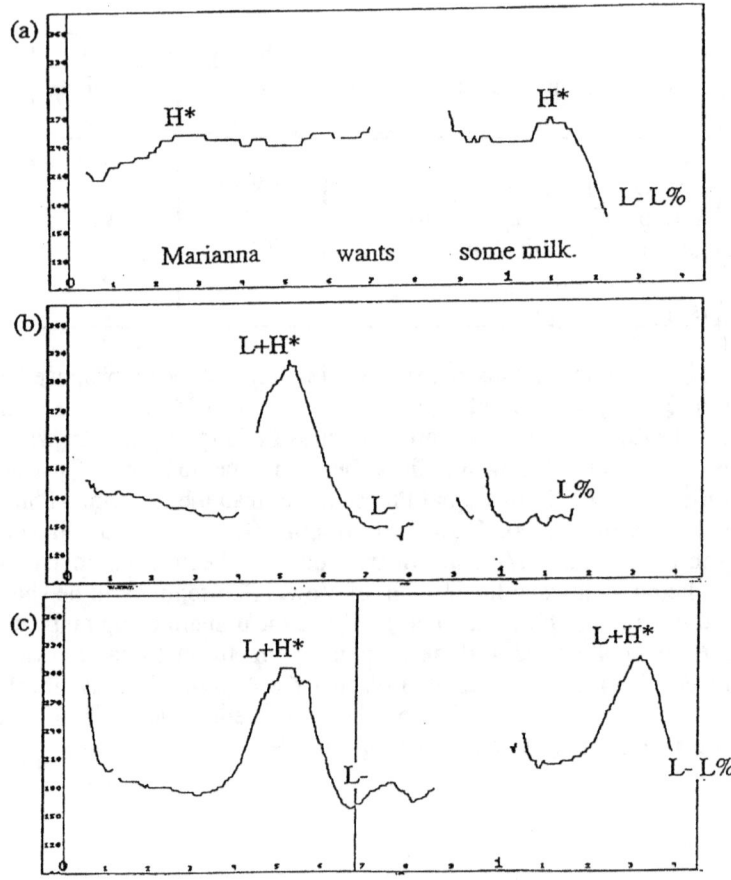

Figure 2.9. Pitch tracks of the English sentence 'Marianna wants some milk.' with different pitch accent placements: (a) with nuclear accent on *milk*, (b) with nuclear accent on *Marianna*, and (c) with a phrase boundary after *Marianna* and nuclear accent on both *Marianna* and *milk*. The L- is a L phrase accent, and the vertical line in (c) marks the medial intermediate phrase boundary.

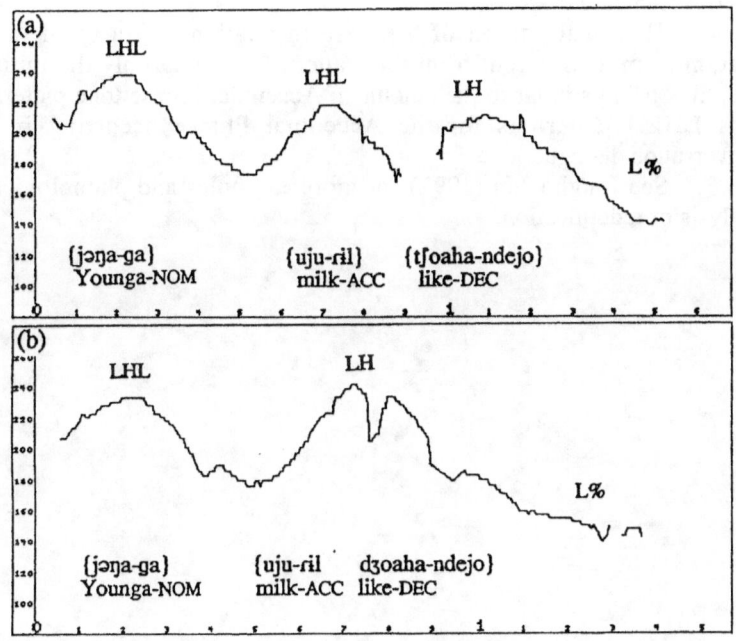

Figure 2.10. Pitch tracks of Korean sentence 'jəŋaga ujuɾil tʃoahandejo' in two different accentual phrasing uttered by a Chonnam speaker: (a) with each word forming one Accentual Phrase and (b) with the second and third word together forming one Accentual Phrase separately from the first word.

NOTES

1. In this thesis, the tonal pattern of Seoul Accentual Phrase is the generalization only based on a phrase beginning with a sonorant sound or a lenis obstruent. (This is also true for the previous studies of Seoul Accentual Phrase. e.g. Lee (1989), deJong (1989)) However, the results of an ongoing research show that Seoul also has an Accentual Phrase which begins with a High tone, i.e., HHLH, when the phrase initial segment is [+spread glottis] or [+constricted glottis] as in the case of the Chonnam dialect (Section 2.2.2) (see Jun 1995b, 1996). Pitch tracks of the same sentences as in (4) but uttered by a Seoul speaker is shown in the Appendix I as an example show the initial H toned Accentual Phrase.

2. The tonal pattern of a phrase in citation, i.e. a word in a citation form, is different from this pattern by having only the initial rise, thus being similar to the Chonnam Accentual Phrase tone pattern. This LHLH pattern is for the Accentual Phrase occurring in a conversation dialogue.

3. See Jongho Jun (1992) for more examples and phonological analysis of reduplication.

III

The Accentual Phrase

The Accentual Phrase is the lowest prosodic level that can be defined in terms of the intonation pattern of an utterance. Its position within the prosodic hierarchy is just below the Intonational Phrase, thus it is structurally the same level as the Phonological Phrase proposed in the theory of Prosodic Hierarchy. As mentioned above, the Phonological Phrase has been claimed to be the domain of several postlexical phonological rules in Korean (Cho, 1987, 1990; Kang, 1992; Silva, 1989, 1991, etc.). For example, the domains of Lenis Stop Voicing and Post Obstruent Tensing have been identified as the Phonological Phrase derived from the syntactic structure of a sentence: Cho(1990) proposed a phonological phrase based on Nespor and Vogel's relation-based prosodic theory and, Silva (1989, 1991) and Kang (1992) proposed a phonological phrase based on Selkirk's end-based theory.

However, informal observation suggests that the domain of these two rules (and of several postlexical phonological rules including Intersonorant /h/-deletion and Long vowel Shortening) are better predicted by the tonal pattern of the Accentual Phrase than by any syntax based algorithm for setting up the Phonological Phrase. That is, all of these syntax-derived approaches to prosodic phrasing predict part of the actual data, but they cannot predict many cases, especially phrasing *within* the maximal category.

Figure 1.2 in Chapter I was based on informal observations. In this chapter, I will describe a set of experiments that fleshes out these earlier informal observations with enough tokens to allow statistical tests of the two accounts.

One of the main results of the experiments is to show that the domain of Lenis Stop Voicing changes due to the non-syntactic or non-linguistic factors such as focus and speech rate. To explain such cases where the output result is different from that could be predicted by the Phonological Phrase formed based on the syntactic structure, Kang (1992) proposes the restructuring rule in (1).

(1) φ-Restructuring rule (Kang 1992:297)

a. A non-branching φ is adjoined to the following φ from left to right. Monosyllabic φ's undergo φ-restructuring more often than polysyllabic φ's.

φ(w( )) φ(w( )..... -> φ(w( ) w( )....

b. If a non-branching φ is followed by a branching φ, the first two ω's may form an independent φ and the remaining ω's form a separate φ.

φ(w( )) φ(w( ) w( ).... -> φ(w( ) w( )) φ(w( )....

c. Any φ containing prosodically prominent words (accented) remains intact.

d. There may be a speaker variation.

The conditions on branchingness or the number of syllables of a phrase in (1a, b) are intended to explain the weight effect on the phrasing and the prosodic prominence in (1c) is to explain the focus effect on the phrasing. However, since the restructuring rule is optional and she provides no guideline for predicting when the rule applies, the predictability of the Phonological Phrase of an utterance is very weak under her formalism based on the syntax.

This problem of restructuring may not arise if we define the phonological phrase based on the tonal pattern, which is the Accentual Phrase, because the Accentual Phrase is the output generated by a speaker influenced by all these non-syntactic factors. But my model will have the same problem as Kang's optionality because we still cannot predict what the accentual phrasing of a given sentence would be. We can only provide possible factors affecting the accentual phrasing or intonational phrasing and provide a syntactic constraint which makes it possible to predict all possible accentual phrasings, good or bad, of a given sentence (see Chapter 5).

My hypothesis is that the grammar can generate φs of different sizes (speakers pick which possible φs to use depending on speech rate and other non-syntactic factors), and assigns a tonal melody to each φ. Thus, I will use the F0 patterns of utterance as diagnostics to determine where φs begin and end. I will show that φs determined in this way account for the data concerning the domain of several phonological rules better than the Phonological Phrase suggested by Cho, Silva and Kang, among others. And furthermore, I will show that the number of the Accentual Phrases changes depending on speech rate; the faster, the fewer the Accentual Phrases within an utterance. Since the domain of the Accentual Phrase changes due to speech rate, the varying domain of phonological rules due to speech rate can be easily explained.

The organization of this chapter is as follows. In Section 3.1, the results of the first experiment showing the domain of the Lenis Stop Voicing rule will be discussed. In Section 3.2, other phonological rules whose domain is the Accentual Phrase, i.e., Post Obstruent Tensing and Vowel Shortening, will be discussed based on more informal observation.

3.1 EXPERIMENT 1: LENIS STOP VOICING

3.1.1 Introduction

It has long been known that the slightly aspirated voiceless stops (or lenis stops) in Korean become voiced intervocalically within a word (Lisker and Abramson, 1964; Kim, 1965; Keating et al., 1983). More recently Cho (1987), Silva (1989, 1991) and Kang (1992) have claimed that, in the Seoul dialect of Korean, the domain of this effect is actually larger: lenis stop voicing happens within the Phonological Phrase but not across Phonological Phrases. Since the Chonnam dialect is the same as Seoul in its syntactic structures (even though it differs from Seoul in its intonation patterns and by some lexical items), the domain of voicing, if we follow their analysis, should be the same for both dialects: it should be the Phonological Phrase as determined by one or the other account of the syntax/prosody mapping.

Since both the Accentual Phrase and the Phonological phrase are a prosodic level higher than the prosodic word but the domain defined by the Accentual Phrase is not always the same as that defined by the Phonological phrase, I designed an experiment to find out whether the domain of lenis stop voicing in both dialects is indeed larger than the prosodic word and if so, whether the domain is the phrase determined by the tonal pattern, my Accentual Phrase or the phrase determined by the syntactic structure, Cho, Silva and Kang's Phonological Phrase.

A formal description of their Intervocalic Obstruent Voicing is shown in (2).

(2) [-son, -voice] -> [+voice] / ϕ(.. [+voice]__[+voice] ..)

That is, Intervocalic Obstruent Voicing is a postlexical phonological rule whereby a voiceless obstruent becomes voiced between voiced segments within a phrase, marked by ɸ. Or, in an autosegmental representation as in (3), [+voice] feature from a voiced segment spreads to the laryngeal node of the following intersonorant consonant (figure from K. H. Kim 1987).

(3)

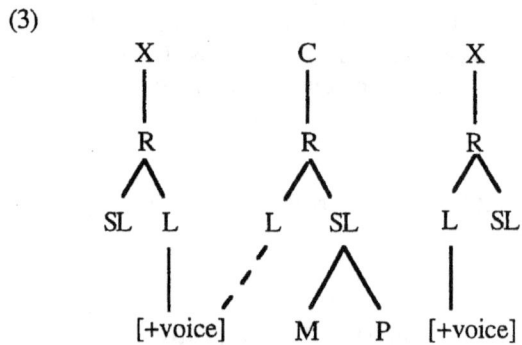

(C: Consonant, X: Skeletal tier, C or V

R: Root, M: Manner, P: Place

SL: Supralaryngeal, L: Laryngeal)

However this rule should be called Lenis Stop Voicing because it is shown by the experiment that there are cases where lenis affricate is not voiced intervocalically even within a word and also intervocalic fricatives, /s/, are rarely voiced within a word (see Jun, 1990b). Thus, the voicing status of the lenis affricate is not reliable in terms of this rule. The formal description of Lenis Stop Voicing is shown in (3). (α is for the Accentual Phrase.)

(3) | -continuant |
    | -const. glot. | -> [+voice] / α(.. [+voice]__[+voice] ..)
    | -spread glot. |

3.2.2 Methods

3.1.2.1 Subjects

Three male and two female speakers of the Chonnam dialect and two male and one female Seoul speakers participated in this experiment.

They were in their twenties. Chonnam speakers C1 and C2, one male and one female, had lived in Kwangju, the main city of Chonnam province, for 26 years and in the United States for about 3 years (C2 is the author). Chonnam speaker C3 had lived in Kwangju for 19 years and moved to Seoul and lived there for 7 years until he came to the States. He had been in the United States for 6 months. This subject sometimes showed a mixed intonation pattern between Chonnam and Seoul intonation. Therefore, to elicit the Chonnam intonation, I talked with him in the Chonnam dialect for about 30 minutes before recording, and gave contexts which included many lexical items typical of the Chonnam dialect for the test phrases and sentences. Chonnam speakers C4 and C5 were in their early twenties and had never been in the United States. All three Seoul speakers, S1, S2 and S3, were born and raised in Seoul and they were in their late twenties and had been in the United States for about half a year.

3.1.2.2 Material

Thirty-five phrases or sentences with various syntactic structures were selected. Most of these were taken from Cho's (1987) and a few from Silva's (1989) corpus of examples but the sentence-final endings were modified somewhat to accord with either Chonnam or Seoul conversational usage in order to get a more natural (colloquial and informal) speech style instead of a reading style. There were also additional sentences or phrases which I devised to test Cho and Silva's predictions. Altogether the corpus included 82 words whose initial segments are lenis obstruents occurring in sentence medial position. These were used to examine whether a lenis obstruent becomes voiced across word boundaries. Each subject was asked to read the phrases or sentences in his or her natural intonational phrasing as if talking to someone in a conversation. To help them produce a conversation style, the test phrases are often embedded in an interogative sentence. For one example, subjects were asked to read the sentence in a specific phrasing intended by the experimenter. In this case, the corresponding meaning was given to help the appropriate phrasing.

The full corpus is given in Table 3.1, in a broad phonetic transcription (in IPA symbols) with word-medial intervocalic lenis obstruents transcribed as voiced. (The material was presented to the subjects in *hangul*.) The word initial lenis obstruents that I examined for voicing are underlined (65 words). The verbal endings given here are the Seoul dialect ones. Corresponding Chonnam renderings were given to Chonnam speakers, but are not shown here.

For each example sentences, the Phonological Phrases predicted by Cho (1990), Silva (1989) and Kang (1992) are marked by {} underneath the glosses. 'All' means that the phrasing given is consistently predicted by all three. For example, the embedded clause in 1 in Table 3.1 is from Cho (1987). By all three accounts, VP of the embedded sentence, ([PP+V] in this example) forms one Phonological Phrase (P-phrase in Cho's term), thus, the PP initial [p] of [paŋ-e] should remain voiceless but the V-initial [t] of [tɨrəgaʃingə] should be voiced. In case when the predicted phrasing is different among them, their name is given separately on the left. Thus, for example, in #12, the voicing status of the relative clause verb initial /p/ or the head noun initial /k/ will differ depending on each account. For #3, the whole phrase is an NP, and thus forms one Phonological Phrase, so the word initial lenis stops of [kojaɲi] 'a cat' and [palmok] 'an ankle' should be voiced, and only the absolutely phrase initial [k] of [kəmɨn] should remain voiceless. The NP phrase in #4 is the same string of words as in #3, but with a different internal structure. Different meanings were given corresponding to the different structures. It was expected to put the Accentual Phrase boundary between *kəmɨn* and *kojaɲi-e*. (The intended phrasing is marked by { } on the example.) That is, in order for the adjective, 'black', to modify the last noun 'the ankle' but not the immediately following noun 'the cat', the preceding adjective is produced in a separate Accentual Phrase. Phrasings of the rest of the sentences or phrases are not specified or given, but each subject choose his or her own phrasing.

Table 3.1. Example Phrases in the Lenis Stop Voicing Experiment

1. [s[NP + VP[PP + V]]+ VP]
    abədʒi-ga   paŋ-e   tɨrəgaʃingə   pwannji?
All :{   }   {   }   {   }   {   }
    'Father-NOM   a room-DAT   to enter-REL   to see-past-int. (Q)'
    => 'Have you seen Father entering the room?'

2.   abədʒi   kabaŋ-e   tɨrəgaʃi-ngə   pwannji?
All :{   }   {   }   {   }   {   }
    'Father-NOM   a bag-LOC   to enter-honor.-REL   to see-past-Q'

3. NP[NP[Adj + N]-gen + NP]
    kəmɨn   kojaɲi-e   palmok => 'the ankle of the black cat'
    {kəmɨn   gojaɲi-e} {palmok}
All :{   }
    'black' 'a cat-GEN' 'an ankle'

4. NP[AP + NP[N-gen + NP] => 'the black ankle of the cat'
   {kəmɨn}{kojaɲi-e balmok}

5. Kjəŋman-iga   tʃal   kat'a.
   All :{   } {   }
      'Kyəŋman-NOM well   to go-past' ==> 'Kyəŋman went safely.'

6. Kjəŋman-iga   tʃal   kat'a.
   All :{   } {   } {   }
      ==> 'It's good for us that Kyəŋman left.'

7. kɨt'e Seoul-esə pon   kɨ   kɨrim-i   katʃ'a-radənde
   All:{   } {   } {   } {   }
      'then Seoul-LOC to see-REL that a picture-NOM fake-they
                                                         said-decl.'
      ==> 'They said the picture (we) saw at Seoul then was fake.'

8. ne   kɨrim-i   tʃeil   nat'adənde
   All:{   } {   }
      'my   a picture-NOM   very   best-they said-decl.'
      ==> 'They said my picture was the very best.'

9. tʃatontʃʰa-hago   kɨrim
   All :{   } {   }
      'a car-and   a pitcure'   ==> 'a car and a picture'

10. kɨgən   adʒu   tʃoɨn   kɨrim-ija
    All :{   } {   } {   }
      'that-NOM   very   good   a picture-decl.'
      ==> 'That is a very good picture.'

11. kɨ   tʃoɨn   kɨrim
    All:{   }
      'the   good   a pitcure' ==> 'the good picture'

12.   Kisu-ga   pon   kɨrim
    Cho: {   } {   }
    Silva: {   } {   }
    Kang: {   } {   } {   }
           'Kisu-NOM   to see-REL   a picture' ==> 'a picture Kisu saw'

13.   Kisu-ga   kɨɾin   kɨɾim-il   pwannɨnde,
Cho: {   }   {   }   {   }
Silva: {   }   {   }   {   }
Kang: {   }   {   }   {   }
       'Kisu-NOM   to draw-REL   a picture-ACC   to see-past-and,

            tʃəŋmal   tʃal   kɨɾjət'ənde.
All :   {   }   {   }
         really   well   to draw-past-decl.'
==> '(I) saw a picture Kisu drew and it was really well drawn.'

14.   na   abədʒi-ga   tʃuʃi-n   kɨɾim   pogois'əs'ə.
Cho : { } {   }   {   } {   }
Silva: { } {   } {   } {   } {   }
Kang : { } {   } {   } {   }   {   }
       'I   Father-NOM   to give-HON-REL   a picture   to look at-
                                                              past prog.'
==> 'I was looking at the picture Father gave to me.'

15.   na   abədʒi-ga   toŋseŋ-hantʰe   tʃuʃi-n   kɨɾim   pogois'əs'ə.
All : { } {   } {   }   {   } {   }
       'I   Father-NOM   brother-DAT   to give-HON-REL   a picture
                                                    to look at-past prog.'
==> 'I was looking at the picture Father gave to my brother.'

16.   ke-ga   tʃa--ni
All : {   }   {   }
       'a dog-NOM   to sleep-Q'   ==> 'Does the dog sleep?'

17.   ke-ga   kɨ-ni
All : {   }   {   }
       'a dog-NOM   to crawl-Q'   ==> 'Does the dog crawl?'

18.   kɨ   kɨɾim   tʃemog-i   adʒu   tʃoin   tʃandi-ɾe
Cho: {   } {   }
Silva: {   }   {   } {   } {   }
Kang: {   } {   }
       'the a picture a title-NOM   very   good   lawn-they say'
==> 'They say the title of the picture was "very good lawn".'

The Accentual Phrase 73

19. Kjəŋsu-ga   ton   padin-gə   pondʒəginni?
    All: {   } {   } {   }
    'Kyəŋsu-NOM   money   to receive-REL   to see-experience-Q'
    ==> 'Have you seen Kyəŋsu received money?'

20. Kjəŋsu-hanʰe   ton   tʃu-ngə   pondʒəginni?
    All: {   } {   } {   }
    'Kyəŋsu-DAT   money   to give   to see-experience-Q'
    ==> 'Have you seen someone gave Kyəŋsu money?'

21. uɾi sənseŋnimin Suni-hanʰe   tʃəmsu-ɾil   tʃal tʃu-ningəgatʰ-e.
    All: {   } {   } {   }{   }
    'our teacher-NOM Suni-DAT   a score-ACC   good to give-is
                                                          likely-decl.'
    ==> 'It seems to be that our teacher gives a good score to Suni.'

22. pabil   tʃadʒu   məgəɾa.
    All: {   } {   }
    'rice-ACC   often   to eat-imperative.'
    ==> 'Eat (your) rice often!'

23. isaŋhage kojaɲi-ga ul-go   ke-ga   tʃisədedəɾa
    All: {   }{   } {   } {   } {   }
    'strangely   a cat-NOM   to cry-and   a dog-NOM   to bark-habitual-
                                                              decl.'
    ==> 'Strangely, a cat has been crying and a dog has been barking.'

24. nə   kojaɲi   palbin   kaɲadʒi   pəltʃu-n   pabo   pwanni?
    All: {   } {   } {   } {   }
    'you   a cat   to step on-REL   a puppy   to punish-REL   a fool
    to see-Q'
    ==> 'Have you seen a fool who is punishing a puppy which
          stepped on a cat?'

25.   Kjəŋsu-nin   pimat-k'oinnin   kojaɲi-ɾil   pwat'e
    Cho/Silva: {   } {   } {   }
    Kang :   {   } {   }   {   }

    'Kyəŋsu-NOM   to be in the rain-REL   a cat-ACC   to see-past.'
    ==> 'They said Kyəŋsu saw a cat in the rain.'

26. na   indʒesa   tʃʰegɨl   tugwən   pwas'ə
All: { }   {   }   {   }   {   }
    'I   now   a book-ACC two   to read-past.'
    ==> 'I now just read two books.'

27. na   indʒesa   tʃʰek   tugwənɨl   pwas'ə
All: { }   {   }   {   }   {   }
    'I   now   a book   two-classifier to read-past.'
    ==> 'I now just read two books.'

28. jədʒa-ga   tu-mjən   tʃinaga-nɨnde
All: {   }   {   }   {   }
    'women-NOM   two-people   to pass by-prog.'
    ==> 'There are two women passing by.'

29. jədʒa   tu-mjən-i   tʃinaga-nɨnde
All: {   }   {   }   {   }
    'women   two-people-NOM to pass by-prog.'
    ==> 'There are two women passing by.'

30.   pap   is'ə.
Cho/Kang:{   }   {   }
 Silva :   {   }
        'rice   to have' ==> '(We) have rice. or (Do you) have a rice?'

31.   abənim   kjesjə / kjesini
Cho/Kang: {   }   {   }
 Silva : {   }
        'Father-honor.   to be-honor.-decl./Q'
        ==> 'Father is inside (or at home)./ Is Father home?'

32. Kosənseŋnim-i   kjesjə/kjesini
All: {   }   {   }
    'Ko teacher-honor-NOM   to be-honor.-decl./Q'
    ==> 'Teacher Ko is inside./ Is Teacher Ko inside?'

33.   abenim   kjesimnik'a?
Cho/Kang: {   }   {   }
 Silva : {   }
        'Father-honor.   to be-honor.-Q'

34.   Kosənseŋnim-i   kjesimnik'a?
All: {   }   {   }
        'Ko teacher-honor-NOM   to be-honor-Q'
        ==> 'Is Teacher Ko inside?'

35.   tʃaŋnjən-e   pjənsan-esə   po-n   kədʒi-ga   kjelhonh-et'e
All: {   } {   }   {   }   {   } {   }
      'last year-in' 'Pyunsan-at' 'to see-REL' 'a beggar-NOM to
                                                              marry-past'
      ==> 'The beggar (we saw) at Pyunsan last year married.'

3.1.2.3 Procedure

For subjects other than C4 and C5, the recording was made in the sound booth of the Linguistics Department of Ohio State University. For these two Chonnam subjects, the recording was made in the sound booth of the Language Research Center of Chonnam National University, Kwangju, Korea. Subjects were given the list of 35 sentences or phrases in *hangul*. In order to get the natural intonational phrasings, subjects were asked to read the list as if they were talking to someone. The list was repeated three times at three self-selected rates, normal, slow, and fast. Utterances were blocked by rate.

In order to ascertain more directly the intended voicing of a stop, an Electroglottograph (henceforth EGG) recording was made (Laryngograph BS5724/ IEC601-1). For EGG, a high frequency electrical current is passed through the larynx, between electrodes placed on the neck surface on the left and the right sides. The electrical impedance (resistance) between the electrodes depends on the glottal area, being small when the vocal folds are pressed firmly against each other and large when the folds are completely separated.

To get EGG data, the EGG band was held tightly around the subject's neck while the subject was reading. The audio wave and EGG signals were simultaneously tracked and digitized. The two signals were separated and viewed synchronically. For every lenis obstruent position, the two signals were examined for sinusoidal periodicity, indicative of voicing. The voicing status of each lenis obstruent was ascertained independently from the audio and the EGG signal. Almost all of the time, the two signals agreed in voicing status: either both showed periodicity or neither did. Figure 3.1. shows sample traces for each type of case.

In this figure, (a) and (b) are from the same utterance of the sentence (4-1) above phrased as {abədʒi-ga} {paŋ-e dɨrəgasiŋgə} {pwannja}. For each picture, the upper two windows are for the audio signal and the lower two windows are for the synchronized EGG signal. The second and the fourth windows are expanded views beginning from the small tick points in the first (audio wave) and the third (EGG wave) window, respectively. The X-axis indicates the time dimension and the Y-axis the amplitude of signal. In Figure 3.1 (b) the /k/ of [abədʒi-**ga**] is shown to be voiced by both the audio and EGG signals — note the periodicity in both signals — whereas in Fig.3.1 (a), the main verb initial lenis stop, /p/, is voiceless, as shown by the lack of periodicity in both audio and EGG waveforms in the second and fourth window.

There were a few cases when the EGG and audio signals disagreed; mostly the audio shows voicing while EGG shows voicelessness. Figure 3.2 shows Audio and EGG waveforms of the example sentence {jouŋsu-nɨn} {<u>h</u>egjəŋi-rɨl} {tʃoahe} (jouŋsu-nɨn 'Youngsu-NOM' + hegjəŋ-irɨl 'Hekyung-ACC' + tʃoahe 'to like') => 'Youngsu likes Hekyung'. The second and fourth window show the waveform around the underlined /h/; voiceless EGG and voiced audio waveform. As we can see, the EGG signal shows weak low-amplitude vibrations for an open glottis while the audio signal shows high-amplitude vibrations continuously through the /h/.

It is already noticed in the literature that the same glottal configuration can produce voiced or voiceless sounds depending on the vocal tract function and air pressure difference. That is, when vocal folds are abducted and supraglottal air pressure is higher due to some constriction within a vocal tract, then vocal folds might not vibrate and a voiceless sound occurs. On the other hand, when there is a high subglottal air pressure and the vocal tract is open, then vocal folds can vibrate while abducted, as in the murmured or breathy [ɦ].

Thus, for those few cases where EGG showed voiceless and audio waveform showed voicing (such cases amounted to about 2% of the overall data (out of 2925 tokens), I assumed the EGG signal to indicate the speaker's intention, since it can give information about glottal adduction and abduction unfiltered by the vocal tract.

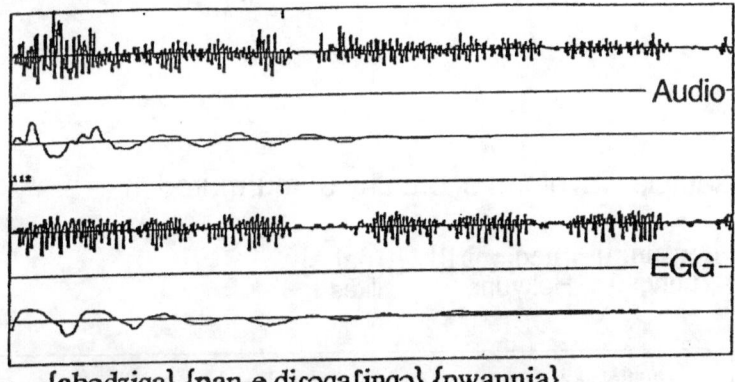

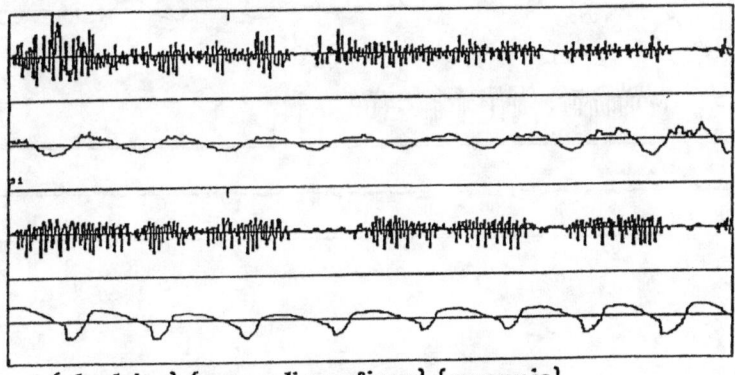

Figure 3.1. Audio & EGG waveforms: (a) When both are voiceless (b) When both are voiced

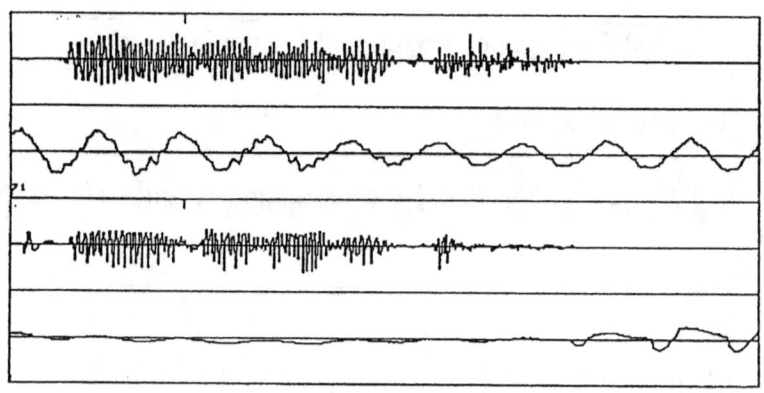

Figure 3.2. Audio and EGG waveforms of *jəŋsunin hegjəɲiril tʃoahe*. The first and the second windows are audio waveforms and the third and fourth window are EGG waveforms. The first window in audio and EGG waveforms shows the whole sentence and the second window of each waveform shows the expanded waveforms around underlined part of the sentence.

3.1.3 Results and Discussion

3.1.3.1 Accentual Phrasing and Lenis Stop Voicing

Accentual Phrase medial lenis stop

Figure 3.3 is the pitch track and audio and EGG waveforms for /kəmɨn kojaŋi-e palmok/, 'the ankle of the black cat', uttered by a Chonnam speaker, C2. The F0 track indicates that only one Accentual Phrase was uttered by this speaker in this instance, because there is only one F0 peak near the beginning for the initial LHL. As would be predicted, both Accentual Phrase medial lenis stops have been subjected to the Lenis Stop Voicing rule, and are voiced. This is clearly shown by the circled parts in both the audio and EGG waveforms. This pattern is what is predicted by Cho (1987, 1990), Kang (1992) and Silva (1989, 1991).

Accentual Phrase initial lenis stop

Figure 3.4 shows the pitch track and audio and EGG waveforms of the same noun phrase /kəmɨn kojaŋi-e palmok/, broken into three Accentual Phrases as {kəmɨn} {kojaŋie} {palmok} — each word forms a separate Accentual Phrase — shown by three F0 peaks for the whole phrase. Since this sentence has the same syntactic structure as that shown in Figure 3.3 above, the voicing of the lenis stop should be the same by the prosodic phonologists' prediction. That is, both noun phrase internal lenis stops — the /k/ of /kojaŋi/ and the /p/ of /palmok/ — should be voiced as they are in Fig.3.3. However, as we can see by the breaks in the F0 track just before the F0 peaks in the pitch track, when the sequence is produced as three Accentual Phrases, the word initial lenis stops are all voiceless at the Accentual Phrase initial position. The voicelessness of /k/ is also shown by the circled part of the EGG and Audio waveforms under the pitch track. This result suggests that the domain of lenis stop voicing cannot be the syntax-determined phonological phrase. Rather, the voicing depends on the accentual phrasing.

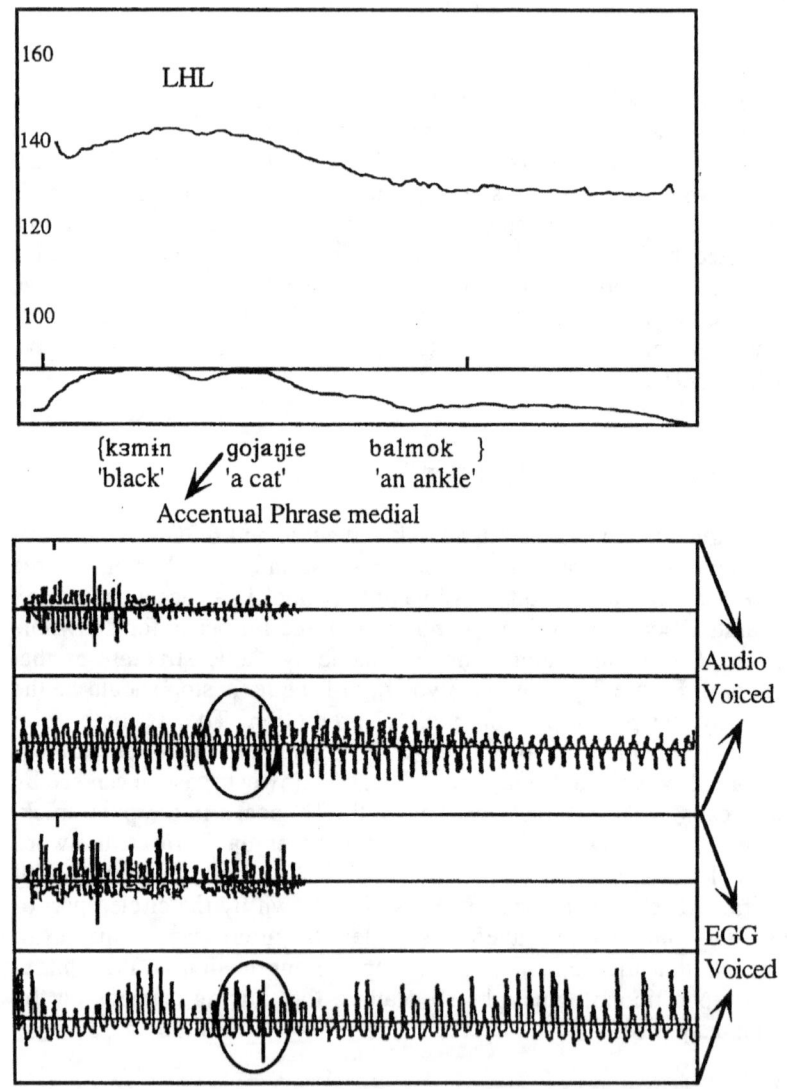

Figure 3.3. Pitch tracks of *kəmin kojaɲie palmok* 'a black cat's ankle' uttered in one Accentual Phrase by C2. Audio & EGG waveforms show a voiced /k/ of *koyaɲie* at the Accentual Phrase medial position.

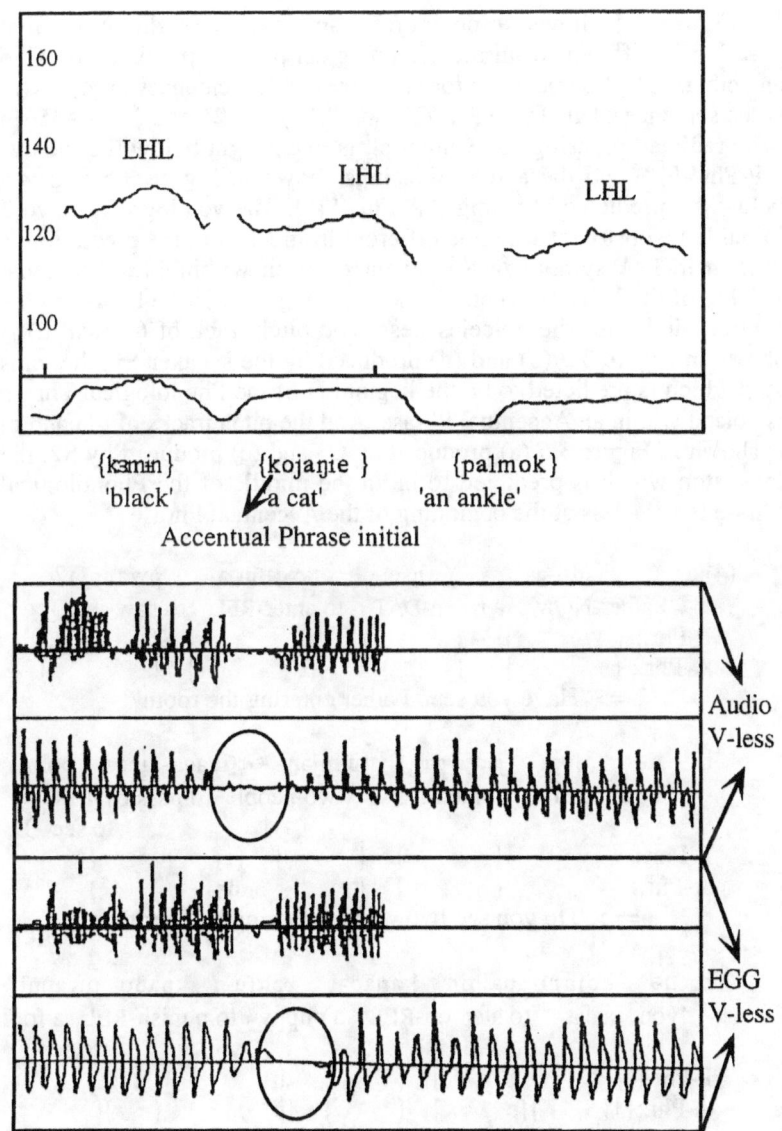

Figure 3.4. Pitch tracks of *kəmin kojaɲie palmok* 'a black cat's ankle' uttered in three Accentual Phrases. Audio & EGG waveforms show a voiceless /k/ of *kojaɲie* at the Accentual Phrase initial position.

Counter-examples to Cho, Silva and Kang's Phonological Phrasing

Figure 3.5 shows some more examples where the Accentual phrasing is different from the Phonological phrases predicted by Cho and others. The F0 tracks are for utterances of the sentences in (4) — (a) is the sentence #1 in Table 3.1, (b) is #28, (c) is # 24 and (d) is #35. In (4), predicted phrasings by Cho et al. is given right below the glosses ("P-Phr.-{ }") and the actual phrasings shown in Figure 3.5 is given below the predicted phrasing ("A-Phr.-{ }"). The voicing of the word initial lenis obstruent which is different from Cho et al.'s prediction is written in IPA symbol in a relevant position within { }. The actual voicing of the lenis obstruent is shown in Figure 3.5: the breaks in the F0 track indicates the voicelessness. The pitch track of (4b and d) is shown in Figure 3.5 (b) and (d) produced by the speaker S1; the lenis stop which is predicted to be the beginning of the Phonological Phrase is voiced within an Accentual Phrase. And the pitch tracks of (4a and c) is shown in Figure 3.5 (a) produced by C3 and (c) produced by S2; the lenis stop which is predicted to be in the middle of the Phonological Phrase is voiceless at the beginning of the Accentual Phrase.

(4) a.   abədʒi-ga   paŋ-e   tɨrəgaʃingə   pwannja?
'Father-NOM a room-DAT to enter-REL to saw-int.Q'
P-Phr.: {   } {   d   } {   }
A-Phr.: {   } {   } {t   } {   }
=> 'Have you seen Father entering the room?'

b. nə   tʃəgi   jədʒa-ga   tu-mjəŋ   tʃinaga-ningə poini
'You' 'there' 'women-NOM two-people to pass by-REL
                                                to see-Q'
P-Phr.:   {   } {   } {tʃ   }
A-Phr.:   {   } {   }   dʒ-   }
==> 'Do you see two women passing by over there?.'

c. nə   kojaŋi   palbɨn   kaŋadʒi   pəltʃu-n   pabo pwanni?
'you a cat   to step on-REL a puppy to punish-REL a fool
                                                  to see-Q'
P-Phr.:{ }{   b   } {   b   } {   }
A-Phr.:{ }{   }{p   } {   } {p   } { }{   }
==> 'Have you seen a fool who is punishing a puppy which stepped on a cat?'

```
     d.  tʃaŋnjən-e    pjənsan-esə     po-n      kədʒi-ga    kjelhonh-et'e
         'last year-in'  'Pyunsan-at'  'to see-REL'  'a beggar-NOM
                                                              to marry-past'
P-Phr.:{            } {                    } {k       }{                    }
A-Phr.:{            } {                       g       }{                    }
     ==> 'The beggar (we saw) at Pyunsan last year married.'
```

In general, the EGG and audio waveforms showed that the lenis stop is voiced in Accentual Phrase medial position but voiceless at the beginning of an Accentual Phrase. The Accentual Phrasing of a sentence, however, is not so straightforwardly predictable. Even though each subject shows his or her own preferred phrasing patterns, the phrasing of the same sentence is not always the same even for different utterances by the same speaker. Syntax does influence the phrasing, as we would predict from the observations that led to Cho's, Kang's and Silva's claims. However, other factors such as speech rate, focus and the length of the phrase must be taken into account as well to explain the tendencies in the accentual phrasing. Before I discuss the effect of rate on the Accentual Phrase and, therefore, on the lenis stop voicing, I will present in more detail the data from the five Chonnam speakers showing the effect of phrasing on the lenis stop voicing.

<u>Status of lenis stop voicing at different prosodic positions for normal rate.</u>

Table 3.2 shows the distribution of the voicing categories for word initial lenis stops for both the Accentual Phrase initial and medial position for normal rate tokens. For each speakers, a total of 195 tokens (three repetitions of 65 words) were examined for the voicing as observed in both EGG and audio signal. Each token of a word initial lenis stop was categorized as either clearly voiced, clearly voiceless, or ambiguous. Ambiguous cases are ones either where the signal showed such weak vibration that the decision was difficult or where vibrations ceased partway through the closure. The value in each cell indicates the number of voiced or voiceless tokens based on the EGG signal. The numbers in parenthesis are based on the audio signal. The number of phrase initial versus phrase medial tokens differs from subject to subject because subjects differed in their Accentual Phrasings: some speakers tend to put more Accentual Phrase boundaries and others tend to put fewer.

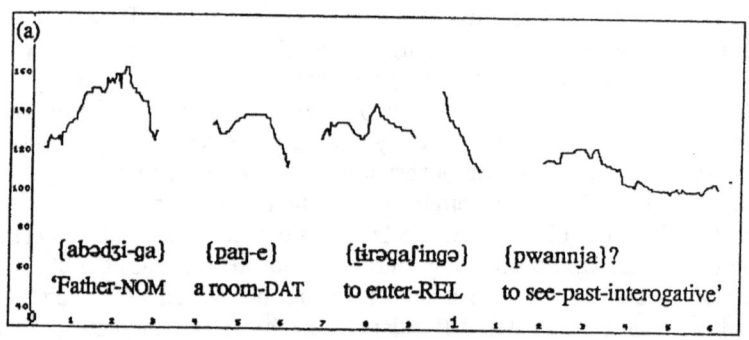

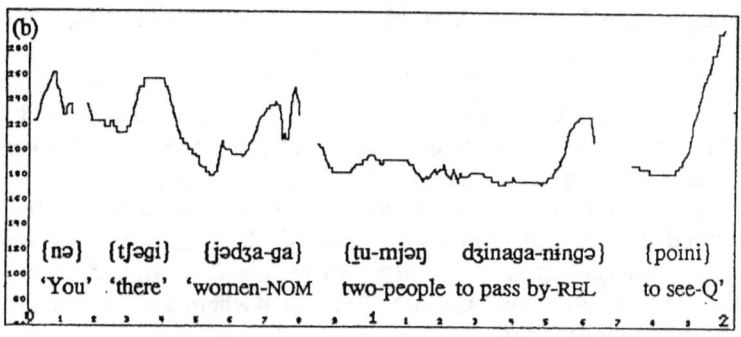

Figure 3.5. Pitch track of (a) #1 by C3 and (b) # 28 by S1 (c) # 24 by S2 and (d) # 35 by S1. (a) {abədʒi-ga}{paŋ-e}{tirəgaʃingə}{pwannja}? => 'Have you seen father entering the room?' (b) {nə}{tʃəgi}{jədʒa-ga}{tu-mjəŋ dʒinaga-nɨngə}{poini}? ==> 'Do you see two women passing by over there?.'

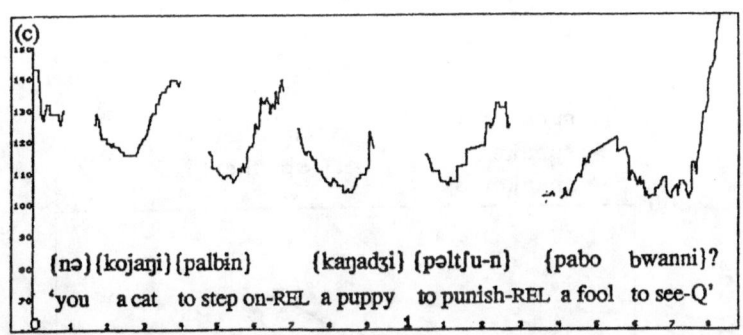

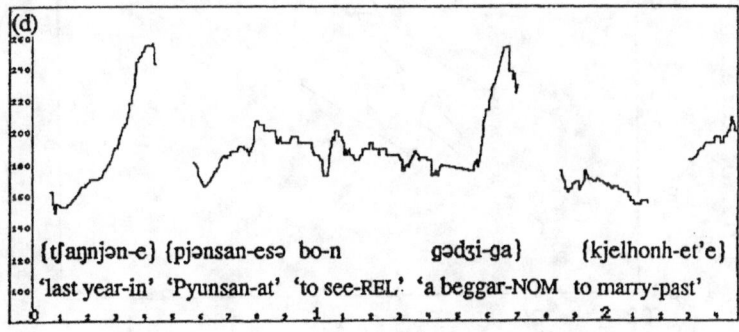

Figure 3.5. (continued)
(c) {nə}{kojaŋi}{palbin}{kaŋadʒi}{pəltʃu-n }{pabo}{pwanni}? => 'Have you seen a fool who is punishing a puppy which stepped on a cat?' (d) {tʃaŋnjən-e}{pjənsan-esə bo-n gədʒi-ga}{kjelhonh-et'e} => 'The beggar (we saw) at Pyunsan last year married.'

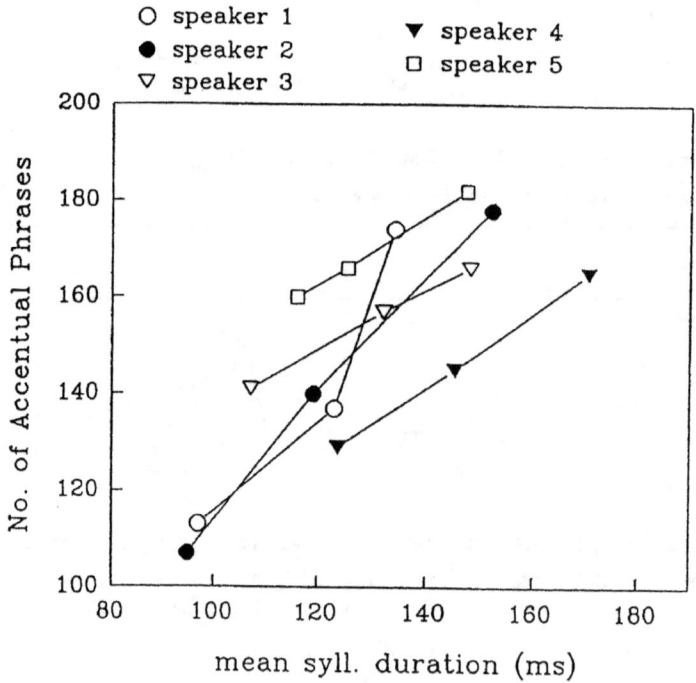

Figure 3.6. The number of Accentual Phrases against the mean syllable duration (in ms) for five subjects. Three points in each line indicate three self-selected speech rate.

Table 3.2. The Voicing Status of the Word Initial Lenis Stop at the Accentual Phrase Initial and Medial Position for 5 Chonnam Speakers

Subj	Accentual Phrase initial			Accentual Phrase medial		
	Clearly Voiced	Ambi-guous	Clearly V-less	Clearly Voiced	Ambi-guous	Clearly V-less
C1	1 (1)	11 (6)	125 (124)	36 (33)	8 (11)	0 (0)
C2	0 (1)	2 (2)	138 (137)	45 (45)	3 (3)	1 (1)
C3	2 (2)	6 (4)	149 (151)	11 (11)	2 (2)	0 (0)
C4	3 (3)	1 (3)	140 (136)	44 (40)	5 (10)	2 (3)
C5	8 (9)	5 (5)	153 (152)	20 (21)	3 (2)	0 (0)

As the table shows, the word initial lenis stop is rarely voiced in Accentual Phrase initial position while it is rarely voiceless in Accentual Phrase medial position. This is also true for the two Seoul speakers, S1 and S2. The third Seoul speaker, S3, showed a very different pattern: she produced each word so deliberately that most of lenis stop were voiceless even within a word. For this subject, it seemed that the Lenis Stop Voicing rule does not exist at all. Except for S3, it is clear that the Accentual Phrasing influences the voicing of the lenis stop.

3.1.3.2 Rate Effect on the Lenis Stop Voicing

Table 3.3 shows the voicing status of the word initial lenis stop at fast and slow rate for five speakers. Each number is the frequency of the voiced or voiceless lenis stop combining Accentual Phrase initial and medial tokens. Again, the numbers in parenthesis are based on the audio waveform data.

Table 3.3. Voicing Status of the Word Initial Lenis Stop at Fast and Slow Rate Combining Accentual Phrase Initial and Medial Tokens.

Subj	Fast rate			Slow rate		
	Clearly Voiced	Ambi-guous	Clearly V-less	Clearly Voiced	Ambi-guous	Clearly V-less
C1	70 (70)	15 (8)	94 (97)	18 (18)	2 (5)	173 (170)
C2	81 (81)	15 (27)	97 (85)	8 (9)	11 (9)	169 (170)
C3	28 (28)	12 (12)	132 (132)	13 (13)	1 (0)	165 (166)
C4	65 (66)	8 (11)	122 (118)	30 (28)	4 (5)	160 (161)
C5	32 (41)	16 (9)	147 (145)	10 (12)	4 (4)	179 (177)

As shown in the table, fast rate utterances tend to have more voiced word initial lenis stop tokens and slow rate utterances tend to have more voiceless ones. But this does not mean the lenis stop voicing is not a phrasal rule. There is an interaction between phrasing and rate.

To show the relationship between phrasing and rate, I calculated the mean syllable duration for each rate by measuring a whole or part of a sentence for each speaker and divided by the number of syllables. The mean results are shown in Figure 3.6. The speakers differ in the actual rates (mean syllable duration) for the three self-selected nominal rates. However, the speakers are alike in that, within each speaker, the number of Accentual Phrases increases as he or she speaks more slowly. This tendency is very clear for all subjects. The slower the rate, the larger the number of Accentual Phrases. This indicates that subjects tend to put more Accentual Phrase boundaries when they speak slowly, while, at fast rate, they tend to produce a longer sequence of segments as one Accentual Phrase. Thus, speech rate influences the formation of Accentual Phrases, and therefore, the lenis stop voicing.

3.1.3.3 Rate and Phrasing and Lenis Stop Voicing

It was shown above that voicing of lenis stop is sensitive to speech rate and Accentual Phrasing. It was also shown that there is an interaction between speech rate and phrasing. Since the number of phrases decreases at fast rate, the number of phrase initial lenis stop also decreases at fast rate, and so does the number of clearly voiceless lenis stops. However, it is not always the case that speech rate affects the lenis stop voicing only indirectly by affecting the number of Accentual Phrases. It also affects the lenis stop voicing even for the same accentual phrasing. That is, even though the lenis stop is almost always voiceless at Accentual Phrase initial position, it is sometimes voiced there at the faster rate. The voicing status of lenis stops only at phrase initial position is shown in Table 3.4. As in Table 3.2, for normal rate, the lenis stop is as a rule almost always voiceless in this position. However, for all subjects, there are a few cases that run counter the rule, and there are more such exceptional cases of clearly or partially voiced lenis stop tokens at faster rate.

The frequency of voicing in Word initial and Accentual Phrase initial lenis stop for five Chonnam speakers in three self selected speech rates is given in Table 7.1 and the frequency of voicing in Word initial and Accentual Phrase medial lenis stop is given in Table 7.2 in the Appendix II.

Table 3.4. The Voicing Status of the Phrase Initial Lenis Stop at Fast and Slow Rate

Subj.	Rate	Clearly Voiced	Ambiguous	Clearly V-less
C1	fast	8 (7)	11 (5)	94 (97)
	slow	0 (0)	1 (4)	173 (170)
C2	fast	4 (4)	7 (21)	96 (82)
	slow	0 (0)	10 (9)	168 (169)
C3	fast	4 (4)	6 (6)	131 (131)
	slow	1 (1)	0 (0)	165 (165)
C4	fast	11 (9)	0 (4)	118 (116)
	slow	3 (2)	2 (2)	160 (161)
C5	fast	6 (9)	7 (7)	147 (145)
	slow	1 (2)	2 (3)	179 (177)

3.1.3.4 Statistics (χ^2 and Cramer's V)

As I have shown the phrasings predicted by Phonological Phrase is not always correct considering the actual data. The phrasings defined by the Accentual Phrase is not perfect either. So, to see if phrasings predicted by both accounts is significantly related to the domain of lenis stop voicing, I calculated χ-square values for speaker C1. And to compare which prediction is closer to the actual data in terms of lenis stop voicing, I calculated Cramer's V. As a representative of Phonological Phrase account, I used Cho's Phonological Phrase. For each of three speech rates, it was found that both the Phonological Phrasing and the Accentual Phrasing are significantly related to the domain of Lenis Stop Voicing, (χ-square was significant).

The result of Cramer's V for normal rate indicates that the Accentual Phrasing is more closely related to the domain of Lenis Stop Voicing than the Phonological Phrasing is; the value of Cramer's V was higher for the Accentual Phrase (0.9085 < 1.1923). For fast rate, the Phonological Phrasing account showed a slightly higher values for Cramer's V (1. 1112 > 1.0965). For slow fate, the Accentual Phrasing account showed a higher value for Cramer's V (0.8257 < 0.9699). Therefore, it is clear that the Accentual Phrasing is more strongly associated with the domain of Lenis Stop Voicing.

Normal rate (expecting 20% voiced and 80% voiceless)

Table 3.5. Observed Data for Normal Rate

	Voiced	Voiceless	Total
Phr. initial	0	50	50
Phr. medial	14	0	14
total	14	50	64

Table 3.6. Cho's Expected 2*2 Contingency Table (N=64)

	Voiced	Voiceless	Total
P-Phr. initial	7.8	31.2	39
P-Phr. medial	5.0	20.0	25
total	12.8	51.2	64

$\chi^2 = 52.836$ (df=1, p <.001) and V = 0.9085

Table 3.7. My Expected 2*2 Contingency Table (N= 64)

	Voiced	Voiceless	Total
A-Phr. initial	10.0	40.0	50
A-Phr. medial	2.8	11.2	14
total	12.8	51.2	64

$\chi^2 = 91.0$ (df=1, p <.001) and V = 1.1923

Fast Rate (expecting 30% voiced and 70% voiceless)

Table 3.8. Observed Data for Fast Rate

	Voiced	Voiceless	Total
Phr. initial	2	36	38
Phr. medial	25	1	26
total	27	37	64

The Accentual Phrase

Table 3.9. Cho's Expected 2*2 Contingency Table (N=64)

	Voiced	Voiceless	Total
P-Phr. initial	11.7	27.3	39
P-Phr. medial	7.5	17.5	25
total	19.2	44.8	64

$\chi^2 = 79.027$ (df=1, p <.001) and V = 1.1112

Table 3.10. My Expected 2*2 Contingency Table (N= 64)

	Voiced	Voiceless	Total
A-Phr. initial	11.4	26.6	38
A-Phr. medial	7.8	18.2	26
total	19.2	44.8	64

$\chi^2 = 76.952$ (df=1, p <.001) and V = 1.0965

Slow Rate (expecting 5% voiced and 95% voiceless)

Table 3.11. Observed Data for Slow Rate

	Voiced	Voiceless	Total
Phr. initial	0	61	61
Phr. medial	3	0	3
total	3	61	64

Table 3.12. Cho's Expected 2*2 Contingency Table (N=64)

	Voiced	Voiceless	Total
P-Phr. initial	1.95	37.05	39
P-Phr. medial	1.25	23.75	25
total	3.2	60.8	64

$\chi^2 = 43.6318$ (df=1, p <.001) and V = 0.8257

Table 3.13. My Expected 2*2 Contingency Table (N= 64)

	Voiced	Voiceless	Total
A-Phr. initial	3.05	57.95	61
A-Phr. medial	0.15	2.85	3
total	3.2	60.8	64

$\chi^2 = 60.2105$ (df=1, p <.001) and V = 0.9699

3.1.4 Summary and Discussion

The lenis stop is almost always voiced within the Accentual Phrase and almost always voiceless at the Accentual Phrase initial position. This makes it seem that the lenis stop voicing rule is categorical. However, when we consider the fact that the voicing of a lenis stop changes depending on speech rate, it indicates that the lenis stop voicing may not be a categorical change. Silva (1992) also found the non-categoricality of lenis stop voicing. Based on variable data of lenis stop closure duration, he interprets that the lenis stop voicing depends on the duration of stop closure and the perception of voicing of the lenis stop is correlated with the percentage of closure voicing; the same duration of closure voicing can be perceived as voiced lenis stop if the total closure duration is short. This variability of voicing is further supported by an experiment on vowel devoicing (Jun and Beckman, 1993, Jun forthcoming) and the measurement data from Jun (1993). In Jun and Beckman (1993), we found that the voicing of the Accentual Phrase medial lenis stop changes depending on the neighboring segmental contexts. When the lenis stop follows an aspirated stop and a high vowel, the lenis stop showed a higher percentage of voicelessness than when it follows a tense or a lenis stop. In this case, the intervening high vowel showed a higher percentage of devoicing than the high vowels in other segmental contexts. Furthermore, in Jun (1993), I found that the duration of the lenis stop is inversely correlated with the duration of the following vowel and the longer the lenis stop, the more often it is voiceless. This phonetic rule of gradation can best be accounted for by using Browman and Goldstein's (1986, 1988) gestural score model.

Browman and Goldstein (1987) assume that the gestures are invariant across different contexts. They also claim that gestures overlap in time because gestures are inherently spatiotemporal in its characteristics. Such overlapping activation of several invariant gestures results in context-varying articulatory trajectories when the gestures involve the same articulators, and in varying acoustic effects even when different articulators are involved. That is, much coarticulation and allophonic variation occurs as an automatic consequence of overlapping invariant underlying gestures.

Since the lenis stop (closure and VOT duration) at the beginning of the Accentual Phrase is significantly longer than that in the middle of the Accentual Phrase and the duration of the lenis stop is negatively correlated with the duration of the following vowel (Jun 1993), the voicing of the lenis stop seems to be the result of the prosodic position effect on segmental duration and coproduction. That is, the intervocalic voicing in casual or fast speech may involve not only reduction of gestural magnitude of the glottal opening-and-closing gesture responsible for the voicelessness but also the blending of closely phased voicing gestures , i.e. overlapping of the consonant's glottal opening gestures with the adjacent vowel's glottal closing gestures.

Moreover, the fact that this intervocalic lenition is very likely to occur within the Accentual Phrase instead of across Accentual Phrases indicates that the glottal opening/closing gesture is influenced by Accentual Phrase boundary. That is, in the middle of the Accentual Phrase, the magnitude of the glottal opening gesture for the [-voice] sound maybe reduced and there will be more overlapping between the glottal opening gesture of the lenis stop and the glottal closing gesture of the adjacent [+voice] sounds, while at the beginning of the Accentual Phrase, the glottal opening gesture may increase and the glottal opening gesture will overlap more with the following glottal closing gesture. This interpretation seems plausible because the Accentual Phrase initial lenis stop is longer and the following vowel is shorter compared to the same segments in the middle of the Accentual Phrase (Jun 1993). There would be enough time for the glottal opening gesture of the lenis stop to reach its target position at the Accentual Phrase initial position and as a result it would be more likely that the glottal opening gesture will overlap more with the following vowel's glottal closing gesture. The variation of lenis stop voicing due to rate, phrasing, segmental and prosodic contexts suggests that the lenis stop voicing rule in Korean is not a categorical phonological phenomenon but gradient phonetic phenomenon.

3.1.5 Conclusion

The experiment shows that the domain of lenis stop voicing is the Accentual Phrase which is marked by the intonational pattern of an utterance, not the phonological phrase which is defined by the syntactic structure of a sentence. Since the voicing of a lenis stop is sensitive to speech rate, it was suggested that the lenis stop voicing rule may not be a categorical rule but gradient phonetic phenomena. This gradient characteristic of rule would be accounted for best by the gestural overlap model proposed by Browman and Goldstein (1988).

3.2. OTHER PHONOLOGICAL RULES

Informal observation shows that other postlexical rules such as Post Obstruent Tensing and Long Vowel Shortening also apply within the Accentual Phrase. I will describe these two rules in the following two subsections.

3.2.1 Post Obstruent Tensing

Post Obstruent Tensing rule is a rule by which a syllable onset lenis obstruent , i.e., [-son], becomes tense after a coda obstruent. This rule has also been claimed to apply within the Phonological phrase by Cho (1987) and Kang (1992) and is formalized as in (5a). Examples following the various syntactic accounts are given in (5b and 5c)

(5) a. [-son] ---> [+constricted glottis] / ɸ(...[-cont]___ ...

   b. mijək 'seaweed' + kuk 'soup'
      -> mijəkk'uk 'seaweed soup'
   c. mijəkk'uk 'seaweed soup' + puəɾa 'pour'
      -> mijəkk'ukp'uəɾa 'Pour the seaweed soup'

The first example, (5b), shows the application of the rule between two nouns within a compound noun and the second example, (5c), shows the application of the rule between an object noun 'seaweed soup' and a verb 'to pour' within a verb phrase. Each of these sequences is predicted to form one phonological phrase by either Cho's relation-based algorithm or Kang's end-based algorithm, thus Post-Obstruent Tensing would apply.

Two utterances of the phrase in (5c) are given in Figure 3.7. However, as the figure shows, the phonological phrasing of the verb phrase is not invariant, and the domain of Post Obstruent Tensing changes depending on the phrasing. That is, as shown in Fig. 3.7(a), the verb and the object noun together can form one Accentual Phrase as in {mijəkk'uk p'uərɑ} 'Pour the seaweed soup.', and in this case, the verb initial lenis stop becomes tense as seen in the spectrogram: The verb initial lenis stop shows the same spectrographic features as the compound medial /k/ of /mijəkk'uk/, showing little or no aspiration at the oral release of /k/ and strong release energy at high frequency. This is the result predicted by either Cho or Kang. Figure 3.7(b) shows an utterance of the same sentence produced in two Accentual Phrases so that each of the object noun and the verb forms its own Accentual Phrase as in {mijəkk'uk}{puərɑ}. In this case, the verb initial lenis obstruent is not tense but remains lenis, showing some aspiration and breathiness and a larger energy roll off, by comparison to the tense compound medial /k/. This result was not predicted by Cho or Kang. Thus, we can see that Cho and Kang's predictions are not always correct. If we look at the pitch tracks for each token, it is clear that this different application of tensing rule is due to the different Accentual Phrasing. If the domain is the phonological phrase as Cho and Kang claimed, both of the examples should have the same result regarding the application of the Post Obstruent Tensing rule since both of them have exactly the same syntactic structure.

Therefore, it is clear that the syntax-derived algorithm for predicting the domain of these postlexical rules is not adequate. Rather, the application of the rule depends more on the actual prosodic phrasing, and the phrasing is not determined only by the syntax.

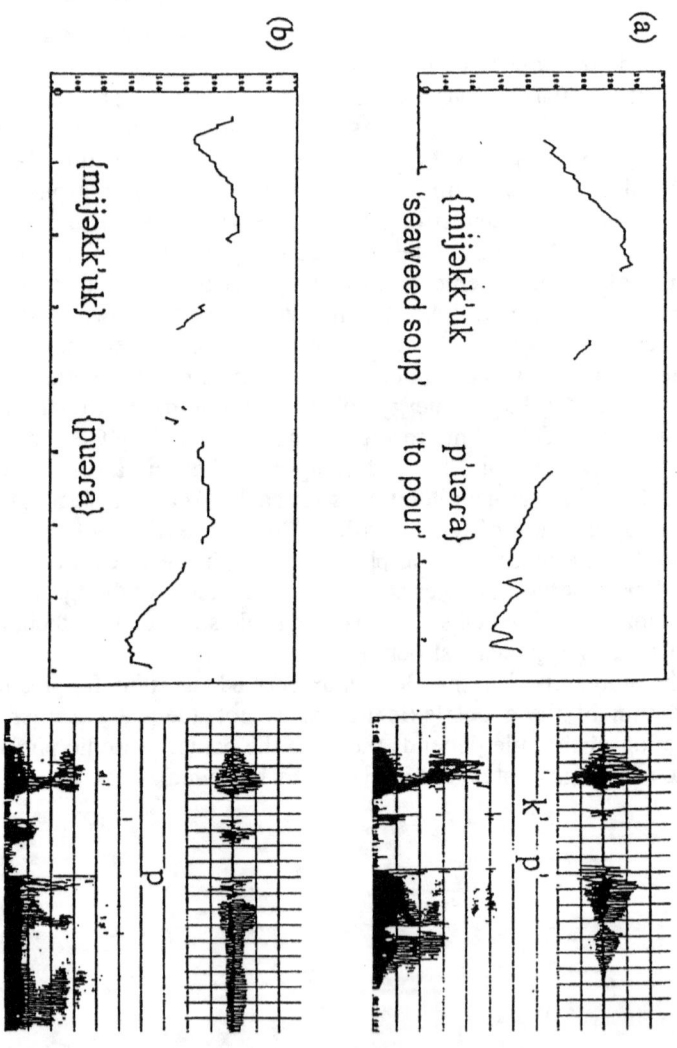

Figure 3.7. Pitch tracks and spectrograms of /mijəkkuk puəra/ 'Pour the seaweed soup.' uttered in two different accentual phrasings: (a) forming one Accentual Phrase and (b) two Accentual Phrases

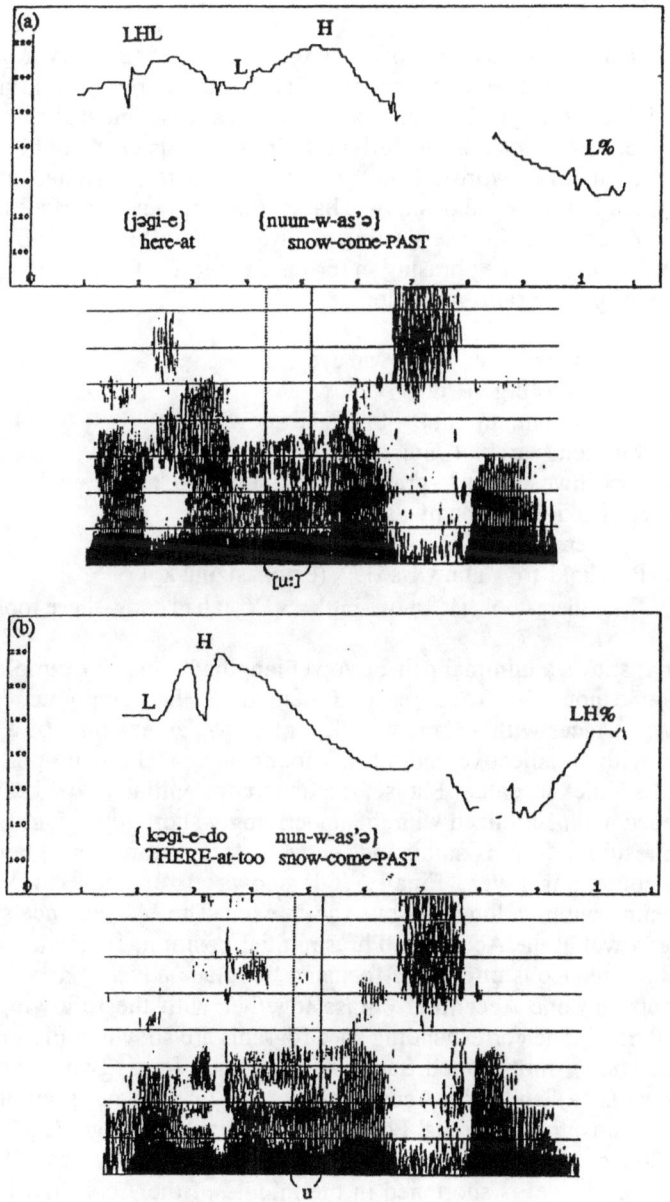

Figure 3.8. Pitch tracks and spectrograms of (6d): (a) {jəgie} {nu:nwassə} and (b) {kəgido nunwassə}

3.2.2 Vowel Shortening

The phonemic contrast in vowel length in the 15 century Middle Korean is being lost in contemporary Seoul, but is preserved in many other dialects such as Chonnam and Kyungsang. In most dialects of Korean (except for Seoul), underlyingly long vowels occur only in the first syllable of a word[1]. But the long vowel is shortened at the Accentual Phrase medial position. That is, the long vowel surfaces only at the Accentual Phrase initial position, as illustrated by the alternations in (6). The phrasing in (6d) is further illustrated using pitch tracks and spectrograms in Figure 3.8.

(6) a. nuːn 'snow' vs. nun 'an eye'
   b. /hampak/ 'big' + /nuːn / 'snow'
      => {hammbaŋnun}[2] 'big flake snow'
   c. /hwesek / 'gray' + /nuːn/ 'snow'
      => {hweseŋnun} 'gray snow' (but can be 'a gray eye')
   d. A: {jəki-e}   {nuːnwassə}
         'here-at'   '(It) snow-past' => 'Here, it snowed.'
      B: {kəki-to   nunwassə}? (emphasizing kəki)
         'there-too' '(It) snow-int.' => 'You had snow there too?

(6a) shows a minimal pair of vowel length. (6b) is an example of a compound noun, where the second element of the compound, /nuːn? 'snow', surfaces with a short vowel. (6c) shows an example of a noun phrase with an adjective and a head noun. Here, if the noun phrase is uttered as one Accentual Phrase, the head noun initial vowel becomes shortened and neutralized with the underlyingly short vowel word. That is, the resulting form is ambiguous between 'gray snow' and 'gray eye' if no context is given. Finally (6d) shows an example of Vowel Shortening within a longer phrase, a sentence. The 'A' sentence shows a long vowel at the Accentual Phrase initial position, {nuːnwassə}. In 'B', the sentence is uttered by focusing the place adverb, kəki 'there', thus forming one Accentual Phrase together with the following VP. The F0 tracks and corresponding spectrograms are shown in Figure 3.8.

As shown in the pitch tracks, the sentence forms two Accentual Phrases in (a) and one Accentual Phrase in (b). As seen in the spectrograms, the Accentual Phrase initial syllable is longer (95.31 ms) than the Accentual Phrase medial one (59.37 ms). In this case, the VP initial long vowel is shortened in the middle of the Accentual Phrase even though it is still in the same syntactic position, the beginning of the Verb Phrase. This VP was claimed to form one Phonological phrase

The Accentual Phrase

when preceded by a VP-external adverb such as time or place adverb by Cho, Silva and Kang (see the posited pattern in Chapter 1, Section 1.1.3). Thus, it is clear that the domain of Vowel Shortening is not the Phonological phrase but should be the Accentual Phrase.

3.3 CONCLUSION

In this chapter, I showed that the Accentual Phrase, a constituent marked by the tonal pattern of an utterance, is a better prediction of the domain of Lenis Stop Voicing, Post Obstruent Tensing and Vowel Shortening in Korean, than the Phonological phrase, a constituent defined by the Prosodic Phonologists (Cho, Silva, and Kang, among others) in terms of the syntactic structure. These three rules generally were observed to apply within the Accentual Phrase but not across the Accentual Phrases. Furthermore, I showed that the number of the Accentual Phrases changes depending on speech rate; the faster the speech rate, the fewer the Accentual Phrases within an utterance. Since the domain of the Accentual Phrase changes due to speech rate, the varying domain of phonological rules due to speech rate can be easily explained by the Accentual Phrase domain but not by the syntax-based domain since the syntactic structure does not change due to speech rate.

NOTES

1. The Kyungsang dialect has a few long vowels in other syllables. Younger (approximately younger than 40) Seoul speakers do not appear to have a phonemic contrast between long and short vowels even though they still pronounce certain words with long vowels.

2. The first word final stop, /k/, is nasalized before the second word initial nasal by Obstruent Nasalization rule. The same is true for (5c).

IV

The Intonational Phrase

4.1 INTRODUCTION

The Intonational Phrase is a prosodic level above the Accentual Phrase. This prosodic level is the domain of the Intonational Phrase contour. The Intonational Phrase contour in Korean includes the tones of one or more Accentual Phrase plus a final boundary tone (L%, H%, LH%, HL%, LHL% or HLH%), which is realized on the last syllable of the phrase. The final syllable of this phrase is lengthened and it is optionally followed by a pause. The Intonational Phrase is characterized by the variability of its domain and by its function of limiting the application of phonological rules.

As with the Accentual Phrasing, the Intonational Phrasing is also influenced by the syntactic structure, but it is not fixed by the syntactic structure and instead varies depending on non-syntactic and non-linguistic factors such as focus, given vs. new information, speech rate, and weight of the phrase (see Chapter 6). In a given context, one Accentual Phrase can form an Intonational Phrase by itself. But, whether an Intonational Phrase contains more than one Accentual Phrase is influenced by the factors mentioned above. An Intonational Phrase boundary is more likely to occur at edges of a maximal category higher in the syntactic hierarchy. That is, based on my and other native speaker consultants' intuitions about likely renderings of many test sentences, I can make the generalization that an Intonational Phrase boundary is very likely to come between a sentential adverb and the modified sentence, between a topic item and the rest of the sentence, between subordinate and main clauses, and so on. At the same time, the Intonational Phrase boundary is less likely to occur between constituents that are within the same maximal category low in the syntactic hierarchy — e.g., between constituents within NP or VP close to the bottom of the hierarchy. These tendencies for placing Intonational Phrase boundaries are similar to those in English: the syntactic domain corresponding to an Intonational Phrase in English includes parenthetical expressions, nonrestrictive relative clauses, tag questions, vocatives, expletives, and certain moved elements (see Selkirk 1978, 1984, Pierrehumbert 1980, and Nespor and Vogel 1986, among others).

The intonational phrasing is also sensitive to rate and weight: the faster the speech rate, the fewer the number of the Intonational Phrases within an utterance, and the more syllables in a sentence or a phrase, the larger the number of the Intonational Phrases. Therefore, it is impossible to predict the intonational phrasing based only on the syntactic structure of the sentence without considering these other aspects of the speech context. This variability of the Intonational Phrase domain has also been noticed by prosodic phonologists (Selkirk 1978, 1986; Nespor & Vogel 1986, Hayes 1989). Thus, they define the Intonational Phrase in a different way from the other prosodic levels above the Prosodic Word/Phonological Word. The prosodic levels lower than the Intonational Phrase are all defined based on the syntactic structure, sometimes directly and sometimes indirectly. The Intonational Phrase, however, has been defined based on many criteria. Selkirk (1984) claims that the Intonational Phrase is syntactically free but semantically constrained and suggested the Sense Unit Condition, according to which the immediate constituents of an Intonational Phrase must form a sense unit (see Chapter 5 for more detail).

By contrast, Nespor and Vogel (1986) try to hold to the principle that every prosodic level is defined based on syntactic information. They therefore suggest a syntactic basis for the Intonational Phrase, but to accommodate to the observed variability in intonational phrasing, they add a restructuring rule at the level of the Intonational Phrase. The factors affecting the application of the restructuring rule include: the length of the resulting phrase, the rate of speech, the style of speech, and contrastive prominence. Restructuring may group any sequence of φs (Phonological Phrases) into a smaller Intonational Phrase as long as the division respects the syntactic and argument structure conditions as well as the general timing conditions (Nespor and Vogel, 1986, p.205).

In addition to the variability of the Intonational Phrase domain, the Intonational Phrase is also characterized as forming a domain of a segmental phonological rule. Since a phonological rule may apply in a given position when the sentence is uttered with one intonational phrasing but not when it is uttered with another, the resulting constituent, the Intonational Phrase, is not isomorphic to any syntactic constituent. Nespor and Vogel (1986:p.216) argue that these facts provide additional evidence for the Intonational Phrase as a constituent in the phonological hierarchy separately from the syntactic constituents which are invariable regardless of their length and other nonstructural considerations.

Examples of phonological rules applying within an Intonational Phrase are further evidence that the Intonational Phrase is a prosodic constituent. Nespor and Vogel (1986) show examples from three languages. They are Gorgia Toscana in Italian (a rule which changes the voiceless stops /p,t,k/ into the corresponding fricatives [f,s,h] between two [-consonantal] segments), Nasal Assimilation in Spanish (a rule which assimilates a nasal in point of articulation to a following obstruent) and s-Voicing in Greek (a rule whereby /s/ is voiced when it is followed by a voiced [+consonantal] segment). Korean also seems to have several phonological rules applying within the Intonational Phrase. In the next two sections, I will describe two experiments showing that the Intonational Phrase in Korean which is defined based on the tonal pattern is also the domain of the postlexical phonological rules: Obstruent Nasalization, Spirantization, and /s/-palatalization.

4.2 EXPERIMENT 2:
THE DOMAIN OF OBSTRUENT NASALIZATION

4.2.1 Introduction

Nasalization of obstruents around nasals is found in many languages. However, the domain of this rule varies between languages; it applies only within a word in Malayalam (Mohanan & Mohanan, 1984), but only across word boundaries in Sanskrit (Whitney, 1889, Selkirk, 1980). Obstruent Nasalization in Korean is a rule where a coda obstruent becomes nasalized before a nasal onset. This rule has been claimed to apply across word boundaries (Ahn 1985), and thus to be a postlexical rule like the Korean Lenis Stop Voicing rule. However, the domain of this rule was not specifically discussed until Cho (1987), who claimed that it is the Phonological Phrase, i.e. Obstruent Nasalization is blocked in environments where a Phonological Phrase boundary intervenes between the trigger and the focus of the rule. In contrast, Kang (1990) claimed this rule applies within the Intonational Phrase, although in Kang (1992), she argued instead that the domain of this rule is the Phonological Phrase. Therefore, it is not clear what the domain of this rule really is. So the rule would be formalized as follows.

(1)   [-son] --> [+nas] / ?(...__[+nas] ...)

Translating Cho's (1987) or Kang's (1992) claim into my prosodic system, the domain of Obstruent Nasalization should be the Accentual Phrase. Based on the phonetic experiment, I will show that the domain of Obstruent Nasalization is neither the syntax-based Phonological Phrase proposed by Cho and Kang (1992), nor the Accentual Phrase that I have proposed here. In fact, instrumental evidence shows that Obstruent Nasalization applies across Phonological Phrase or Accentual Phrase boundaries. That is, the domain of application of Obstruent Nasalization is the Intonational Phrase for these speakers of Seoul and Chonnam Korean. Furthermore, the categoricality of the postlexical rule of Obstruent Nasalization is investigated based on the duration measurement data. If the duration data of the derived nasal or preceding vowel show any graduality, the rule would be a phonetic rule, following Pierrehumbert (1990).

4.2.2. Procedures

Subjects

4 Chonnam speakers (2 females and 2 males) and 4 Seoul speakers (1 female and 3 males) participated in the experiment. Information on each subject is in Table 4.1. For S1, only oral/nasal airflow data were collected and no separate audio recording was made.

Table 4.1. Background of Each Subject

Subj.	Age (sex)	Years in USA	from	Major
C1	30 (M)	4 yrs. 3 mos.	Kwangju	Chemical Eng.
C2	25 (M)	7 mos.	Mokpo	Agricul. Eco.
C3	25 (F)	7 mos.	Mokpo	N/A
C4	30 (F)	4 yrs. 3 mos.	Kwangju	Linguistics
S1	29 (M)	2 mos.	Seoul	Linguistics
S2	26 (F)	1 yr. 2 mos.	Seoul	Linguistics
S3	30 (M)	2 yrs. 2 mos.	Seoul	Linguistics
S4	31 (M)	2 yrs. 2 mos.	Seoul	Linguistics

Material

The corpus was the list of 40 sentences in Table 4.2 and the 62 words in Table 4.3. Among the 40 sentences in Table 4.2, there were 8 pairs of sentences contrasting two different kinds of consonant-nasal sequences across a word boundary: in one sentence of the pair a coda obstruent was followed by an onset nasal to give a 'derived nasal' sequence and, for the other sentence of the pair, a coda nasal was followed by an onset nasal to give an 'underlying nasal' sequence. A representative example is shown in (3). A coda obstruent before an onset obstruent within a word or at the end of a word is neutralized to a lenis stop by Coda Neutralization. Thus, in (3a) and in all other similar examples of coda /s/ in Table 4.2 and 4.3, if the underlying /s/ does not surface as [n], it will surface as a lenis stop [t], as shown by the alternate output in (3a). In addition, there were two sentences (#B1c and B2c) where the first word ends in a nasal and the second word starts with a lenis stop. These sentences are added to compare the domain of the lenis stop voicing with that of Obstruent Nasalization. The other sentences have a stop and nasal sequence across a word boundary with no contrasting nasal-nasal. Table 4.2 lists the sentence corpus. The text given in (3) and Table 4.2 is for Seoul speakers. The verbal endings were changed for Chonnam speakers to analogous dialect forms. For example, the declarative verbal ending '-kɨman' or '-nti' was replaced with '-(nɨ)ntɛ' and the interogative verbal ending '-nja' was replaced with '-ni'.

(3) a. a derived nasal sentence
    sɛutʃə<u>s</u> +   <u>n</u>ɛmsɛka + isaŋhantɛ
    'pickled shrimp' 'smell'   'is stange'
    = 'The smell of the pickled shrimp is strange.'
        => [sɛudʒə<u>n</u> nɛmsɛga isaŋhandɛ] or
        => [sɛudʒə<u>t</u> nɛmsɛga isaŋhandɛ]

 b. an underlying nasal sentence
    sɛutʃə<u>n</u> +   <u>n</u>ɛmsɛka + isaŋhantɛ
    'shrimp pancake' 'smell'   'is stange'
    = 'The smell of the shrimp pancake is strange.'
        => [sɛudʒə<u>n</u> nɛmsɛga isaŋhandɛ]

The 40 sentences were divided into two blocks and 10 paired sentences (#A1a-A5b in Table 4.2) were in the first block. The subjects were asked to produce these 10 sentences in two different phrasings: first, making two segments in the sequence of concern belong to separate Accentual Phrases and second, making them belong to the same Accentual Phrase. The first phrasing was obtained by asking subjects to put focus on both words and the second phrasing by asking them to put focus on the first word. Thus, for example, subjects read the sentence '#A1a' six times total, three times in the first phrasing and three times in the second phrasing. Within each phrasing, each sentence is pseudo-randomly ordered in a way not to be put the paired sentences next to each other. This ordering is to avoid subject's putting a contrastive focus and to make it hard for subjects to guess the purpose of the experiment. The accentual phrasing of the rest of the sentences except for #C17 and #C18 was not given in a fixed way and left free so that each subject would produce whatever phrasing they felt to be natural. The subjects were asked to produce sentences #C17 and #C18 using two different intonational phrasings. In the first phrasing, the first 2nd and 3rd nouns, *kwangjut'ak mims'iga,* were pronounced as one Accentual Phrase, thus within an Intonational Phrase (for this phrasing, no comma was given in the text); in the second phrasing, the two nouns were separated by an Intonational Phrase boundary. This was accomplished by asking the subject to treat the first of the two nouns as a topic separated from the rest of the sentence, as indicated by comma in the text. The author provided a model pronunciation in order to make sure that the subjects understood the intended phrasing. All subjects had no difficulty producing these two types of intonational phrasings.

Table 4.2. List of Sentences

==
A. Pairs contrasting Consonant-Nasal with Nasal-Nasal

A1a. otʃiŋətʃəs nɛmsɛka isaŋhantɛ
    otʃiŋə-tʃəs   nɛmsɛ-ka   isaŋha-ntɛ
    'squid pickle' 'smell-NOM' 'strange-declarative'
    => 'The smell of the squid pickle is strange.'

A1b. otʃiŋətʃən nɛmsɛka isaŋhantɛ
    otʃiŋə-tʃən   nɛmsɛ-ka   isaŋha-ntɛ
    'squid pancake' 'smell-NOM' 'strange-declarative'
    => 'The smell of the squid pancake is strange.'

A2a. sɛutʃəs masi isaŋhantɛ
    sɛu-tʃəs   mas-i   isaŋha-ntɛ
    'shrimp pickle' 'taste-NOM' 'strange-declarative'
    => 'The taste of the shrimp pickle is strange.'

The Intonational Phrase

A2b. sɛutʃən masi isaŋhantɛ
      sɛu-tʃən   mas-i   isaŋhantɛ
      'shrimp pancake' 'taste-NOM' 'strange-declarative'
      => 'The taste of the shrimp pancake is strange.'

A3a. wəlkɨp manhɨmjən mwəhani
      wəlkɨp   manh-ɨmjən   mwə-hani
      'salary'   'much - if'   'what use-Q'
      => 'It's no use even if (they) have a large salary.'

A3b. tʃakɨm manhɨmjən mwəhani
      tʃakɨm   manh-ɨmjən   mwə-hani
      'money'   'much - if'   'what use-Q'
      => 'It's no use even if (they) have a lot of money.'

A4a. nə nurinpap məkəpwassni => 'Have you tried a scorched rice?'
      nə   nurin-pap   mək-əpwass-ni
      'you' 'scorched rice' '(have you) tried-Q'

A4b. nə nurinpam məkəpwassni
      nə   nurin-pam   mək-əpwass-ni
      'you' 'scorched chestnut' '(have you) tried-Q'
      => 'Have you tried a scorched chestnut?'

A5a. noransɛk motʃaka tʃeil kʰintɛ
      noran   sɛk   motʃa-ka   tʃeil   kʰintɛ
      'yellow' 'color' 'a hat-NOM' 'the most' 'big'
      => 'The yellow hat is the most big.'

A5b. nosənsɛŋ motʃaka tʃeil kʰintɛ
      no-sənsɛŋ   motʃa-ka   tʃeil   kʰintɛ
      'Mr.No teacher' 'a hat-NOM' 'the most' 'big'
      => 'Teacher No's hat is the biggest.'

A6a. i hopak masissnintɛ => 'This pumpkin is delicious.'
      i   hopak   masiss-nintɛ
      'this' 'pumpkin' 'delicious-DEC'

A6b. i kapaŋ məsissnintɛ => 'This bag is beautiful.'
      i   kapaŋ   məsiss-nintɛ
      'this' 'bag' 'beautiful-DEC'

A6c. i hop'aŋ masissnɨntɛ => 'This bean paste bread is delicious.'
    i   hop'aŋ   masiss-nɨntɛ
    'this' 'bean paste bread' 'delicious-DEC'

B. Pairs contrasting Cons-Nasal vs. Nasal-Nasal vs. Nasal-Consonant

B1a. tʃakɨnpak nɛmsɛka isaŋhantɛ
    tʃakɨn   pak   nɛmsɛ-ka   isaŋha-ntɛ
    'small' 'a gourd' 'smell-NOM' 'strange-DEC'
    => 'The smell of small gourd is strange.'

B1b. tʃakɨnpaŋ nɛmsɛka isaŋhantɛ
    tʃakɨn   paŋ   nɛmsɛ-ka   isaŋha-ntɛ
    'small' 'a room' 'smell-NOM' 'strange-DEC'
    => 'The smell of small room is strange.'

B1c. tʃakɨnpaŋ kutʃoka isaŋhantɛ
    tʃakɨn   paŋ   kutʃo-ka   isaŋha-ntɛ
    'small' 'a room' 'structure-NOM' 'delicious-DEC'
    => 'The structure of small room is strange.'

B2a. i tʃakɨnpak nɛmsɛka isaŋhantɛ
    => 'The smell of this small gourd is strange.'
    i   tʃakɨn   pak   nɛmsɛ-ka   isaŋha-ntɛ
    'this' 'small' 'a gourd' 'smell-NOM' 'strange-DEC'

B2b. i tʃakɨnpaŋ nɛmsɛka isaŋhantɛ
    i   tʃakɨn   paŋ   nɛmsɛ-ka   isaŋha-ntɛ
    'this' 'small' 'a room' 'smell-NOM' 'strange-DEC'
    => 'The smell of this small room is strange.'

B2c. i tʃakɨnpaŋ kutʃoka isaŋhantɛ
    i   tʃakɨn   paŋ   kutʃo-ka   isaŋha-ntɛ
    'this' 'small' 'a room' 'structure-NOM' 'strange-DEC'
    => 'The structure of this small room is strange.'

C. Simple Consonant-Nasal

C1. taɨm tal wəlkɨp nɛɾimjən ətʃ'ətʃi
    taɨm   tal   wəlkɨp   nɛɾimjən   ətʃ'ətʃi
    'next' 'month' 'salary' 'to cut down' 'what if'
    => 'What if next month's salary is reduced?.'

The Intonational Phrase

C2. kɨ twɛntʃaŋkuk masi isaŋhɛ
    kɨ   twɛntʃaŋkuk   mas-i   isaŋh-ɛ
    'that' 'bean paste soup' 'taste-NOM' 'strange-DEC'
    => 'The taste of the bean paste soup is strange.'

C3. kɨ kwaŋtʃutɛk maɨms'ika nəmu tʃoa
    kɨ   kwaŋtʃutɛk   maɨms'i-ka   nəmu   tʃoa
    'that' 'woman from Kwangju' 'personality-NOM' 'too' 'good'
    => 'The personality of the woman from Kwangju is very good.'

C4. jaŋnjəmtʰoŋtalk məkkosipɨmjən tʃənhwahɛ
    jaŋnjəm-tʰoŋtalk   məkko-sɨp-ɨmjən   tʃənhwah-ɛ
    the seasoned-fried chicken' 'to eat-want-if' 'call-IMP'
    => 'Call if you want to eat the seasoned fried chicken.'

C5. kɨ kjorənpok matʃʰunkəni => 'Is that drill suit custom made?'
    kɨ   kjorənpok   matʃʰu-nkə-ni
    'that' 'drill suit' 'custom-made-REL-Q'

C6. hapkjək moshɛsstako tʃasalhɛsste
    hapkjək moshɛ-ss-tako   tʃasalhɛ-ss-te
    'pass' 'not-past-because of' 'to commit suicide-past-DEC'
    => '(He/She) committed suicide because they/she didn't pass'

C7. nə jaŋnjəmtʰoŋtalk nəmu tʃoahanɨnkuna
    rə   jaŋnjəm-tʰoŋtalk   nəmu   tʃoaha-nɨnkuna
    'you' 'the seasoned-fried chicken' 'too much' 'to like-EXCL'
    => 'You like the seasoned fried chicken too much.'

C8. nə kamasotʰ mwəntʃi ani => 'Do you know what is 'kamasotʰ'?'
    nə   kama-sotʰ   mwə-ntʃi   ani
    'you' 'an iron pot' 'what-REL' 'to know-Q'

C9. nə kimsaskas nukuntʃi ani
    nə   kim-saskas   nuku-ntʃi   ani
    'you' 'Mr.Kim-reed hat' 'who-REL' 'to know-Q'
    => 'Do you know who is 'kimsaskas'?'

C10. nə kamasotʰ mojaɲi kɨəknani
    nə   kamasotʰ   mojaɲ-i   kɨəkna-ni
    'you' 'an rion pot' 'shape-NOM' 'to remember-Q'
    => 'Do you remember the shape of an iron pot?'

C11. kɨ kwaŋtʃutɛk̲ ̲m̲aɨmɨn amuto molla
    kɨ   kwaŋtʃutɛk   maɨm-ɨn   amu-to   molla
    'that' 'woman from Kwangju' 'personality-TOP' 'anybody-EMP'
                                                 'don't know'
    => 'Nobody knows the personality of woman from Kwangju.'

C12. i mitətək̲ ̲n̲ɛmsɛka isaŋhantɛ
    i   mitətək   nɛmsɛ-ka   isaŋha-ntɛ
    'this' 'kind of shell' 'smell-NOM' 'strange-DEC'
    => 'The smell of this 'mitətək' shell is strange.'

C13. i sujəŋpok̲ ̲n̲əmu tʃakɨntɛ => 'This swimsuit is too small.'
    i   sujəŋpok   nəmu   tʃak-ɨntɛ
    'this' 'swimsuit' 'too'   'small-DEC'

C14. kɨ jənkɨk̲ ̲n̲əmu tʃɛmiəpstɨɾa => 'That play was too boring.'
    kɨ   jənkɨk   nəmu   tʃɛmi-əps-tɨɾa
    'that' 'a play' 'too'   'fun-no-past DEC'

C15. juhaksɛŋ suka putʃ'ək̲ ̲n̲ɨləsstɛ
    juhaksɛŋ   su-ka   putʃ'ək   nɨl-əss-tɛ
    'student studying oversea' 'the number-DEC' 'rapidly' 'to-increase-
                                                         past -DEC'
    'The number of students studying oversea increased rapidly.'

C16. kɨ tonɨl kakkak̲ ̲n̲anwəkatʃjəsstɛ
    kɨ   ton-ɨl   kakkak   nanwə-katʃj-əss-tɛ
    'that' 'money-DEC' 'each'   'to divide-to have-past-DEC'
    => 'They divided the money with each other.'

C17. kɨ twɛntʃaŋkuk̲.̲ ̲m̲asi tʃəŋmal isaŋhɛ
    kɨ   twɛntʃaŋkuk   masi   tʃəŋmal   isaŋh-ɛ
    'that' 'bean paste soup' 'taste-NOM'   'really'   'strange-DEC'
    => 'The bean paste soup, taste is really strange.'

C18. kɨ kwaŋtʃutɛk̲,̲ ̲m̲aɨmssika nəmu tʃoa
    kɨ   kwaŋtʃutɛk   maɨms'i-ka   nəmu   tʃo-a
    'that' 'woman from Kwangju' 'personality-NOM' 'too'   'good-DEC'
    => 'The woman from Kwangju, her personality is very good.'

C19. kɨ jənkɨk naonɨn saɾam kiəkhani
    kɨ   jənkɨk   nao-nɨn   saɾam   kiəkha-ni
    'that' 'a play' 'to appear-REL' 'a man' 'to remember-Q'
    => '(Do you) remember actors in that play?'

C20. nə totʰoɾimuk mantɨltʃul ani
    nə   totʰoɾimuk   mantɨ-ltʃu-l   ani
    'you' 'acorn starch paste' 'to cook-a way-REL' 'to know-Q'
    => 'Do you know how to cook acorn starch paste?'

In addition, to compare nasalization within a sentence with that within a word in isolation, 31 minimal pairs of words contrasting word medial stops or nasals with word final stops or nasals were recorded with 3 repetitions. The recordings were digitized and some of sentences were analyzed further with pitch tracks to confirm the accentual phrasing. The word list is given in Table 4.3.

Table 4.3. List of Word Internal and Final Stop vs. Nasal

Word internal stop vs. nasal	Word final stop vs. nasal
1. masnata 'tasty'	1. otʃiŋətʃəs 'pickled squid'
2. mitʰməɾi 'original hair'	2. sɛutʃəs 'pickled shrimp'
3. kətʰmjən 'the exterior'	3. noɾaŋsɛk 'yellow'
4. pəpnje 'enactments'	4. pak 'a gourd'
5. hakmun 'studies'	5. upak 'hail'
6. sapmok 'inserting tree'	6. wəlkip 'salary'
7. səknjə 'sterile woman'	7. nuɾinpap 'scorched rice'
8. sakmakhata 'dreary'	8. halpok 'disembowelment'
9. kjəkmjəl 'annihilation'	9. sotʰ 'a pot'
10. kokmultʃʰaŋko 'a granary'	10. ipultʃip 'blanket shop'
11. pakmul 'natural history'	11. hopak 'pumpkin'
12. tokmul 'poison water'	12. sakjək 'shooting'
13. kakmak 'the cornea'	13. sapəp 'judicature'
14. mokma 'a hobbyhorse'	14. sukap 'handcuffs'
15. tʰapmun 'a tower door'	15. isak 'grain'
16. mannata 'to meet'	16. otʃiŋətʃən 'squid pancake'
17. minməɾi 'a bare head'	17. sɛutʃən 'shrimp pancake'
18. kənmjən 'dried noodles'	18. nosənsɛn 'Mr. No-teacher'

19. pəmɾjɛ 'explanatory notes'
20. ha<u>nm</u>un 'the anus'
21. sa<u>mm</u>ok 'a Japanese cedar'
22. sə<u>nn</u>jə 'a saintess'
23. sa<u>nm</u>akhata 'faint'
24. kjə<u>nm</u>jəl 'contempt'
25. ko<u>nm</u>ultʃʰaŋko
      'a tribute storehouse'
26. pa<u>nm</u>ul 'fancy goods'
27. to<u>nm</u>ul 'an animal'
28. ka<u>nm</u>ak no meaning
29. mo<u>nm</u>a no meaning
30. tʰa<u>mm</u>un 'indirect inquiry'
31. kət̪ʰ<u>m</u>ojaŋ 'appearance'

19. pa<u>n</u> 'a room'
20. jupa<u>n</u> 'breast'
21. wənki<u>m</u> 'the principal sum'
22. nuɾɨnpa<u>m</u> 'scorshed chestnut'
23. tʃʰəlpo<u>n</u> 'an iron rod'
24. so<u>n</u> 'a hand'
25. ipultʃi<u>m</u> 'blanket baggage'
26. hop'a<u>n</u> 'bean paste bread'
27. sakjə<u>ŋ</u> 'the brink of death'
28. sapə<u>m</u> 'a crime'
29. suka<u>m</u> 'confinement'
30. isa<u>n</u> 'an ideal'
31. kənmoja<u>n</u> 'a shape of a
      tendon'

Method

Audio recordings of all Chonnam speakers and Seoul speakers S2-S4 reading the 40 sentences in Table 4.2 were made in a sound-treated booth of the Dept. of Linguistics, Ohio State University using a microphone and a cassette tape-deck. The recordings were digitized in 10kHz sampling rate for waveforms and pitch track analysis, and spectrogram data were examined on Kay Sona-Graph (model 5500). In addition, oral and nasal airflow recordings of all speakers reading the first 10 sentences in Table 4.2. were made. All the sentences were repeated 3 times. In order to get natural phrasings, speakers were asked to read as if they were talking to someone in a conversation. In a few cases, a context was given to elicit the desired phrasing.

    To assess the degree and timing of nasalization, nasal and oral air flow were recorded using a Rothenberg split airflow mask with an oral flow transducer and a nasal flow transducer. The oral flow signal was passed through 3 kHz anti-aliasing low-pass filter; and the nasal flow signal was passed through a 30 Hz low-pass filter. The nasal flow signal was preamplified by 20 dB in order to make the signal large enough for easy analysis. The signals from the flow transducers were digitized with a 6 kHz sampling rate using CSPEECH (a multi-channel speech analysis program developed by Paul Milenkovic, U. of Wisconsin). Subjects were asked to read sentences 1-10 in Table 4.2, while holding the mask firmly against their faces, covering both their nose and their mouth, with the foam-padded mask divider over the upper lip in order to record the oral and nasal flows separately. After every two sentences they were asked to breathe briefly. Two repetitions of each of the two different phrasings were recorded. (Due to the mechanical problem, airflow data of subject C4, S2, S3 and S4 could not be obtained.)

To see if there is any phonetic difference between phrases with derived nasals and those with underlying nasals, several measurements were taken from the audio and airflow waveforms. Figure 4.1 shows a sample set of waveforms for an utterance 'otʃiŋət*ʃəs n*ɛmsɛka isaŋhantɛ', meaning 'The smell of the squid pickle is strange.' with each measurement marked. The italicized part is shown in the upper signal and the underlined part is shown in the lower signal. The upper signal is the audio waveform showing the duration of the vowel before the coda consonant, ('V' in the figure) and the duration of the nasal sequence, (the target derived or underlying coda nasal plus the following onset nasal ('N' in the figure). The lower picture is the oral and nasal airflow waveform showing the four measurements:
1. the duration of the nasalized portion of vowel before the derived or underlying nasal, which is the time from the point when the nasal flow starts rising within a vowel until the end of the vowel.
    (=time between 'A' and 'B' in the figure).
2. baseline nasal air flow before the nasal flow starts
    (= 'A' in the figure).
3. nasal air flow at the end of the vowel
    (= 'B' in the figure).
4. nasal air flow at the peak of the nasal flow
    (= 'C' in the figure).

4.2.3 Results

4.2.3.1 The Results of Measurements

The results of measurements from audio waveforms and from the air flow data did not show any statistically significant difference between the utterances with an underlying nasal and the utterances with a derived nasal. Figure 4.2 shows the results from the audio waveforms. That is, for each subject, the mean duration of the vowel (the left panel in Fig.4.2) and the mean duration of the nasal (the right panel) were very similar between phrases with a derived nasal and those with an underlying nasal.

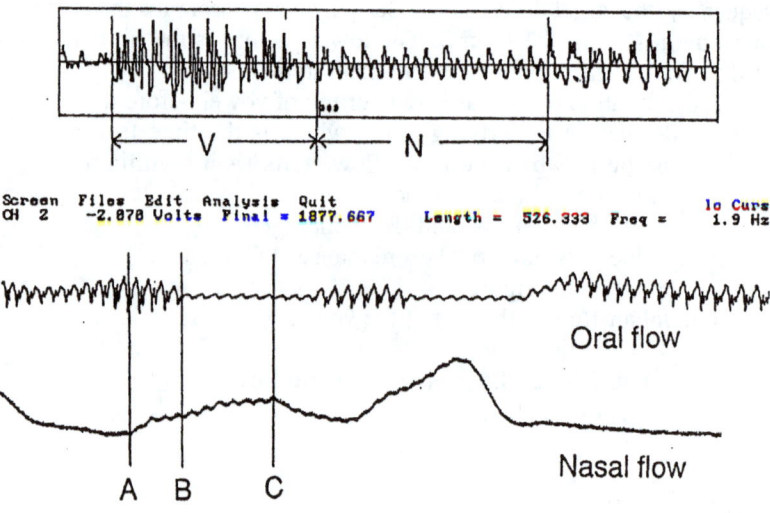

Figure 4.1. Two measurements from the audio waveform (duration of vowel and duration of coda plus onset nasal) and three measurements from oral /nasal air flow waveform. Three places of nasal airflow were marked: A for the baseline nasal airflow just before rising. B for the nasal airflow at the end of a vowel. C for the peak of a nasal airflow.

The Intonational Phrase

The air flow data for subjects for whom air flow was successfully recorded also showed not much difference between phrases with derived and underlying nasal. Figure 4.3 shows that, for each subject, the duration of a nasalized vowel before derived nasal was not significantly different from that before underlying nasal. The time between A and B in Figure 4.1 is measured for the duration of nasalized vowel in ms. The nasal flow transducer signal (Volts) at three places, before the nasal rise (A), at the vowel offset (B), and at the peak (C), also shows very similar values between phrases as shown in Figure 4.4. (The base line for the nasal flow transducer signal is arbitrary.) Each subject has 20 tokens for each conditions, derived or underlying nasal (5 sentences * 2 phrasings * 2 repetitions).

These results show that there is no detectable significant phonetic difference between a derived nasal and an underlying nasal. That is, the change from a stop to a nasal is a categorical one rather than a gradual one. This confirms that the rule of Obstruent Nasalization in Korean is a phonological as opposed to a phonetic rule. Then, the next question is what is the domain of obstruent nasalization. To find out the domain of obstruent nasalization, the nasalization within a Phonological Phrase (either the Phonological Phrase or the Accentual Phrase) and that between Phonological Phrases and that between Intonational Phrases are examined.

4.2.3.2 *Nasalization within and across Phonological Phrases and Accentual Phrases*

First, to examine the obstruent nasalization within the Phonological Phrase, sentences containing 'object NP + Verb' or 'Poss N + head Noun' were examined. There are 15 sentences which have the target consonant-nasal sequence in these contexts (#A1a, A2a, A4a, A5a, B1a, B2a, C2, C3, C4, C6, C10, C11, C12, C15 and C20 in Table 4.2). And, at the same time, sentences where the Consonant-Nasal sequence are uttered in one Accentual Phrase is examined for nasalization. Figure 4.5 shows an example pitch track of a sentence #A4a, *nə nurinbap* + V *məgəbwanni*, where the object NP, *nurinpap*, and the verb, *məgəbwanni*, form one Phonological Phrase and one Accentual Phrase, a LHLH tonal pattern for the Seoul dialect. The spectrogram and waveform data below the pitch track show that the object NP final /p/ becomes nasalized to [m] before [m] of the following verb, as indicated by an arrow. The same is true for the Chonnam dialect as shown in (b), where the Accentual Phrase has a LHL tonal pattern before the High boundary (H%) tone.

Thus, this example clearly shows that the obstruent is nasalized within the Phonological Phrase or the Accentual Phrase. This was almost always true for all subjects. Table 4.4 shows the percentage of nasalized obstruents within the Phonological Phrase and Accentual Phrase. There were 45 token sentences which have the consonant-nasal sequence within the Phonological Phrase (15 sentences * 3 repetitions = 45 tokens). Since the Accentual Phrasing is not fixed except for the first 10 sentences, the number of tokens of nasalized obstruents within the Accentual Phrase varied from subject to subject. The number of nasalized tokens out of the total token number is in parenthesis. Subjects C3 and S2 each has one case where the obstruent coda stop is not nasalized within the Phonological Phrase, thus 97.8%.

Table 4.4. The Percentage of Nasalized Obstruents within the Phonological Phrase and Accentual Phrase. (Nasalized Token/Total Token Numbers) is in the Parenthesis.

Subjects	Phonological Phrase	Accentual Phrase
C1	100.0% (45/45)	100% (16/16)
C2	100.0% (45/45)	100% (18/18)
C3	97.8% (44/45)	100% (19/19)
C4	100.0% (45/45)	100% (18/18)
S2	97.8% (44/45)	100% (22/22)
S3	100.0% (45/45)	100% (42/42)
S4	100.0% (45/45)	100% (24/24)

Now, I will show nasalization across the Phonological Phrases or the Accentual Phrases. First, nasalization across the Accentual Phrases is examined. Figure 4.6 shows pitch tracks of tokens of sentences #B1c ({tʃagɨnbaŋ}{kudʒo-ga}{isaŋhandɛ} 'The structure of small room is strange') and #B1a ({tʃagɨnbak}{nɛmsɛga}{isaŋhandɛ}) 'The smell of small gourd is strange'), uttered by a Seoul speaker, where the possessive Noun and the head noun each forms a separate Accentual Phrase with a LH or LHLH tonal pattern. #B1c is in the upper picture to show the Accentual phrasing relative to the domain of lenis stop voicing. Here, the head noun's initial lenis stop /k/ of [kudʒoga] 'the structure-NOM' is not voiced after the possessive noun's final voiced segment [ŋ] of [tʃagɨnbaŋ] 'small room', as shown by the broken line of the pitch track. Thus, the Accentual Phrase boundary is confirmed by the F0 pattern. The pitch track of #B1a is in the lower

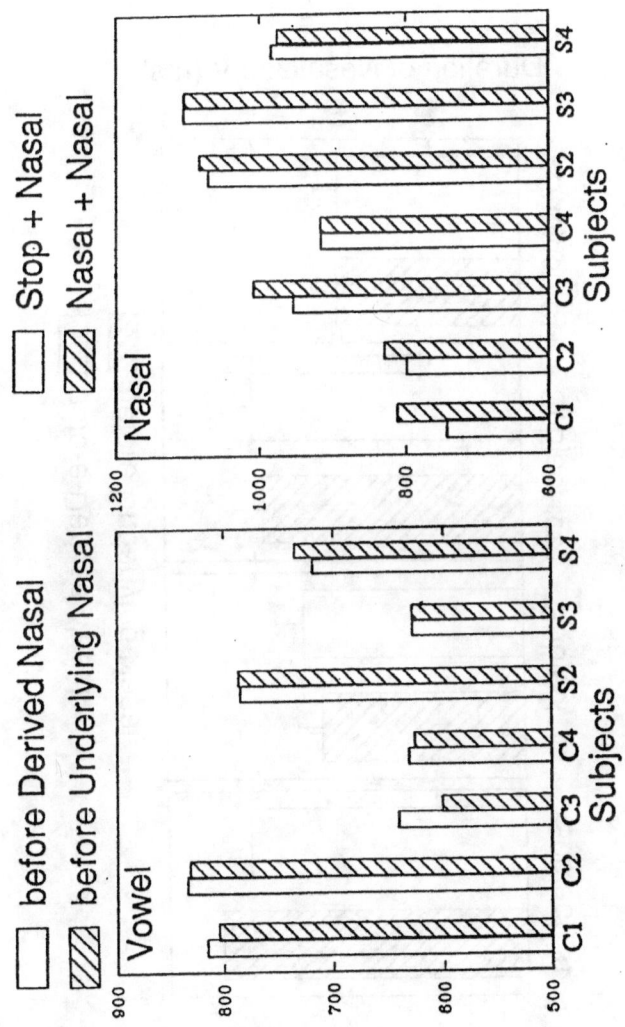

Figure 4.2. Mean duration of vowel and of the nasal measured from audio waveforms and averaged over the tokens for each subject.

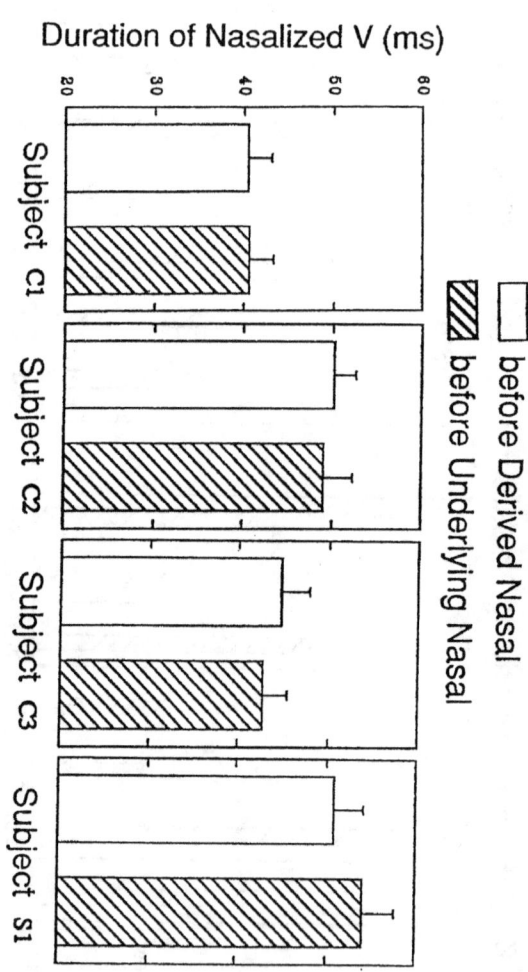

Figure 4.3. Mean durations of the nasalized portion of the preceding vowel from airflow waveforms. (N=20, A Standard Error is shown on top of each bar.)

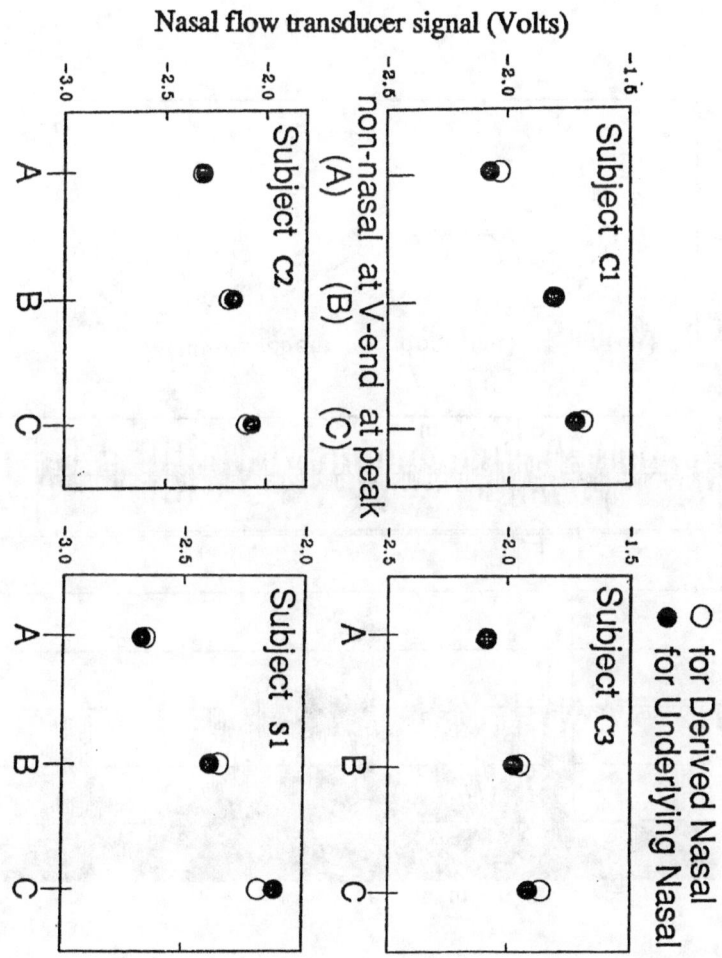

Figure 4.4. Mean nasal flow transducer signal (Volts) at three different places (base line arbitrary) : A, B, and C as defined in Figure 4.1.

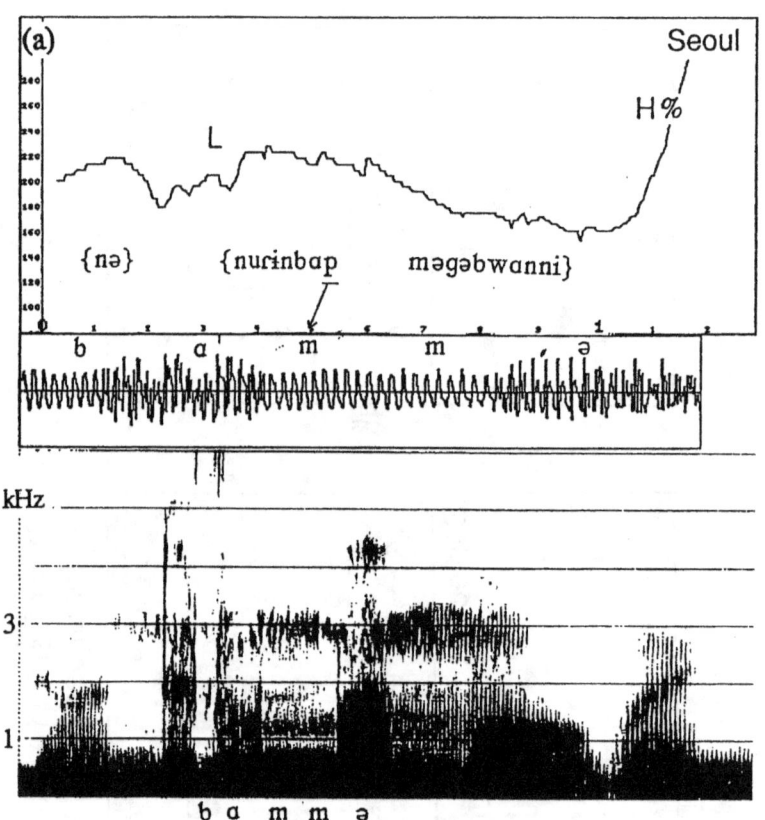

Figure 4.5. A pitch track of a sentence, Subj.NP nə +Obj. NP nuɾinbap + V məgəbwanni, meaning 'Have you tried scorched rice?', uttered (a) by S3 and (b) by C1. The waveform below the pitch track shows a part of a sentence spanning the boundary between the Obj. NP and the verb, and the spectrogram shows the stop is nasalized.

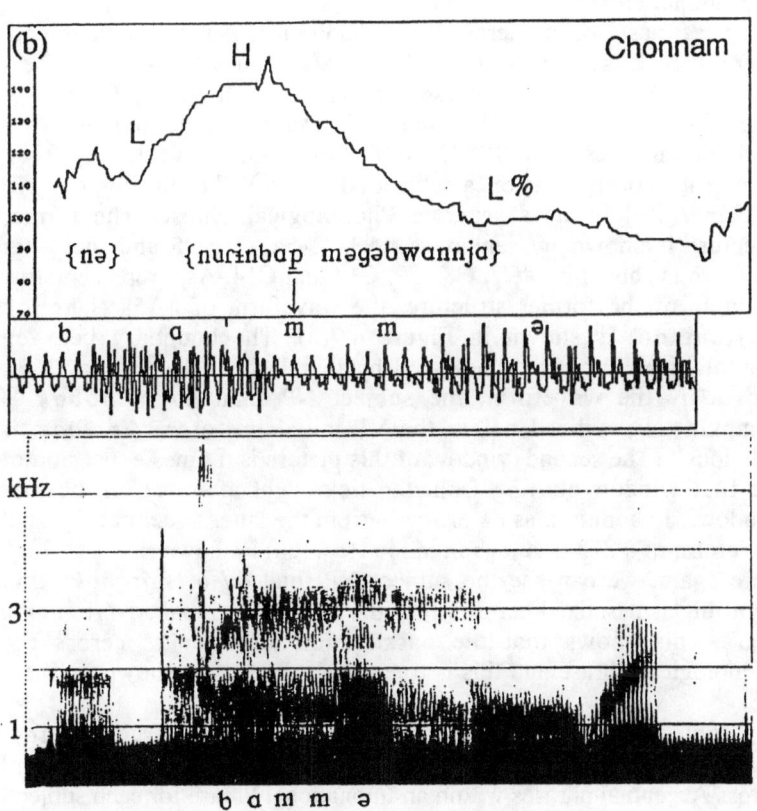

Figure 4.5. (continued)

picture which has exactly the same accentual phrasing as that of #B1c above: The same structure with the same Accentual phrasing, but with different lexical items to test the nasalization; a Poss. N ending with a stop, [tʃaginbak], and the head N beginning with a nasal, [nɛmsɛ]. The waveform and spectrogram below show that the Poss. N final /k/ is nasalized at the end of the Accentual Phrase before the nasal of the following head N which belongs to a separate Accentual Phrase. This shows that nasalization occurs across the Accentual Phrases within an Intonational Phrase.

Next, nasalization across the Phonological Phrases is examined. There were 13 sentences where the target stop-nasal sequence occurs across the Phonological Phrases: #A3a, A5a, C1, C5, C7, C8, C9, C13, C14, C16, C17, C18, and C19. According to the previous prosodic analyses (Cho 1987, 1990; Kang 1992, Silva 1989, 1990), each of the constituents of [a subject NP and a VP] or [a subj./obj. NP and an Adv.] forms a separate Phonological Phrase. The former structure is shown by sentences #A3a, A5a, C1, C5 and the latter structure is shown by #C7, C8, C9, C13 and C14. As a representative example of the former structure, the waveform of #A5a (i hobak maʃinnindɛ) is shown in Figure 4.7(a). The boundary between Phonological Phrases is indicated by the slashed line. However, as shown by the waveform, the subject NP final /k/ of *hobak* 'a pumpkin' is nasalized before the VP initial [m] of *maʃinnindɛ* 'is delicious'. (The second window of this picture is 6 times expansion of the first window starting from the tick, right after [a], in the first window.) In addition, as an example from the latter structure, a partial waveform of #C13 (i sujəŋbok nəmu tʃagindɛ) is shown in Fig. 4.7(b). Here again, we can see the subject NP final /k/ of *sujəŋbok* 'this swimsuit' is nasalized before [n] of the following verbal adverb, *nəmu* 'too'. This shows that the nasalization also occurs across the Phonological Phrase and this is true for all subjects as shown in Table 4.5.

Table 4.5 shows the percentage of nasalized obstruents across Phonological Phrases (out of 39 tokens: 13 sentences * 3 times), and across Accentual phrases within an Intonational Phrase for each subject. Again, the nasalized token number of tokens out of the total token number of tokens is in parenthesis.

Table 4.5. The Percentage of Nasalized Obstruents Across the Phonological Phrases and Accentual Phrases. (Nasalized Token/Total Token Numbers) is in the Parenthesis.

Subjects	Phonological Phrases	Accentual Phrases
C1	100.0% (39/39)	100.0% (72/72)
C2	100.0% (39/39)	100.0% (71/71)
C3	94.9% (37/39)	97.3% (72/74)
C4	100.0% (39/39)	100.0% (75/75)
S2	97.4% (38/39)	97.2% (69/71)
S3	97.4% (38/39)	98.0% (50/51)
S4	100.0% (39/39)	100.0% (69/69)

Like C3 and S2 in Table 4.4, Subject C3, S2 and S3 have one or two tokens of a non-nasalized coda stop. These subjects tended to produce segments more clearly and carefully. Since this much exception was also found in the stop-nasal sequence even within a word, I consider this as an exception to the rule. Thus, we can say that the obstruent nasalization occurs across the Phonological Phrase defined according to the syntactic structure or the Accentual Phrase defined according to the tonal pattern.

4.2.3.3 Nasalization across Intonational Phrases

Since nasalization occurs between Phonological Phrases or Accentual Phrases, a higher prosodic level, the Intonational Phrase, was examined as the domain of nasalization. Figure 4.8 shows the sentence #C18 uttered by a Seoul speaker (S2) with two different intonational phrasings. The upper picture is a sentence with two Intonational Phrases, meaning 'The woman from Kwangju, her personality is very good.'. The structure is "Topic NP (*kɨ kwaŋdʒut'ɛk* 'The woman from Kwangju') + a subject NP (*maɨms'i-ga* 'personality-NOM') + a VP (*nəmu* 'really' + *tʃotɨra* 'nice')". The topic NP forms the first Intonational Phrase ending with a HL boundary (HL%) tone followed by a pause. The waveform below shows that the obstruent coda at the end of the first Intonational Phrase, /k/, is not nasalized. It also shows the last syllable of the topic noun, *t'ek* , is lengthened compared to the same syllable in the lower picture which is in the middle of an Intonational Phrase.

On the other hand, the lower picture is a pitch track of a sentence where the same segmental sequence is uttered with one Intonational Phrase, meaning 'The personality of the woman from Kwangju is very good.' The structure is "a subj. NP (Det *i* + a Poss. N *kwaŋdʒut'ɛk* + a head N-NOM *maɨms'i-ga*) + a VP (a verbal Adv. *nəmu* + a Verb *tʃoa*)." Here, the vertical line in the picture indicates the end of the Poss. N, /k/, and it matches the Accentual Phrase final High tone in Seoul. The high F0 drops right after /k/ because the following Accentual Phrase starts with a Low tone, i.e. *L*(H)L*H*. The waveform below covers the same time scale as in (a), showing this utterance is shorter than the utterance (a) with two Intonational Phrases. It also shows that the final vowel of the first noun is shorter than that in (a) and this noun's final /k/ is nasalized before [m].

The same sentence uttered by a Chonnam speaker (C1) is shown in Figure 4.9. As in Figure 4.8 above, the upper picture is of an utterance with two Intonational Phrases, with a HL boundary tone at the end of the first Intonational Phrase (HL%). Here, again we can see the lengthening of the last vowel of the topic noun in (a) followed by a pause, indicating the Intonational Phrase boundary in addition to the existence of the boundary tone. The lengthening can be seen by comparing with the vowel duration in the lower picture, which is the same sentence uttered in one Intonational Phrase, thus shorter than the utterance in (a). Here, /k/ ends in a Low tone, the Accentual Phrase final tone in Chonnam, L*HL* or HH*L*, and is immediately followed by a High F0, the initial rising pattern of the Chonnam Accentual Phrase. Also, the waveform shows the final vowel of the first noun is short and the following /k/ is nasalized. Therefore, we can see that nasalization does not occur between the Intonational Phrases but does occur within the Intonational Phrase. Thus, it is clear in both dialects that Obstruent Nasalization occurs within the Intonational Phrase larger than the Accentual Phrase, but not across the Intonational Phrases.

In data I observed, the Intonational Phrase in Korean is generally followed by a pause. Thus, most of the tokens across Intonational Phrases showed a clear pause as shown in Figure 4.8 and 4.9 and in many cases the stop was even released. However, since the pause is not obligatory following the Intonational Phrase boundary, some tokens showed no pause. In this case, the vowel at the end of the Intonational Phrase is lengthened and generally followed by a brief stop closure. An example spectrogram is shown in Figure 4.10 (a) without a pause but with a stop release. Figure 4.10 (b) is given to compare the duration of the Intonational Phrase final vowel in (a) with that of the Accentual Phrase final but Intonational Phrase medial vowel. Only the underlined part of #C18 is shown on the spectrogram. Thus, even without pause, the stop is not nasalized across the Intonational Phrase boundary in this corpus[1].

4.2.4 Conclusion of Experiment 2

The domain of obstruent nasalization in Korean is the Intonational Phrase which is larger than a Phonological Phrase, whether we understand this to be Cho's syntactically derived Phonological Phrase or my tonally derived Accentual Phrase. This also suggests that the Intonational Phrase in Korean serves as the domain of a postlexical phonological rule. Also, the measurements from the audio waveform and the oral and nasal waveforms confirm that the rule of Obstruent Nasalization in Korean is a phonological rule as opposed to a phonetic rule.

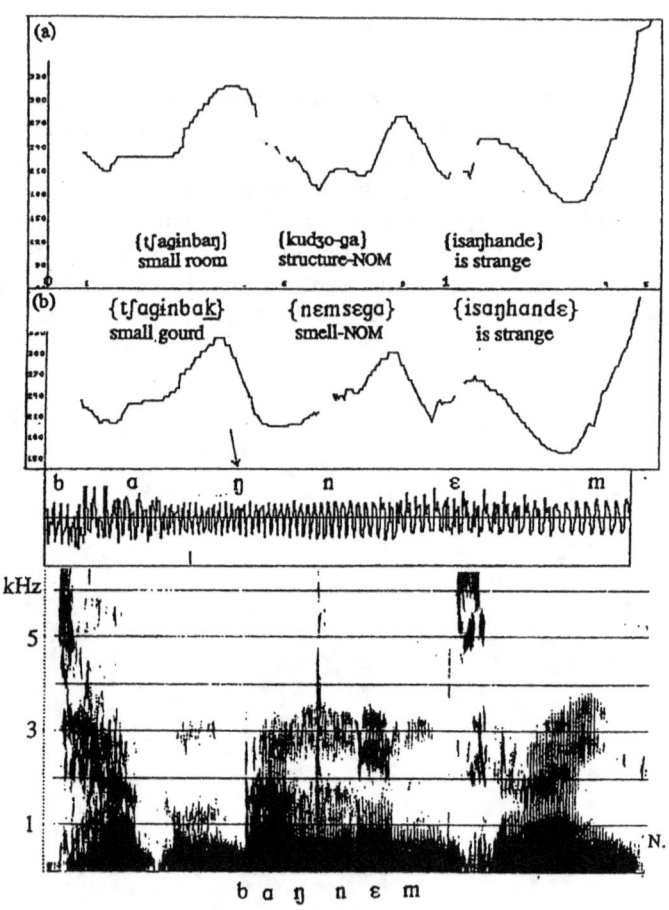

Figure 4.6 Pitch tracks of sentences (a){tʃaginbaŋ}{kudʒo-ga}{isaŋhandɛ} (Poss. N. tʃaginbaŋ , a head N-NOM kudʒo-ga, VP isaŋhandɛ) and (b) {tʃaginbak} {nɛmsɛga}{isaŋhandɛ} (Poss. N. tʃaginbak, a head N.-NOM nɛmsɛ-ga , VP isaŋhandɛ), both uttered by S2. Waveforms and spectrogram show segments around the stop-nasal sequence.

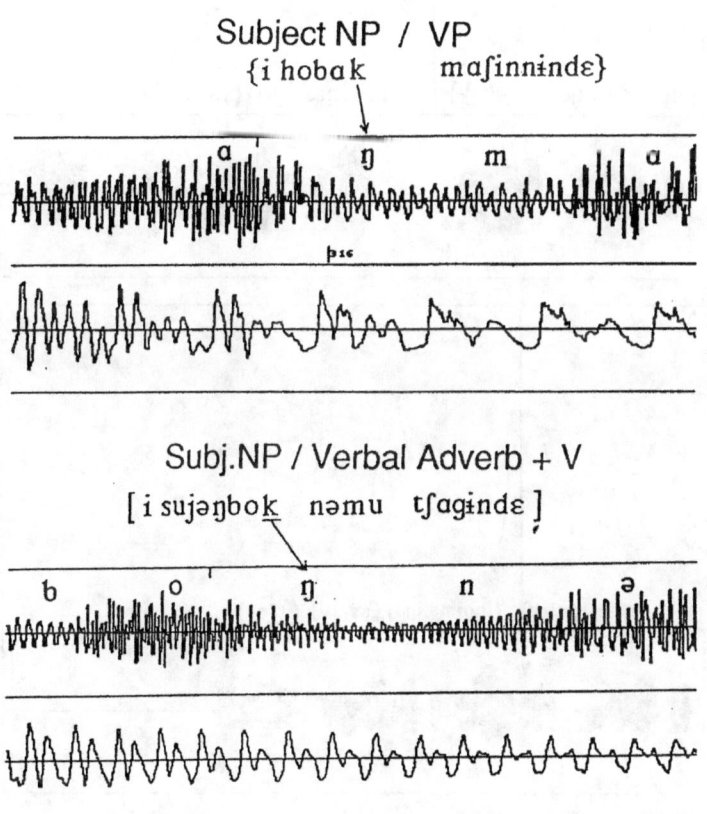

Figure 4.7. An waveform of spanning the boundary between (a) the subj. NP *i hobak* and the VP *maʃinnɪndɛ*. and (b) the subject NP *sujəŋbok* and the verbal adverb *nəmu*.

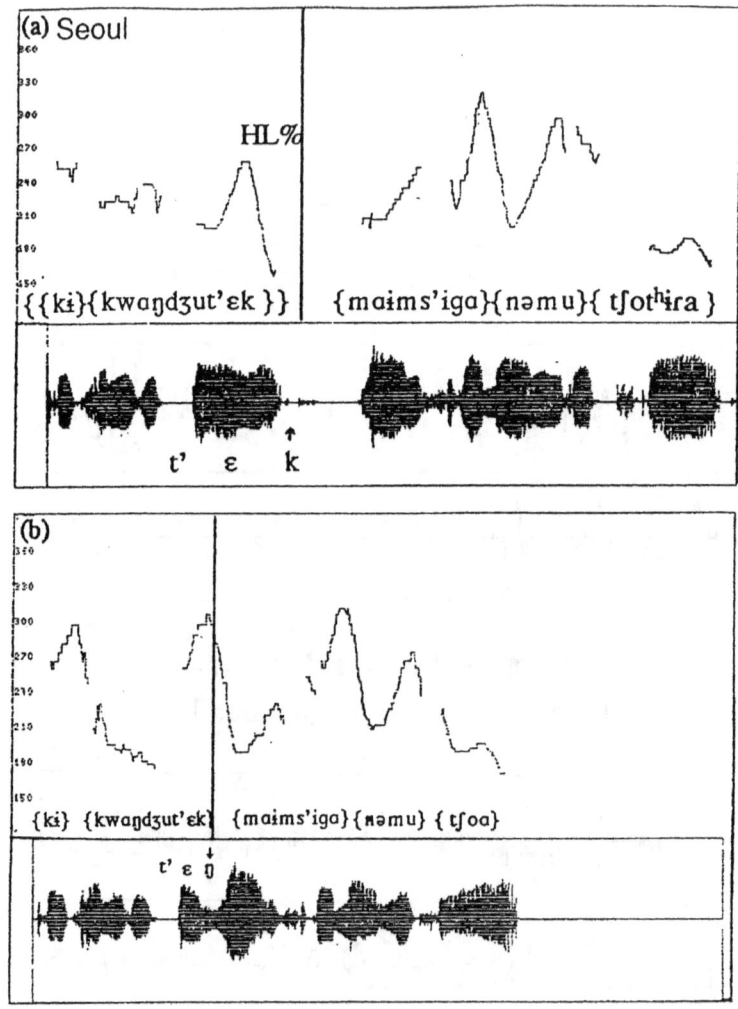

Figure 4.8. Pitch tracks of a sentence in two different intonational phrasings uttered by a Seoul speaker (S2): (a) in two Intonational Phrases and (b) in one Intonational Phrase. The vertical line in the upper picture indicates the boundary between two Intonational Phrases and that in the lower picture indicates the end of the Poss. N, *kwaŋdʒut'ɛk*.

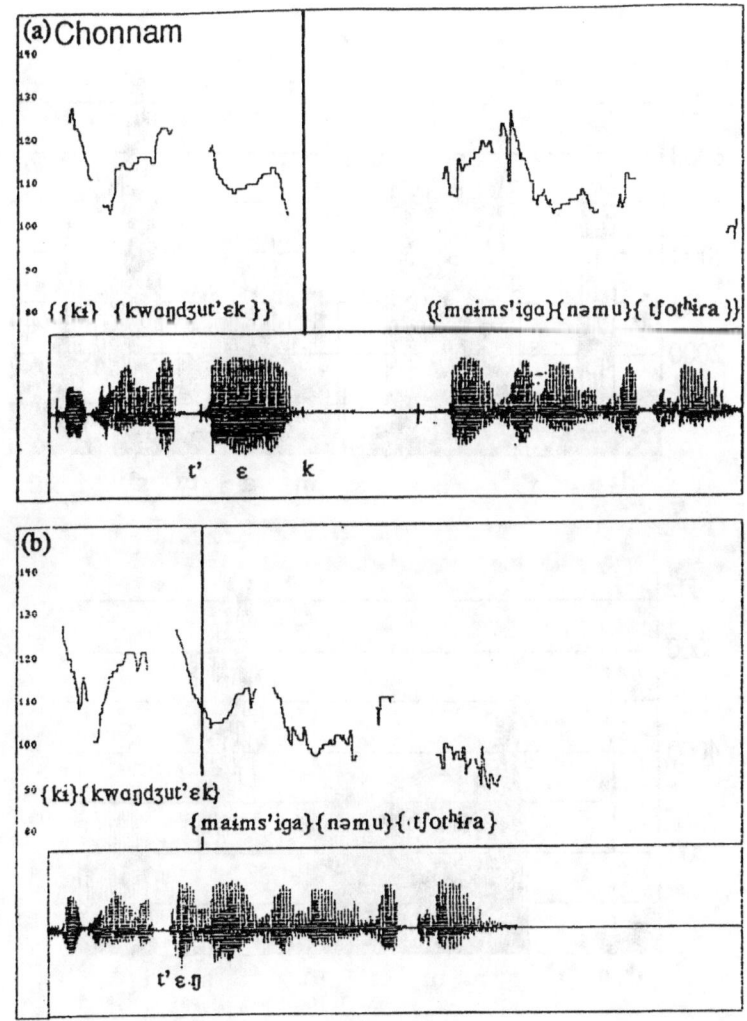

Figure 4.9. Pitch tracks of the same sentence in two different intonational phrasings as in Figure 4.8, but uttered by a Chonnam speaker (C1).

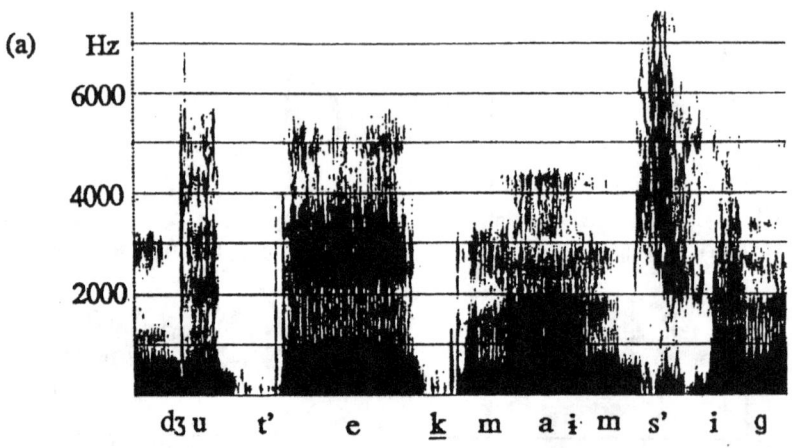

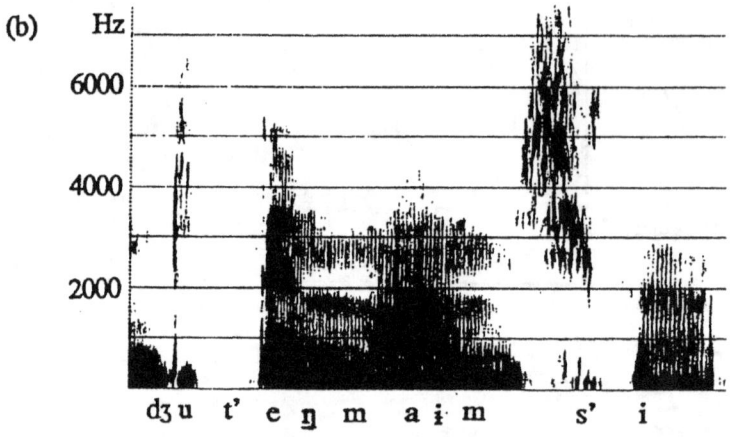

Figure 4.10. Spectrograms of [kɨ kwaŋtʃut'ɛk, maɨms'ika nəmu tʃoa] in (a) the Intonational Phrase boundary after 'ḵwaŋtʃut'ɛk' without a pause but only with the stop release. (b) produced in one Intonational Phrase. (Only the underlined part is shown.)

4.3 EXPERIMENT 3 :
THE PROSODIC DOMAIN OF SPIRANTIZATION AND /S/-PALATALIZATION

4.3.1. Introduction

This section introduces the experiment run to find out the domain of Spirantization and /s/-palatalization. It was shown above that the prosodic constituent such as the Accentual Phrase and the Intonational Phrase serve as the domain of postlexical phonological rules such as Lenis Stop Voicing rule and the Obstruent Nasalization rule. The domain of Spirantization in Korean has never been explicitly identified by phonologists. Spirantization is a rule where a dental obstruent in a coda position followed by an onset /s/ becomes a fricative, [s], creating a geminate [ss]. The formalization of the rule is as in (4a) and examples are given in (4b, c).

(4) a. [-cont, +cor] -> [+cont] / ____[+cons, +cont]
 b. kut [kut̪] + so -> [ku<u>ss</u>o] 'harden+declarative ending'
 c. tʃʰatʃ [tʃʰat̪] + se-> [tʃʰa<u>ss</u>ɛ] 'search for+declarative ending'

This phenomenon has been recognized by some phonologists but called by different names: Assibilation or Spirantization by Martin et al. (1967), Kim (1972) and by Cho (1990), Neutralization (i.e. assimilation) by Cook (1988), etc. However, the domain of this phenomenon has not been explicitly defined.

By contrast, the rule of palatalization, especially the non-neutralizing cases of palatalization (Kim, 1972), where /s, n, l/ become palatalized before /i, j/, has been described in the literature as applying across word boundaries as well as within a morpheme. A formal statement of the /s/-palatalization is given in (5a) and examples in (5b,c).

(5) a. [+cont, +ant] -> [-ant] / ____[-cons, -ant, +high]
 b. sikje [ʃigʲe] 'a watch'
 c. os 'cloth' + i 'NOM' -> [oʃi] 'cloth-NOM'
 d. os 'cloth' # irim 'name' -> [odirim] 'the name of cloth'

Example (5b) shows the application of the rule morpheme internally, i.e. to an underived word and (5c) shows the application of the rule between morphemes, a noun and a case marker. Ahn (1985) and Cho (1987) claim that this rule is a postlexical rule but they do not give any specific domain for it. However, as shown in (5d), /s/-palatalization does not seem to apply across word boundaries. This is because the word final /s/ is surfaced as [t] by Coda Neutralization (this [t] becomes [d] by Lenis Stop Voicing.). By Coda Neutralization, a word final obstruent such as /s/, /tʰ/, /t'/, /tʃ/ is neutralized to [t]. That is, due to the way Korean phonology works, we can't have data where the first word ends with [s] and the second word begins with [i, j]. The only possible way to get palatalized /s/ in this environment is by looking at data where the second word begins with /si/; i.e., the first word final /s/ may become spirantized due to the following /s/ and the fricatives together may become palatalized due to the following /i/. Or, it may work in the other order. That is, the second word initial /s/ may become palatalized due to the following /i/ first and then the palatalized /s/ may trigger the preceding coda /t/ to become [ʃ]. If the latter alternative is true, the palatalization rule would be triggered by the palatalized segment and we may find a palatalized consonant before non-homoganic palatalized consonant. For example, [n] or [l] -> [nʲ] or [lʲ]/ _ [ʃ] (/punsin/ 'impersonation'-> [punʲʃin] or /pʰalsip/ '80'-> [pʰalʲʃ'ip] or /kɨgəl sirəhe/ '(I) hate that' -> [kɨgəlʲ ʃirəhe]). These are possible outputs but since no study of phonetic experiment of palatalization using palatography is available now, I will not attempt to conclude any further but leave as an open issue for further research. Of course, if we look at /n/ or /l/-palatalization, we can tell if the postlexical palatalization rule applies across a word boundary or even the boundary of a larger prosodic categories.

For now, since I examined only spectrogram data, I designed the corpus to get a case where a word final [s] is followed by /si/ across a word boundary. This way, we can tell at least whether the domain of Spirantization is also the domain of /s/-palatalization, but not vice versa.

4.3.2 Procedures

<u>Subjects</u>
7 speakers (3 Seoul speakers and 4 Chonnam speakers) participated in the experiment. All subjects except for one Chonnam speaker (C3) and one Seoul speaker (S4) from the previous nasalization experiment

participated in this experiment. The new Chonnam subject was a twenty-four year old female speaker from Henam city, who had been in the United States for six months.

Materials

Fifty one sentences with different syntactic structures were recorded with five repetitions. Among these, forty were pairs of sentences minimally contrasting 'dental obstruent coda + /s/-onset + /i/' vs. 'sonorant coda + /s/-onset + /i/' between word boundaries as in (b). The target sequence is underlined. A word final /s/ is realized as [t] by Coda Neutralization as mentioned earlier.

(6) a. i + seutʃəs[t] + sikʰɨmha-nte =>[i sɛudʒəʃ ʃikʰɨmhandɛ]
 'this' 'pickled shrimp' 'sour-DEC'
 =>'This pickled shrimp is sour'
 i + seutʃən + sikʰɨmha-nte =>[i sɛudʒən ʃikʰɨmhandɛ]
 'this' 'shrimp pancake' 'sour-DEC'
 => 'This shrimp pancake is sour'
 b. i + patʰ[t] + sir-ini => [ibaʃ ʃirɨni]
 'this' 'a field' 'hate+Q' = '(Do you) hate this field?'
 i + pan + sirini => [iban ʃirɨni]
 'this' 'class' 'hate+Q' = '(Do you) hate this class?'

The target sequence with a dental obstruent coda is to see if the word final obstruent is spirantized or not, and the counterpart sentence with a word final sonorant is to compare the duration of frication of the spirantized coda plus onset /s/ against the duration of a single /s/ when spirantization does not occur. The 'onset /s/ + /i/' condition is to see if the frication is palatalized: /s/-palatalization.

To compare frequency values of fricatives, palatalized vs. non-palatalized, 11 sentences with the onset /s/ followed by vowels other than /i/ were included. In addition, 24 words were also recorded with 5 repetitions to compare these phenomena between words with those within a word. The full list of the sentence is given in Table 4.6 and a list of words is in Table 4.7. The first two sentences in Table 4.6 is again to see the accentual phrasing in terms of the lenis stop voicing. Subjects were asked to contrastively emphasize the words in italic, and as in the other experiments the author modeled contrastive emphasis if needed. Also, subjects were asked to produce any material followed by a comma within a sentence, i.e. the first NP in sentences 41, 44, 47, 49, 51, in one Intonational Phrase. Except for these cases, subjects were allowed to phrase the sentences as they wanted. Generally, all the subjects chose the same Accentual Phrasing for each sentence.

Table 4.6. List of Sentences

1. nə *minaɾi* kiəknani 'Do you remember parsley (but nothing else)?'
    nə   minaɾi   kiəkna-ni
    'you'   'parsley'   'to remember-Q'
2. nə minaɾi kiəknani 'Do you remember parsley ?'
    nə   minaɾi   kiəkna-ni
    'you'   'parsley'   'to remember-Q'

3. nə tʃaŋmik'otʃʰ[t] siɾənwassni 'Have you loaded a rose (but nothing else)?'
    nə   tʃaŋmik'otʃʰ[t]   siɾə-nwass-ni
    'you'   'a rose'   'to load-perfect-Q'
4. nə tʃaŋmik'otʃʰ[t] siɾənwassni 'Have you loaded a rose?'
    nə   tʃaŋmik'otʃʰ[t]   siɾə-nwass-ni
    'you'   'a rose'   'to load-perfect-Q'
5. nə isatʃim siɾənwassni 'Have you loaded the baggage for moving?'
    nə   isatʃim   siɾə-nwass-ni
    'you'   'the baggage for moving'   'to load-perfect-Q'

6. nə *kamasotʰ[t]* s'issənwassni 'Have you washed the iron pot (but nothing else)?'
    nə   kamasotʰ[t]   s'issə-nwass-ni
    'you'   'an iron pot'   'to wash-perfect-Q'
7. nə kamasotʰ[t] s'issənwassni 'Have you washed the iron pot?'
    nə   kamasotʰ[t]   s'issə-nwass-ni
    'you'   'an iron pot'   'to wash-perfect-Q'
8. nə tʃutʃəntʃa s'issənwassni 'Have you washed the tea pot?'
    nə   tʃutʃəntʃa   s'issə-nwass-ni
    'you'   'a tea pot'   'to wash-perfect-Q'

9. i tʃaŋmik'otʃʰ[t] siŋsiŋhantɛ 'This rose (but not other flower) is fresh'
    i   tʃaŋmik'otʃʰ[t]   siŋsiŋha-ntɛ
    'this'   'a rose'   'fresh-DEC'
10. i minaɾi siŋsiŋhantɛ 'This parsley is fresh'
    i   minaɾi   siŋsiŋha-ntɛ
    'this'   'parsley'   'fresh-DEC'

11. i tʃaŋmik'otʃʰ[t] siŋsiŋhantɛ 'This rose is fresh'
    i   tʃaŋmik'otʃʰ[t]   siŋsiŋha-ntɛ
    'this'   'a rose'   'fresh-DEC'

12. nan *tʃaŋmik'otʃʰ[t]* silhtɨra 'I hate roses, but not other flowers'
    nan   tʃaŋmik'otʃʰ[t]   silh-tɨra
    'I'   'a rose'   'to hate-DEC'
13. nan tʃaŋmik'otʃʰ[t] silhtɨra 'I hate roses'
    nan   tʃaŋmik'otʃʰ[t]   silh-tɨra
    'I'   'a rose'   'to hate-DEC'
14. nan minaɾi silhtɨra 'I hate parsley'
    nan   minaɾi   silh-tɨra
    'I'   'parsley'   'to hate-DEC'

15. nə kɨ tʃamos[t] siɾəhani 'Do you hate the nightgown?'
    nə   kɨ   tʃamos   siɾəha-ni
    'You' 'that'   'nightgown' 'to hate-Q'
16. nə kɨ tʃampa siɾəhani 'Do you hate the jacket?'
    nə   kɨ   tʃampa   siɾəha-ni
    'You' 'that'   'jacket'   'to hate-Q'
17. nə *musinos[t]* siɾəhani 'Which cloth do you hate?'
    nə   musin   os   siɾəha-ni
    'You'   'what'   'cloth'   'to hate-Q'

18. tʃikɨm mjətʃʰ[t] sini 'What time is it now?'
    tʃikɨm   mjətʃʰ[t]   si-ni
    'now'   'what'   'time-Q'
19. nə tʃikɨm naika mjətʃʰ[s]ini 'How old are you now?'
    nə   tʃikɨm   naika   mjətʃʰ[s]-i-ni
    'You'   'now'   'age-NOM'   'how old-Copular-Q'

20. nan sotʰ[t]—s'issnɨnke tʃɛil silhtʰɨra
                            => 'I hate washing a pot the most.
    nan   sotʰ   s'iss-nɨn-ke   tʃɛil   silhtʰɨra
    'You'   'a pot'   'to wash-PROG-REL' 'the most' 'to hate-DEC'
21. nan son s'issnɨnke tʃɛil silhtʰɨra
                            => 'I hate washing hands the most.
    nan   son   s'iss-nɨn-ke   tʃɛil   silhtʰɨra
    'You'   'a hand'   'to wash-PROG-REL' 'the most' 'to hate-DEC'

22. onilɨn kamasotʰ [t] s'isstʃianhato twɛntɛ
　　　　　　　=> '(We) don't have to wash an iron pot today.'
　　onilɨn　　　kamasotʰ　　　s'iss-tʃianha-to　　　twɛ-ntɛ
　　'today'　　'an iron pot'　'to wash-NEG-EMPH'　'to be okay-DEC'

23. nə kɨ katʃukos[t] siɾini 'Do you hate the leather cloth?'
　　　nə　　　kɨ　　　katʃukos　　　siɾ-ini
　　　'You'　'that'　'leather cloth'　'to hate-Q'

24. nə kɨ tʃʰəŋpatʃi siɾini 'Do you hate the blue jean pants?'
　　　nə　　　kɨ　　　tʃʰəŋpatʃi　　　siɾ-ini
　　　'You'　'that'　'blue jean pants'　'to hate-Q'

25. kɨ sampɛos[t] siwənhatəntɛ 'That hemp cloth was cool'
　　　kɨ　　　sampɛos　　　siwənha-təntɛ
　　　'that'　'hemp cloth'　'to cool-DEC'

26. kɨ tʃʰəŋpatʃi siwənhatəntɛ 'That blue jean pants was cool'
　　　kɨ　　　tʃʰəŋpatʃi　　　siwənha-təntɛ
　　　'that'　'blue jean pants'　'to cool-DEC'

27. kɨ tʃas[t] sippunɨi ilman tʃullɛ 'Will you give me just a tenth of
　　　　　　　　　　　　　　　　　　the pine nuts?'
　　　kɨ　　　tʃas　　　sippun-ɨi　　　il-man　　　tʃullɛ
　　　'that'　'pine nutthat'　'tenth-GEN'　'one-only'　'to give-Q'

28. kɨ tʃaŋ sippunɨi ilman tʃullɛ 'Will you give me just a tenth of
　　　　　　　　　　　　　　　　　　the soy sauce?'
　　　kɨ　　　tʃaŋ　　　sippun-ɨi　　　il-man　　　tʃullɛ
　　　'that'　'soy sauce'　'tenth-GEN'　'one-only'　'to give-Q'

29. jotʃɨm soŋipəsəs[t] sisɛka ət'əni 'How is the market price of a pine
　　　　　　　　　　　　　　　　　　mushroom thesedays?'
　　　jotʃɨm　　　soŋipəsəs　　　sisɛ-ka　　　ət'ə-ni
　　　'thesedays'　'a pine mushroom'　'a market price-GEN'　'how-Q'

30. jotʃɨm twɛtʃikoki sisɛka ət'əni 'How is the market price of a
　　　　　　　　　　　　　　　　　　pine mushroom thesedays?'
　　　jotʃɨm　　　twɛtʃikoki　　　sisɛ-ka　　　ət'ə-ni
　　　'thesedays'　'pork'　'a market price-GEN'　'how-Q'

31. nan kɨ tʃamos[t] siltʰɨɾa 'I don't like the nightgown'
    na-n   kɨ   tʃamos   siltʰɨɾa
    'I-TOP' 'that' 'a nightgown' 'to hate-DEC'
32. nan kɨ motʃa siltʰɨɾa 'I don't like the hat'
    na-n   kɨ   motʃa   siltʰɨɾa
    'I-TOP' 'that' 'a hat' 'to hate-DEC'

33. kɨ tʃas[t] sɛkk'ali isaŋhantɛ   'The color of the pine nuts is strange'
    kɨ   tʃas   sɛkk'al-i   isaŋha-ntɛ
    'that' 'pine nuts' 'color--NOM' 'strange-DEC'
34. kɨ tʃaŋ sɛkk'ali isaŋhantɛ   'The color of the soy sauce is strange'
    kɨ   tʃaŋ   sɛkk'al-i   isaŋha-ntɛ
    'that' 'soy sauce' 'color--NOM' 'strange-DEC'

35. kɨ tʃamos[t] satʃima 'Don't buy the nightgown'
    kɨ   tʃamos   sa-tʃima
    'that' 'nightgown' 'to buy-NEG IMP'
36. kɨ patʃi satʃima 'Don't buy the pants'
    kɨ   patʃi   sa-tʃima
    'that' 'pants' 'to buy-NEG IMP'

37. kɨ ɛka tʃʰəs[t] sontʃuɾɛ 'That child is the first grandchild'
    kɨ   ɛka   tʃʰəs   sontʃu-ɾɛ
    'that' 'child-NOM' 'first' 'grandchild-DEC'
38. kɨ ɛka maknɛ sontʃuɾɛ 'That child is the last grandchild'
    kɨ   ɛka   maknɛ   sontʃu-ɾɛ
    'that' 'child-NOM' 'last' 'grandchild-DEC'

39. kɨ sɛutʃəs[t] siŋsiŋhatəntɛ 'That pickled shrimp is fresh'
    kɨ   sɛutʃəs   siŋsiŋhatəntɛ
    'this' 'pickled shrimp' 'fresh-DEC'
40. i sɛutʃən sikʰɨmhantɛ 'This shrimp pancake is sour'
    i   sɛutʃən   sikʰɨmha-ntɛ
    'this' 'shrimp pancake' 'sour-DEC'
41. kɨ sɛutʃəs[t] siŋsiŋhatəntɛ   'That pickled shrimp, it is fresh' (two I-phrases)
    kɨ   sɛutʃəs   siŋsiŋhatəntɛ
    'this' 'pickled shrimp' 'fresh-DEC'

42. kɨ tʃʰəmamitʰ[tʰ] siwənhatəntɛ 'It was cool under that eaves'
    kɨ   tʃʰəmamitʰ   siwənha-tən-tɛ
    'this' 'the eaves'   'cool-EXP-DEC'
43. kɨ toŋtʃʰimi siwənhatəntɛ 'The chopped radishes pickled in salt
                                water were cool'
    kɨ   toŋtʃʰimi   siwənha-tən-tɛ
    'this' 'chopped radishes pickled in salt water'   'cool-EXP-DEC'
44. kɨ tʃʰəmamitʰ[tʰ] siwənhatɨɾa 'Under that eaves, it was cool '
                                    (two I-phrases)
    kɨ   tʃʰəmamitʰ   siwənha-tɨɾa
    'this' 'the eaves'   'cool-EXP-DEC'

45. kɨ katʃukos[tʰ] sutʃʰika nəmu kʰɨntɛ   'The size of the leather
                                            cloth is too big'
    kɨ   katʃukos   sutʃʰi-ka   nəmu   kʰɨ-ntɛ
    'this' 'leather cloth' 'size-NOM'   'too'   'big-DEC'
46. kɨ tʃʰəŋpatʃi sutʃʰika nəmu kʰɨntɛ   'The size of the blue jean
                                          pants is too big'
    kɨ   tʃʰəŋpatʃi   sutʃʰi-ka   nəmu   kʰɨ-ntɛ
    'this' 'blue jean pants' 'size-NOM' 'too'   'big-DEC'
47. kɨ katʃukos[tʰ] sutʃʰika nəmu kʰɨtəɾa   'The leather cloth, the size
                                             is too big' (two I-phrases)
    kɨ   katʃukos   sutʃʰi-ka   nəmu   kʰɨ-ntɛ
    'thi   'leather cloth' 'size-NOM'   'too'   'big-DEC'

48. kɨ oɾitʰəlos[tʰ] silhɨmjən toŋsɛŋ tʃutʃa   'If (you) don't like the
                                                down cloth, let's give it to (your) borther'
    kɨ   oɾitʰəlos   silh-ɨmjən   toŋsɛŋ   tʃu-tʃa
    'that' 'down cloth'   'to hate-if'   'brother'   'to give-let's'
49. kɨ oɾitʰəlos[tʰ] silhɨmjən toŋsɛŋ tʃutʃa   'The down cloth, let's
    give it to (your) borther if (you) don't like it' (two I-phrases)
    kɨ   oɾitʰəlos   silh-ɨmjən   toŋsɛŋ   tʃu-tʃa
    'that' 'down cloth'   'to hate-if'   'brother'   'to give-let's'
50. kɨ soŋipəsəs[tʰ] sɛkk'ali isaŋhatɨɾa   'The color of the pine
                                             mushroom is strange'
    kɨ   soŋipəsəs   sɛkk'al-i   isaŋhatɨɾa
    'that' 'pine mushroom' 'color-NOM'   'strange-DEC'
51. kɨ soŋipəsəs[tʰ] sɛkk'ali isaŋhatɨɾa   'The pine mushroom, the
                                             color is strange' (two I-phrases)
    kɨ   soŋipəsəs   sɛkk'al-i   isaŋhatɨɾa
    'that' 'pine mushroom' 'color-NOM'   'strange-DEC'
==

Table 4.7. List of Words

==

1. tʃasu	'self surrender'
2. tʃassu	'the number of pine nuts'
3. kɛsu	'revision'
4. kɛssu	'the number of articles'
5. miso	'smile'
6. mitso	'to believe-suffix'
7. pʰatʰ[t]s'i	'red bean seed'
8. pʰasi	'fish market (seasonal)'
9. kasi	'a thorn'
10. hoŋs'i	'a red-ripe persimmon'
11. tasi	'again'
12. as'i	'madam (old honorific)'
13. jəsɛŋ	'the rest of one's life'
14. jəssɛ	'six days'
15. kusəlsu	'macicious gossip'
16. tʃasu	'embroidery'
17. tʃassu	'to sleep-Q'
18. poɾis'al	'a barley corn'
19. kɛsalku	'a wild apricot'
20. massalku	'tasty apricot'
21. kasu	'a singer'
22. kassu	'to go-Q'
23. s'iɾim	'wrestling'
24. siɾim	'anxiety'

Method

Figure 4.11 illustrates the measures used to determine rules. It shows a wideband spectrogram of the region around the target sequence and an average power spectrum calculated over the initial 20 ms of the fricative. For spirantization, the wide-band spectrogram of each of these utterances were examined for the existence of a stop closure right after the preceding vowel and the duration of frication was measured in ms. This is measure (a) in Figure 4.11. For /s/-palatalization, since [ʃ] has its fricative peak at a value considerably lower than that of [s], and since any assimilation effect from the following palatalized fricative onset should be the smallest in the initial part of the coda frication, the lowest peak frequency at the initial 20 ms of the coda frication was measured in Hz, as shown in (b) in Figure 4.11. Second, the power spectrum is used to measure the lowest peak frequency during the duration (the initial 20 ms) of frication, as shown in (c) in Figure 4.11. The dotted horizontal line in the spectrogram (upper figure) refers to the same frequency value as that referred to by the dotted vertical line in power spectrum (lower figure). T-tests were performed on the measurements to check whether the difference in the duration measurement, between [s] and [ss], and the difference in the frequency measurement, between [ʃ]+[i] or [s]+other vowel, is statistically significant or not.

In addition, the pitch track of each sentence was also examined to confirm the Accentual Phrasing.

4.3.3. Results and Discussion

In general, Spirantization and /s/-palatalization occur across Accentual Phrase boundaries as well as within a word, but they do not occur across Intonational Phrase boundaries. The obstruent coda was almost always spirantized before an onset /s/ within a word, resulting in a geminate fricative. The only exceptions were 14 tokens (out of a total 766), when the test word was produced very deliberately, and Spirantization was blocked even within a word resulting in a clear stop closure for [t]. For example, Figure 4.12 shows spectrograms for (a) /miso/ 'a smile' and (b) /mitso/ 'believe+declarative ending' and a rare case of (c) /mitso/ with a stop closure. The spectrogram for /mitso/ shows a longer frication and the frication starts right after the preceding [i]. Figure 4.13 shows spectrograms for (a) /kasi/ 'a thorn' and (b) /kasa/ 'house work'; the lowest peak frequency for /kasi/ is lower, about 3500 Hz, than that for /kasa/.

Spirantization and /s/-palatalization are also found to apply across word boundaries and even across Accentual Phrase boundaries. Figure 4.14 shows example pitch tracks and spectrograms of tokens of the sentences where the target obstruent coda and onset at a word boundary are produced (a) in the same Accentual Phrase and (b) in two different Accentual Phrases: /tʃangmik'otʃʰ[t] sirənwanni/ 'Have you loaded the rose?'. (An object noun and the following verb can form either one or two Accentual Phrases but always form one Accentual Phrase if the object noun is focused. The initial high F0 pattern in (a) indicates that the object noun is emphasized (see Chapter 2.). The spectrogram in (a) shows no stop closure at the end of the object noun and the lowest frequency peak is seen to begin right after the /o/ of 'rose' and to continue all the way through the onset of the following verb; i.e. the object noun final obstruent is spirantized and palatalized. Fig. 4.14b shows the sentence produced as two Accentual Phrases. (See the very high initial peak for the last Accentual Phrase, which is focused.) The last H is a boundary tone of the question intonation. The spectrogram under the pitch track shows the same pattern of frication as that in (a) indicating the application of Spirantization and palatalization. Fig. 4.14c is a part of the spectrogram of a sentence, /nə isatʃʻim sirənwanni?/ 'Have you loaded baggage for moving?' (isatʃʻim 'a baggage for moving' + sirənwanni 'Have (you) loaded+question'), showing the palatalized /s/ in the middle of an Accentual Phrase. The frication in (c) is shorter in duration but has the same peak frequency as the frication in (a) and (b). Thus, the spectrogram in Figure 4.14a shows that, within one Accentual Phrase, the word final [t] of tʃaŋmik'otʃʰ [tʃaŋmik'ot] becomes spirantized before the word initial /s/ of sirənwanni, creating a longer frication compared to that of Figure 4.14c, which has a word final sonorant coda followed by a word initial /s/.

However, Spirantization and /s/-palatalization do not occur across Intonational Phrase boundaries. As an example, Figure 4.15 shows pitch tracks and spectrograms of a sentence #44, a structure of 'Subject NP + VP' (ki tʃʰəmamitʰ siwənhatɨra. 'It is cool under the eaves.'), produced by the Chonnam speaker (C1) in two different intonational phrasings: One in one intonational phrasing and the other in two intonational phrasings putting a phrase boundary right after the subject NP, tʃʰəmamitʰ. X-axis covers the same time for both (a) and (b). Figure 4.15(a) shows an utterance with one Intonational Phrase with two Accentual Phrases inside and a High boundary tone, ({HHL}{HHL}H%). Each Accentual Phrase has a HHL tonal pattern because the initial segment of each phrase has a laryngeal feature of [+spread], [tʃʰ] and [s]. ( ) is used as an Intonational Phrase marker. Figure 4.15(b) shows a pitch track and spectrogram of the same sentence uttered in two Intonational Phrases with a HL boundary tone and a pause in between, ({HHL}HL%) ({HHL}H%).

Fig. 4.15a shows that within the Intonational Phrase, frication starts right after [i] of 'tʃʰəmamitʰ' and merges with the following onset /s/ and the spirantized fricative coda is palatalized together with the onset /s/ before /i/ as in [ki tʃʰəmamiʃʃiwənhadɨra]. On the other hand, as in Figure 4.15b, a stop closure for [t] (shown by the burst line after the vowel [i] between 3000 and 4000Hz) and a pause are seen between the Intonational Phrases blocking Spirantization. Since there is no Spirantization, there is also no /s/-palatalization.

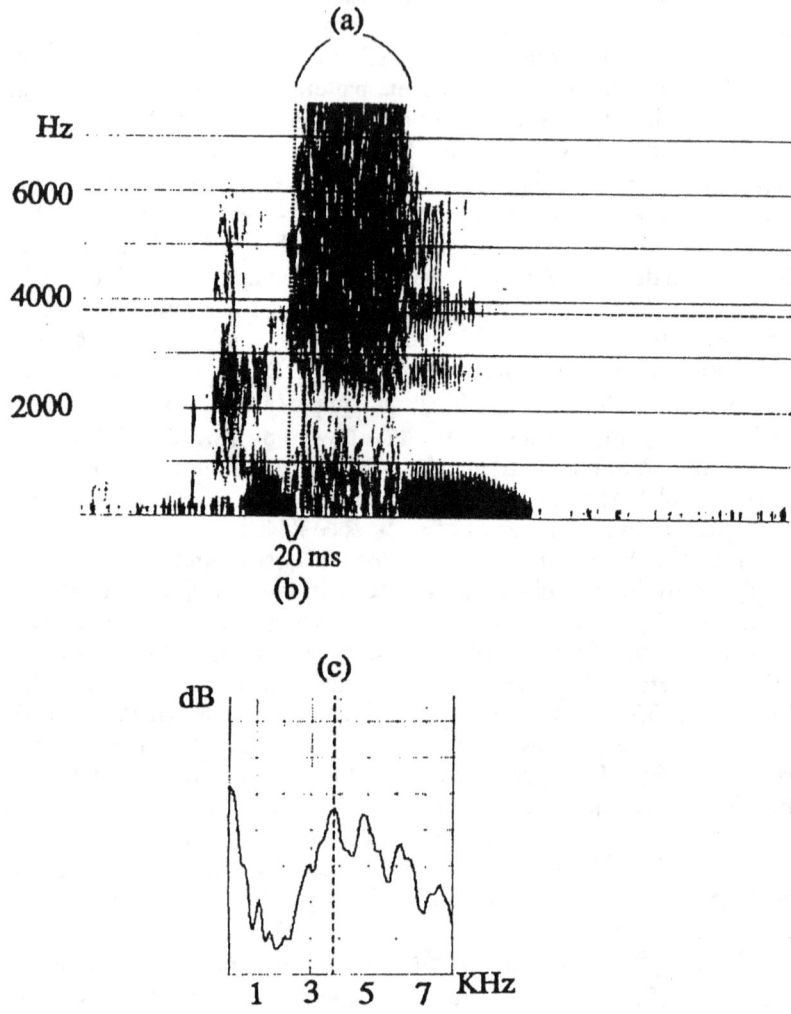

Figure 4.11. A sample spectrogram and a power spectrum showing measurements. (a) the duration of frication, (b) the initial 20 ms of the frication and (c) the lowest peak frequency during the 20 ms of the frication. Both the vertical line on the spectrum and the horizontal line on the spectrogram refer to the same frequency value.

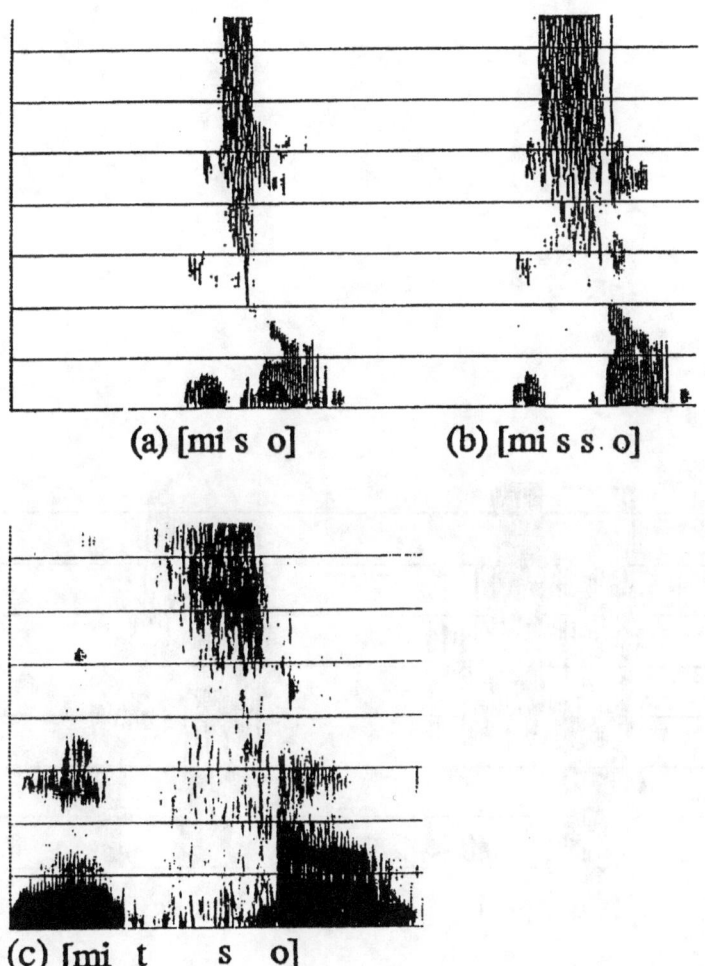

Figure 4.12. Spectrograms for (a) /miso/ 'a smile' and (b) /mitso/ 'believe' without stop closure and (c) /mitso/ with stop closure

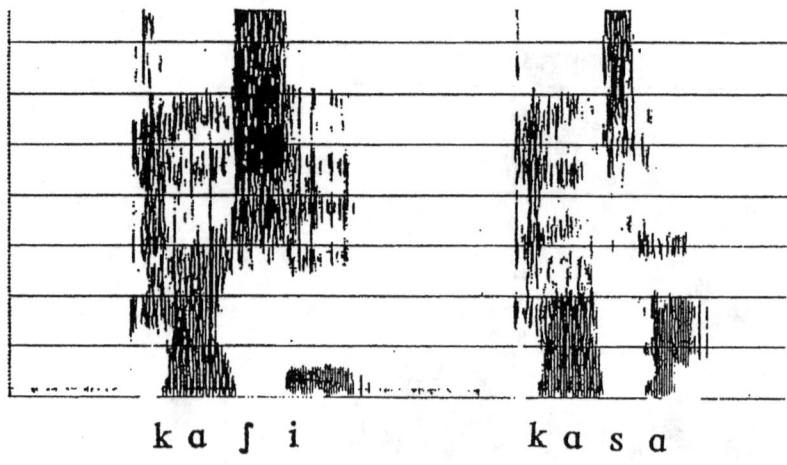

Figure 4.13. Spectrograms of palatalized /s/ in *kasi* 'a thorn' vs. non-palatalized /s/ in *kasa* 'house work'

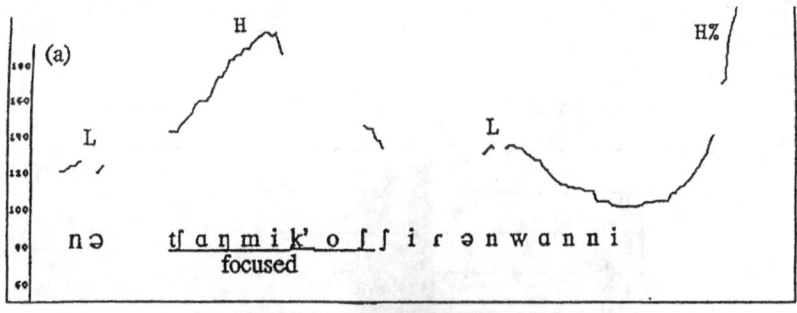

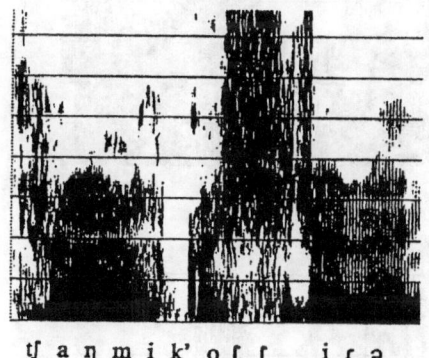

Figure 4.14. Pitch tracks and spectrogram of /tʃangmik'otʃʰ sirənwassni?/ [tʃaŋmik'oʃ ʃirənwɑnni] 'Have you loaded a rose?', uttered by the Seoul speaker (S1) in two accentual phrasings: (a) in one Accentual Phrase and (b) in two Accentual Phrases. (c) is spectrogram of [isatʃ'im sirənwanni?] 'Have you loaded baggage for moving?' uttered by S2 in two Accentual Phrases. Only the underlined parts of the sentence are shown in the spectrograms.

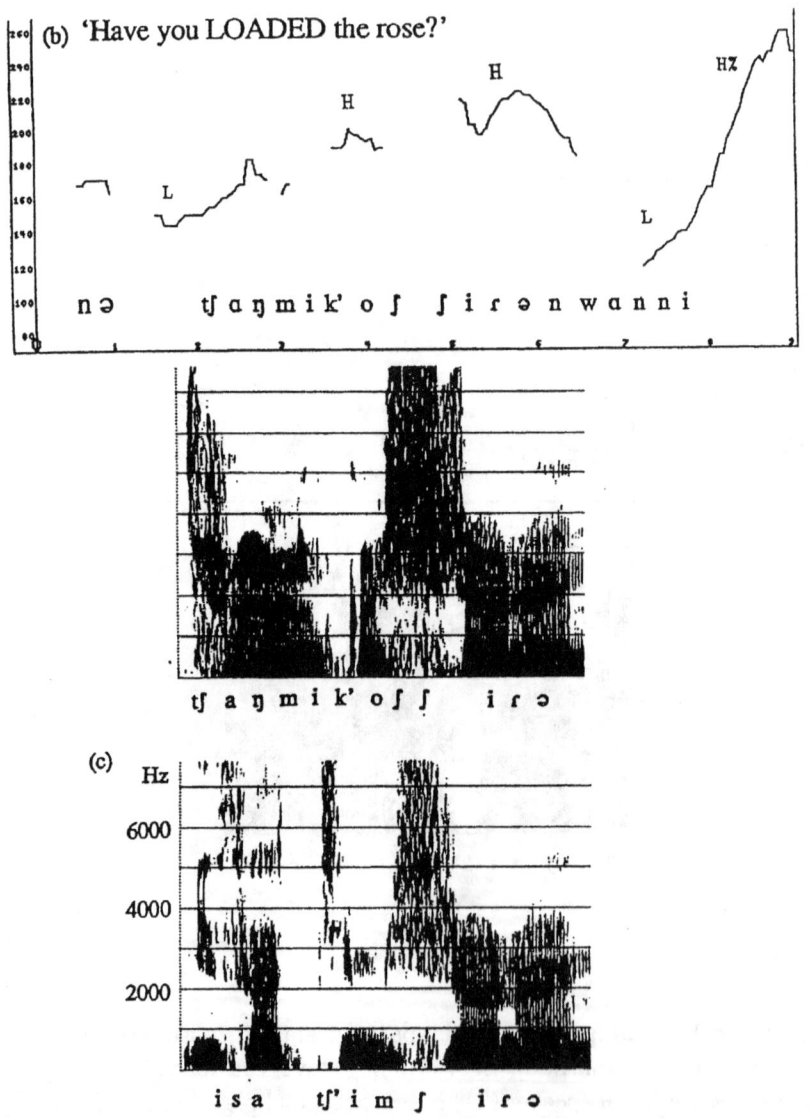

Figure 4.14. (continued)

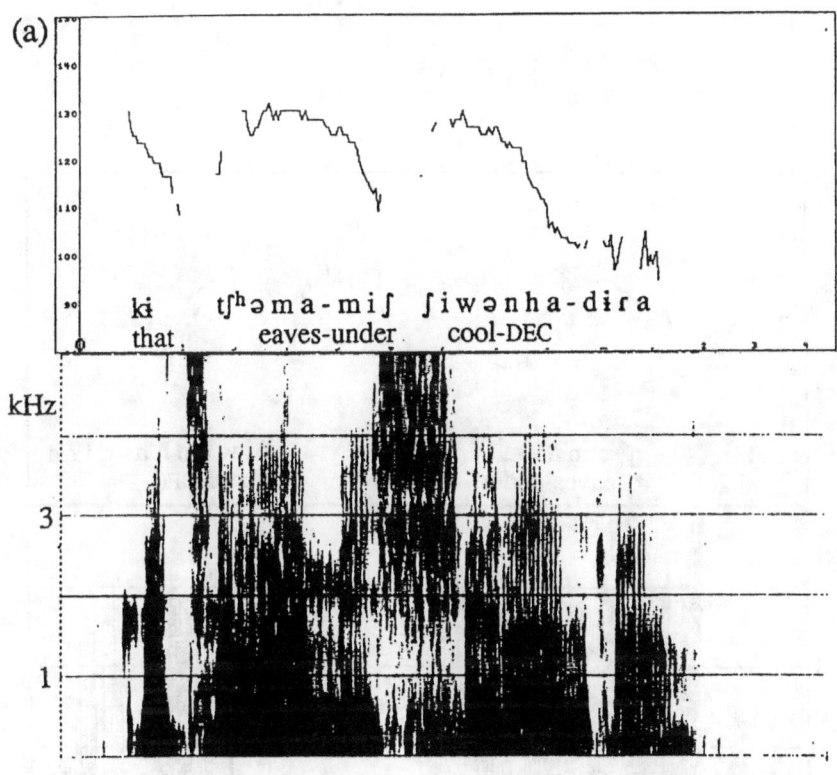

Figure 4.15. Pitch tracks and spectrograms of [kɨ tʃʰəmamitʰsiwənhatɨra.] in two different Intonational phrasings produced by the Chonnam speaker, C1. (a) in one Intonational Phrase, ({kɨ tʃʰəmamiʃ ʃiwənhadɨra}), meaning 'It is cool under the eaves'. (b) in two Intonational Phrases, ({kɨ tʃʰəmamit}) ({ʃiwənhadɨra}), meaning 'Under the eaves, it is cool'.

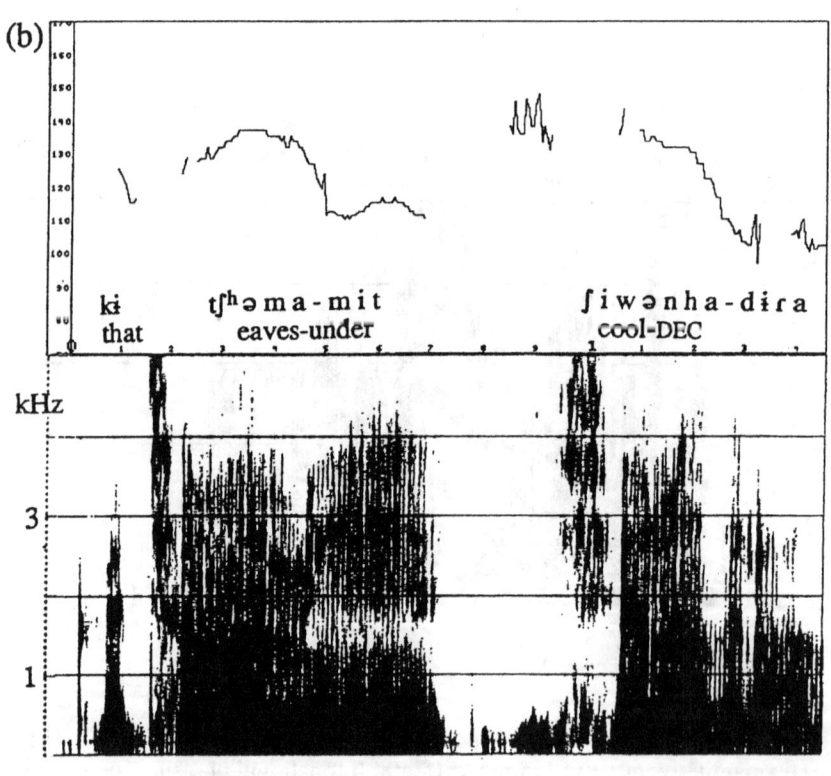

Figure 4.15. (continued)

In summary, word final obstruents followed by a word initial /s/ becomes spirantized almost all the time within an Intonational Phrase with a very few exceptions, and Spirantization is blocked across Intonational Phrase boundaries even when there is no intervening pause. (And when Spirantization occurred, the frication always showed palatalization before the following /i/.) Table 4.8 shows the number of tokens in different prosodic conditions for each subject: first, the number of tokens where the stop-fricative sequence occurs across an Intonational Phrase boundary with pause; second, the number of tokens where the stop-fricative sequence occurs across an Intonational Phrase boundary without pause; third, the number of tokens where the stop-fricative sequence occurs across word boundaries. There were about 80% of Accentual Phrase boundary and 20% Accentual Phrase medial tokens for each subject. The numbers within the parenthesis is the number of tokens combining both across and within an Accentual Phrase condition. (Due to several missing tokens, the number differs from speaker to speaker.). Lastly, the last column shows the number of tokens where the stop-fricative sequence occurs within a word. For each speaker, there were 25 tokens of sentences where the sequence occurs across an Intonational Phrase boundary and there were 120 tokens of words with an obstruent coda followed by a fricative onset. 'No Spirantization' means when the coda stop was not spirantized and a stop closure was shown in the spectrogram.

Table 4.8. The Number of Spirantized and non-spirantized Tokens of the Stop-Fricative Sequence Occurring in Four Different Prosodic Conditions for Each Speaker.

	After I-Phrase			Across words within IP	Within a word	
	with pause	without pause				
Subj.	No spirant	No	Yes	Spirant.	No	Yes
C1	24	1	0	219(219)	0	110
C2	25	0	0	215(215)	3	107
C3	17	6	2	206(209)	1	107
C4	17	8	0	220(220)	8	102
S1	21	4	0	213(220)	2	107
S2	22	3	0	118(119)	0	110
S3	25	0	0	210(216)	0	109

For the stop-fricative sequences produced across word boundaries, at least 97% of them were spirantized for all subjects. (The difference between the token number and the number in parenthesis is the cases where the coda stop is not spirantized.) A similar proportion of Spirantization was found in the word medial tokens. There were a very few sentences which were produced without pause after the Intonational Phrase. But still in this prosodic condition, all subjects except for C3 produced with a stop closure, blocking Spirantization. C3's two tokens were produced in a very fast and sloppy way. I considered this as an exception to the rule as in the rare case of blocking of Spirantization even within a word when the word is deliberately produced. Of course, when there was a pause across Intonational Phrase boundaries, there were no tokens where a coda stop was spirantized. Sometimes, a stop closure was often noticed by the burst of stop release in the spectrogram. Thus, it is clear that Spirantization is blocked across an Intonational Phrase boundaries.

Duration Data for Spirantization

To see if the coda stop is really spirantized but not deleted, the mean duration of the frication was measured in within a word and across Accentual Phrase boundaries. Table 4.9 shows the mean duration for the frication for each subject. For each subject, there were 35 tokens for within-a-word tokens and 90 tokens for across-Accentual Phrase tokens. The standard deviation is in parentheses.

Table 4.9. The Mean Duration and Standard Deviation of Derived and Underlying Frication (in ms) of Word Medial and Across Accentual Phrase Condition.

Subj	within a word		across Accentual Phrases	
	derived : [ss]	underlying : [s]	derived : [ss]	underlying : [s]
C1	178.12 (28.74)	76.52 (22.14)	92.96 (15.30)	68.72 (18.58)
C2	200.20 (33.07)	102.24 (21.04)	116.76 (13.74)	89.04 (17.96)
C3	176.50 (33.99)	88.6 (22.33)	98.35 (18.87)	80.43 (20.48)
C4	183.14 (34.28)	94.88 (22.67)	105.02 (15.95)	79.08 (19.29)
S1	137.48 (41.06)	73.90 (24.35)	91.50 (23.16)	76.16 (25.15)
S2	208.59 (26.32)	117.26 (25.56)	96.98 (17.89)	82.16 (14.93)
S3	156.51 (26.80)	78.18 (23.32)	120.77 (32.68)	96.97 (36.68)

For all 7 speakers, the duration of frication for the spirantized coda plus an onset [s] was significantly longer than that of an onset [s] only (p <.001). In fact, it was usually about twice as long as that of the onset [s], indicating that the stop was indeed spirantized and not merely deleted. The duration of [ss] was also significantly (p < .001) longer than [s] across Accentual Phrase boundaries. However, the difference between the derived and underlying frication duration is not as big as that in word medial pairs. At the same time, the duration of the single frication is in general a little shorter than that within a word, while the duration of the derived frication is in general quite shorter in Accentual Phrase boundary position than that in word medial position.

This is maybe because the derived geminate fricative in word medial position is actually a derived fricative [s] plus a tense fricative [s']. (Based on my data, the underlying /s'/ is significantly longer (p < .001) than the underlying /s/ except for one subject.) This tenseness of the onset /s/ is due to other phonological rule of tensing: [s] -> [s'] after lenis stop. But this rule does not seem to apply across word boundaries and less so across Accentual Phrase boundaries. However, since this is only based on informal observation, we need a further experiment to clarify this durational difference. Or, it may be due to the fact that a segment is fully pronounced in a word in citation form but shortened in a sentence level: i.e., a word in citation form is generally produced deliberately and slowly compared to a word within a sentence. Or, the shortened derived fricative could be due to some kind of phrase level degemination process, but since all subjects produced the sentence corpus mostly in two Accentual Phrases but rarely in one Accentual Phrase, I don't have enough data to test this hypothesis.

Peak Frequency Data for /s/-palatalization

/s/ before /i, j/ in Korean has a lowest peak frequency around 2000-3000Hz, clearly different from /s/ before other vowels which has a lowest peak frequency around 4000-5000Hz. (The range here is due to the fact that adult male voices have lower peak frequencies than adult female voices.) Table 4.10 shows the mean peak frequency values of /s/ before /i/ and before other vowels in word medial and across Accentual Phrase boundaries for each subject. The standard deviation is in parentheses.

Table 4.10. The Mean Peak Frequency Value and Standard Deviation of /s/ before /i/ and before Other Vowels in Word Medial and across Accentual Phrase Boundary Position for Each Subject.

	/s/ within a word		/s/ across Accentual Phrases	
Subj	before /i/	before other V	before /i/	before other V
C1	2837.3 (44.0)	4574.1 (503.3)	2734.6 (80.1)	4443.3 (733.3)
C2	2837.3 (123.3)	4407.4 (341.5)	2874.2 (110.5)	4112.5 (524.4)
C3	3216.0 (202.2)	5330.0 (480.6)	3188.8 (139.7)	4981.8 (622.9)
C4	2822.9 (81.2)	5185.5 (174.6)	2805.4 (114.4)	5227.7 (117.1)
S1	3023.3 (71.3)	6240.0 (678.8)	2980.0 (161.7)	4440.0 (180.0)
S2	2606.2 (134.5)	5152.0 (456.4)	2648.7 (162.9)	4760.0 (103.3)
S3	1920.0 (42.8)	3577.8 (385.8)	1897.7 (92.5)	3208.9 (476.1)

For all subjects, the frequency of fricative (at the initial 20 ms) before /i/ was significantly lower than that before other vowels ($p < .001$) in both positions, indicating the derived fricative is palatalized across Accentual Phrase boundaries. However, since Spirantization does not occur across Intonational Phrase boundaries and we cannot have data to /s/-palatalization alone, we cannot tell at this moment if the domain of /s/-palatalization is larger than an Intonational Phrase. To find out the domain of postlexical palatalization rule, we need to test /n/ and /l/ palatalization using palatography.

4.3.4 Conclusion of Experiment 3

The domain of Spirantization in Korean is the Intonational Phrase, larger than the Accentual Phrase. That is, there is almost always no stop closure for the dental obstruent coda before /s/ within the word and between words across Accentual Phrases as well as within the Accentual Phrase. Instead, the neutralized coda becomes a fricative [s] before the following onset /s/, and the frication continues to the following onset /s/. Therefore, the duration of the frication combining the derived fricative coda and the onset /s/ is significantly longer than that of onset /s/ only. However, this spirantization does not occur between the Intonational Phrases.

/s/-palatalization in Korean also occurs within the Intonational Phrase right after Spirantization. The lowest peak frequency value of the initial 20 ms of spirantized frication shows the frequency value adequate to a palatal fricative. However, since examining /s/-palatalization between words was possible only when there is Spirantization between words, and Spirantization does not occur between the Intonational Phrases, it is not clear whether the domain of /s/-palatalization itself is the Intonational Phrase or larger than that. We can only say at this moment that /s/-palatalization occurs within the Intonational Phrase. A further experiment is needed to find out the domain of the other two, /n, l/, non-neutralizing cases of palatalization.

4.4 CONCLUSION

The Intonational Phrase is a prosodic level above the Accentual Phrase and the domain of the intonational contour. The Intonational Phrase is characterized by the variability of its domain and by its function of limiting the application of phonological rules, in particular of the rules for Obstruent Nasalization and Spirantization. As in the case of the Accentual Phrase, the Intonational Phrase varies depending on non-syntactic and non-linguistic factors such as semantic and pragmatic factor, speech rate and weight of the phrase. This variability of the Intonational Phrase domain has been noticed by prosodic phonologists but they had to restructure the domain of Phonological Phrase to preserve the Strict Layer Hypothesis. Since the intonational contour includes the tonal pattern of the Accentual Phrases in this model, we do not need any restructuring rule of the Accentual Phrase after the Intonational Phrase is formed.

Based on the phonetic experiments, I show that the Intonational Phrase, in addition to being the domain of the intonational contour, is also the domain of postlexical phonological rules in Korean like Obstruent Nasalization, Spirantization and /s/-palatalization. Even though the variability of the domain of the Intonational Phrase has been noticed and incorporated in the prosodic hierarchy, the domain of Phonological Phrase has not been yet. In the next chapter, I will discuss cases when the prosodic phrasing, especially the Accentual Phrase, is influenced by non-syntactic factors such as focus, lexical meaning, speech rate and heaviness of a phrase, etc.

NOTES

1. Even though I could not find any tokens against this conclusion based on the data in this experiment, I found, through an informal observation, a case where an intonational phrase final stop is nasalized before a nasal when there is no pause intervening the intonational phrases and when sentence is produced in a very fast and sloppy way.

V

Factors Affecting Prosodic Phrasing

The essential unifying claim of Prosodic phonology is that prosodic structure is not isomorphic to the syntactic structure, thus necessitating a hierarchy of phonological constituents separate from the syntactic constituents. However, despite the separation of the two structures, in most accounts within Prosodic Phonology, the definitions of the prosodic constituents are fundamentally dependent on syntactic structure. That is, the algorithms for building the prosodic units, especially that for building Phonological Phrases, depends on information about syntactic structure — information such as the location of edges of maximal projections or about whether syntactic structure is branching (Selkirk 1984, 1986; Nespor and Vogel 1986; Hayes 1989). The Phonological Phrase defined in such a way has been justified as the domain of phonological rules in many languages, including the Lenis Stop Voicing, Post Obstruent Tensing, Obstruent Nasalization rule in Korean (Cho 1987, 1990; Kang 1992; Silva 1989, 1992, etc.). However, as shown in phonetic experiments in previous chapters, these syntactic algorithms for building Phonological Phrases cannot always predict the domain of these phonological rules, at least in Korean. Rather, the domain of Lenis Stop Voicing and so on is better predicted by prosodic units determined from the intonational pattern of an utterance: the Accentual Phrase and the Intonational Phrase. The Accentual Phrase is a prosodic unit that comes between the Prosodic Word and the Intonational Phrase. Since the choice of where to put Accentual Phrase boundary is part of the intonational structure of an utterance, it is influenced by factors which determine the intonation pattern. These include several factors other than the syntactic factors such as focus, speech rate and the weight of the resulting Accentual Phrase.

To be sure, syntax also plays a role. One common example is the typical Accentual Phrasing between a subject noun and a predicate verb phrase. Prosodic phonologists working on Korean have claimed that a subject NP and a following predicate VP do not form one Phonological Phrase, whereas the object NP and following predicate V do form a single Phonological Phrase. In utterances which I have examined, it is indeed often true that a subject and a predicate do not form one Accentual Phrase. But when the rate is fast or when either or both of the resulting phrase would be short, as in (1), the subject and the predicate instead tend to group together to form one Accentual Phrase, thus becoming the domain of the lenis stop voicing rule.

(1) negɑ pəɾjəs'ə.   => {negɑ bəɾjəs'ə}
     'I'   'to throw-past'   'I threw (it).'

To account for these kinds of exceptions to the basic Phonological Phrase formation rules, Prosodic Phonologists propose restructuring rules that are sensitive to the rate and weight, as already discussed above in Chapter 4. Since their restructuring rule is too powerful, the introduction of this restructuring rule weakened their proposal.

In addition to the rate and weight effect, the accentual phrasing is influenced by semantic and pragmatic factors — e.g., the semantic complexity of word (or Bolinger's (1972) semantic emptiness), the relative informativeness or predictability of the meaning of the word, and attentional focus. The Intonational Phrase is another prosodic unit which varies in size depending on these non-syntactic factors, but the variability of the Intonational Phrase has been noted by other Prosodic Phonologists, as already discussed in Chapter 4. In this chapter, I will focus on factors affecting the Accentual Phrasing of an utterance, for two reasons. First, it is at this prosodic level that my view of prosodic structure differs most from other proposals in which phrasing is based primarily based on the syntactic structure. Second, the factors affecting the accentual phrasing are the same as those affecting the Intonational Phrasing. In sections 5.1 through 5.4, I will discuss nonsyntactic factors affecting the Accentual Phrase: speech rate, phonological weight, focus and semantic weight. In section 5.5, I will discuss the Accentual Phrasing patterns of phrasal compounds which are not always isomorphic to the syntactic structure of the compound. Finally in section 5.6, I will describe the relationship between Accentual Phrasing and syntactic structure and formulate a syntactic constraint on Accentual Phrasing that may be the source of the impression that phonological phrasing can be predicted almost entirely from the syntax. All accentual phrasings of examples given in this chapter are based on native speaker judgements about the acceptability of various Accentual Phrasings for the example sentences. The native speakers include myself and eight other Chonnam speakers and ten Seoul speakers. The degree of consent

Factors Affecting Prosodic Phrasing 157

among my consultants about any particular Accentual Phrasing varied across speakers and across example sentences. All examples and accentual phrasings shown in this chapter are agreed upon by most of the 18 consultants, from about 80 to 100 percent depending on the example sentence.

5.1 SPEECH RATE FACTOR

The effect of rate on accentual phrasing was explored in detail in Chapter 3 in the experiment on the domain of the Lenis Stop Voicing Rule. For different utterances of the same text material, the number of Accentual Phrases tends to decrease as the speech rate increases. That is, at faster rates one Accentual Phrase often contains more words. The number of Accentual Phrases as a function of the speech rate was shown in Figure 3.5.

Figure 5.1 is another illustration of this speech rate effect. The upper figure is the sentence /ikən atʃu tʃoin kɨlimija/ 'This is a very good picture.', uttered at a normal rate by a Seoul speaker with four Accentual Phrases: {igən} 'this', {adʒu} 'very', {tʃoin} 'good', and {kɨrimija} 'a picture-be'. The lower figure is the same sentence uttered at a faster rate with two Accentual Phrases: {igən}{adʒu dʒoin gɨrimija}.

Both pitch tracks are shown with the same time scale to compare the speech rates. The blank space after the pitch track in (b) shows the time difference between the two. At fast rate, because the whole predicate is uttered as one Accentual Phrase, the word initial lenis stops in {tʃoin} and {kɨrimija} are all voiced. This rate effect is very similar to the effect that has been claimed for the Intonational Phrase by Selkirk (1984) and Nespor and Vogel (1986), etc. That is, it is generally believed to be true cross linguistically that the faster the rate, the fewer the Intonational Phrases for a given number of words. Since both the Intonational Phrase and the Accentual Phrase are defined in terms of the intonational structure of utterances, it is not surprising that both prosodic levels are sensitive to rate. That is, the effect is fundamentally the same for both levels. This is further supported by the fact that the Accentual Phrase is sensitive to the weight of the phrase, a factor which is also known to affect the intonational phrasing.

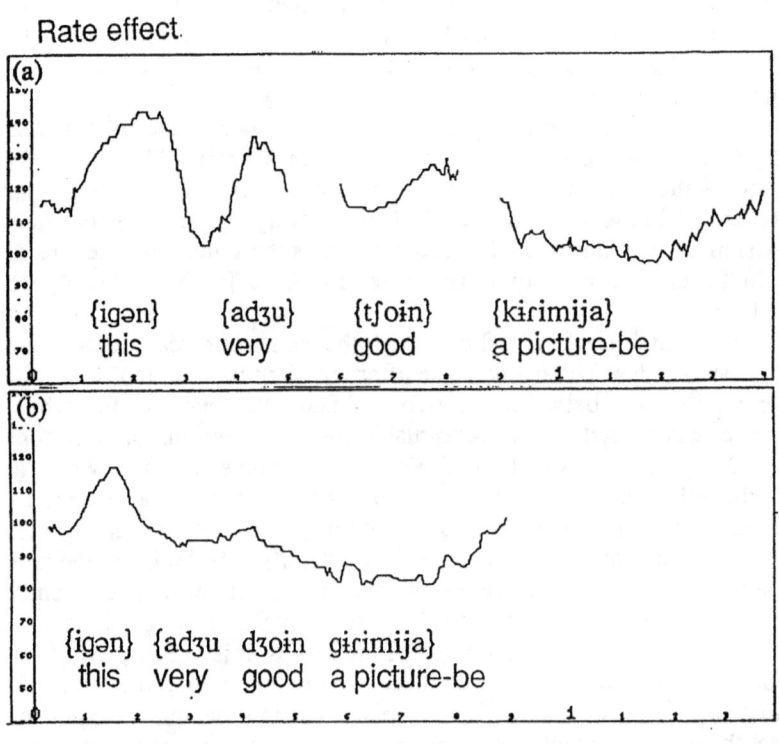

Figure 5.1 Rate effect on the Accentual Phrase (a) a sentence uttered at normal rate as in {igən}{adʒu}{dʒoin}{kiɾimija} and (b) at fast rate as in {igən}{adʒu dʒoin giɾimija} 'This is a very good picture'.

5.2 PHONOLOGICAL WEIGHT FACTOR

The Accentual Phrase is also sensitive to the heaviness of the phrase, that is, to the number of syllables within the phrase. In general, when the resulting Accentual Phrase would have more than five syllables, a sentence of words that otherwise would be phrased together tends to break into two phrases. Figure 5.2 illustrates this weight effect. The top panel shows the pitch track of a sentence /miwun kaɲinin tʃakin kjəŋmilil tʃoahe/ (*miwun* 'ugly' + *kaɲinin* 'Kangi-NOM' + *tʃakin* 'small' + *kjəŋmi-lil* 'Kyungmi-ACC' + *tʃoahe* 'to like') 'Ugly Kangi likes small Kyungi.' The subject noun and its adjective form one Accentual Phrase and so do the object noun and its adjective. However, when the number of syllables within the subject and the object noun increases, as in *kaŋmaninenin* and *kjəŋmanineril,* respectively , each of the preceding adjectives forms its own Accentual Phrase separate from its head noun, thus making five Accentual Phrases within the utterance, as in the utterance in the lower panel.

Another related example of this weight effect can be found in the relationship between the verb of a relative clause and its following head noun. When the head noun is short, a monosyllable or disyllable, it tends to form one Accentual Phrase together with the preceding verb. But when the head noun is four syllables or longer, it tends to form an Accentual Phrase by itself, separate from the preceding verb of the relative clause. An example is shown in (2).

(2) a. kikə-1   ha-1   <u>e</u>-ka   əti-iss-ni
    'that-ACC'   'to do-REL' 'a child-NOM' 'where-be-INT'
    =>{kigəl}{harega}{ədiinni} or {kigəl harega}{ədiinni}

b. kikə-1   ha-1   <u>əlini</u>-ka   əti-iss-ni
   'that-ACC'   'to do-REL' 'a child-NOM' 'where-be-INT'
   =>{kigəl}{hal}{əriniga}{ədiinni} or
      {kigəl hal}{əriniga}{ədiinni}
    'Where would be a child to do it ?
    - i.e.What kind of child would do a thing like that?'

c. jəɲi-ja,   nɨ   tʃak-in   <u>pi</u>   pwa-ss-ni
   'Youngi-VOC' 'you' 'small-REL' 'a broom' 'to see-past-Q'
   => {jəɲija,}{nə}{tʃagin <u>bi</u>}{pwanni }
   'Youngi, did you see a small broom ?

d. jəɲi-ja,　　　nə　　tʃak-ɨn　　pitʃ'aɾu　　pwa-ss-ni
　　　　　　　　　　　(tʃ'ok'ɨman)　(pitʃ'iɾak)
'Youngi-VOC' 'you' 'small-REL' 'a broom' 'to see-past-Q'
=> {jəɲija,}{nə}{tʃagɨn}{pitʃ'aɾu}{pwanni}
'Youngi, did you see a small broom ?
(words in parenthesis are Chonnam)

Both sentences in (2a,b) have the same meaning, but differ in the number of syllables of the head noun of the relative clause. The head noun in (2a) is a monosyllabic word, [e] 'a child', and does not form its own Accentual Phrase but forms one Accentual Phrase together with the preceding verb of the relative clause, resulting in a three syllable Accentual Phrase {haɾega}, or together with the all the preceding words of the relative clause {kigəl haɾega}. On the other hand, the head noun in (2b) is a three-syllable noun, /əlini/, and it forms one Accentual Phrase with the case marker, separately from the preceding verb. The pair (2c,d) is similar; (2c) also has the same meaning as (2d) but differs in the number of syllables for the object noun. The object noun in 'broom' is a monosyllabic word, [pi] in (2c), but a three syllable noun, [pitʃ'aɾu] in Seoul (or [pitʃ'iɾak] in Chonnam) in (2d). The most common accentual phrasing of these sentences shows that the short object noun tends to form one Accentual Phrase together with the preceding adjective, [tʃagɨn], while the longer object noun tends to form its own Accentual Phrase as shown above.

Of course, these are not the only possible Accentual Phrasings: even the short head noun in (2a) or the short object noun in (2c) would form its own Accentual Phrase if it is focused or newly introduced to the discourse to which we now turn.

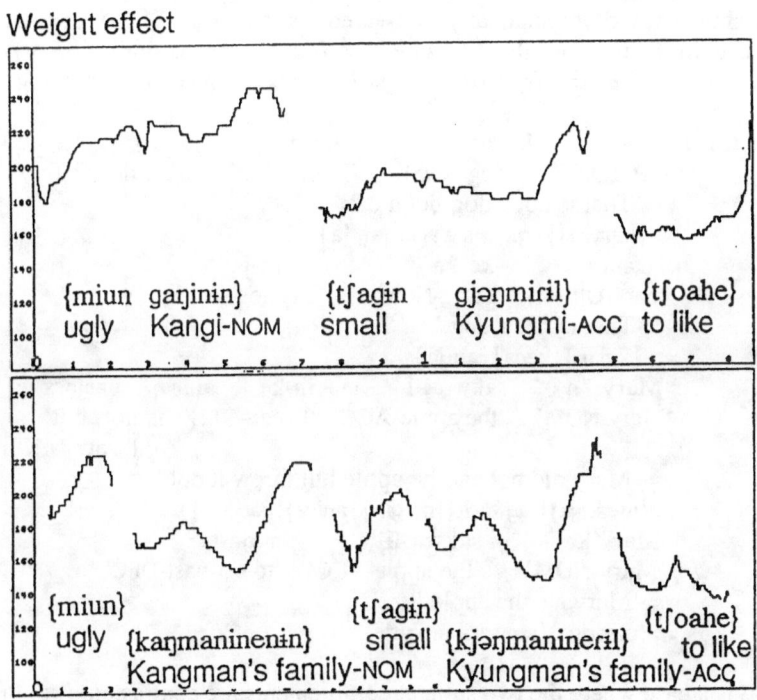

Figure 5.2. Weight effect on the Accentual Phrase. (a) a pitch track of a sentence with three syllable head nouns: {miwun gaɲinɨn}{tʃagɨn gjəŋmiɾil}{tʃoahe}. 'Ugly Kangi likes small Kyungmi' and (b) a sentence with five syllable head nouns: {miwun}{kaŋmaninenɨn} {tʃagɨn} {kjəŋmanineɾil}{tʃoahe} 'Ugly Kangman's mom (or Kangman's family) likes small Kyungman's mom (or Kyungman's family).'

5.3 FOCUS FACTOR

Focus has long been noticed by phonologists as a factor affecting the Phonological Phrasing as well as the Intonational Phrasing. Kanerva (1990) discusses the influence of focus on the formation of prosodic domains in Chichewa: the prosodic constituent lower than the Intonational Phrase, which may be larger than the Phonological Phrase (called Focal Phrase), can be formed into several alternate groupings and this indeterminacy can be resolved by taking into account the semantically and pragmatically motivated feature focus. The Accentual Phrase in Korean is also affected by focus. The examples in (3) illustrate the similar effects of contrastive focus on Accentual Phrasing.

(3) a. kikə-n   ke-ka   aniɾa   kojaŋi-ja
    'that-TOP'   'a dog-NOM'   'is not, but'   'a cat-declarative'
    = 'That is not a dog but a cat'
    =>{kigən}{kega aniɾa}{kojaŋija}
  b. kikə-n   ke-ka   ani-ja
    'that-TOP'   'a dog-NOM'   'is not-decl.'
    = 'That is not a dog.'
    => {kigən}{kega}{anija}
  c. Mary-ka   sakwa-lil   məgin-ke   aniɾa   pərjəsst'e
    'Mary-NOM'   'the apple-ACC' 'to eat--REL' 'is not, but'
                                                        'to throw-DEC'
    = 'Mary did not eat the apple but threw it out.'
    =>{meəɾiga}{sagwaɾil}{məginge aniɾa}{pərjət'e}
  d. Mary-ka   sakwa-lil   məgəste
    'Mary-NOM'   'the apple-ACC' 'to eat-past-DEC'
    = 'Mary ate the apple.'
    =>{meəɾiga}{sagwaɾil məgət'e}

(3a) is a case where the two subject complements are contrasted: [ke] 'a dog' vs. [kojaŋi] 'a cat'. (3b) is given to show that a similar sentence with no contrastive focus has a different phrasing from (3a): i.e. the subject noun and the predicate generally do not form one Accentual Phrase. (3c) is a case where the two verbs are contrasted: 'to eat' vs. 'to throw out'. (3d) is given to show that a sentence similar to (3c) but without the contrastive part has a different Accentual phrasing: i.e. the object noun and the verb, especially pragmatically closely related to the object noun (see Section 5.4), tend to form one Accentual Phrase. In both sentences having the contrastive phrases, (3a) and (3c), each contrasting word initiates an Accentual Phrase and include the following word(s) before the contrastive word. Therefore, in (3c), the object noun, {sagwaɾil} 'an apple-ACC', and the following verb, {məginge-} 'to eat', do not belong to the same Accentual Phrase even though they belong to the same VP, a maximal projection. Instead, each contrasting verb forms one Accentual Phrase, thus the second verb initial lenis stop, /p/, does not become voiced. Since the voicing of the /p/ is not accounted for by the basic rules of the Phonological Phrase formation, the prosodic phonologists add a restructuring rule due to focus to adjust the domain of the Phonological Phrase (see Ch. 3 (1)) or add the focus condition as one of the defining factors of the Phonological Phrase formation rule (Cho 1990).

The fact that focus can change Phonological Phrasing has been observed in other languages: Modern Greek (Condoravdi 1990), Bengali (Hayes and Lahiri 1991), Hausa (Inkelas 1988), and Chichewa (Kanerva 1990). Cho (1990) and Kang (1992) in particular have noticed the focus effect on phonological phrasing in Korean. Cho describes the rule as follows: "Most notably, interrogative pronouns and words with an emphatic or contrastive accent form a Phonological Phrase with the following word, even when the two words are contained in different maximal projections. This happens only when the following word itself is not accented, as in the multiple question construction, and only when the following word has not been incorporated into a Phonological Phrase with some other element . Thus, words with the feature [+accent] form a Phonological Phrase with an unphrased word (Cho 1990, p.56-57)." Here by emphatic or contrastive "accent", Cho means "narrow focus". She seems to be adopting the term "accent" from the literature on pitch accent placement and focus in English.

Cho's description implies that the formation of Phonological Phrase due to focus applies to a sentence after all the phrasing rules have been applied, and that the string of words affected by focus is fairly short. That is, only the immediately following word is dephrased. However, actual data seem to suggest that focus affects longer strings of words and dephrasing due to focus is more ubiquitous. As we can see in the following examples, the effect of focus is to dephrase all following words within the same Intonational Phrase unless one of those following words itself is focused.

The following examples in (4) show the effects on Accentual Phrasing of focus. Corresponding pitch tracks produced by a Chonnam speaker are given in Figure 5.3. (Here, % is a marker for an Intonational Phrase boundary.)

(4) '(They said) A cucumber grown in winter is delicious, but is it really true?'
/kjəuɾe tʃepeha-n oi-ka masit'a-nɨnte, tʃəŋmal kɨlə-nte/
'winter-LOC + to grow-REL + a cucumber-NOM + delicious-but + really + so-Q'
=> [kjəuɾe tʃebehan oiga matit'anɨnte, tʃəŋmal kɨɾənte]
a. neutral focus
{kjəuɾe dʒebehan}{oiga}{masit'anɨnte}%{tʃəŋmal gɨɾənte}%
b. subject within the relative clause is focused
{<u>kjəuɾe</u> dʒebehan oiga masit'anɨnte}%{tʃəŋmal gɨɾənte}%
c. verb within the relative clause is focused
{kjəuɾe}{<u>tʃebehan</u> oiga masit'anɨnte}%{tʃəŋmal gɨɾənte}%
d. the head noun is focused
{kjəuɾe dʒebehan}{<u>oiga</u> masit'anɨnte}%{tʃəŋmal gɨɾənte}%
e. main verb is focused
{kjəuɾe dʒebehan}{oiga}{<u>masit'anɨnte</u>}%{tʃəŋmal gɨɾənte}%

Example (4a) and Fig. 5.3a give the phrasing for the sentence uttered in neutral focus by this speaker: two Intonational Phrases with three Accentual Phrases in the first Intonational Phrase and one Accentual Phrase in the second Intonational Phrase. Other speakers from among my Seoul and Chonnam consultants, produced different phrasings for the matrix clause in neutral focus — phrasings such as {kjəuɾe}{tʃebehan}{oiga} {masit'anɨnte}, ... or {kjəuɾe dʒebehan oiga}{masit'anɨnte}. However, all 18 of my consultants showed the same phrasings when asked to produce one word in narrow focus. Example (4b) and Fig. 5.3b show this consistent phrasing when the time adverb of the relative clause is narrowly focused: the first Intonational Phrase has only one Accentual Phrase while the second Intonational Phrase remains intact. This illustrates how far reaching are the effects of focus, combining all the following words within the Intonational Phrase into one Accentual Phrase. Example (4c) and Fig. 5.3c show the case where the verb of the relative clause is focused. Here, focus has a similar effect as in (b): it makes the focused verb initiate an Accentual Phrase and dephrases all the following Accentual Phrases within the Intonational Phrase. Thus, focus sets off a word from preceding material, creating a phrase boundary between the focused word and the preceding word, and dephrasing the words following it. We interpret this pattern as showing that prosodically the Accentual Phrase is head initial.

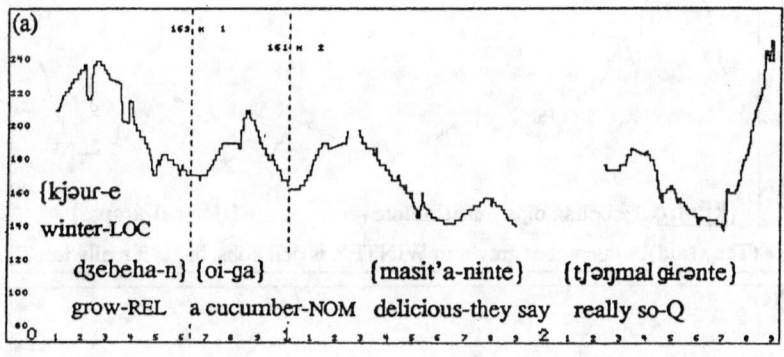

Figure 5.3. Pitch tracks of sentences in (4a-e) produced by a Chonnam speaker
(a) neutral focus
(b) first word [kjəuɾe] is focused
(c) second word [tʃebehan] is focused
(d) third word [oiga] is focused
(e) fourth word [masit'aninte] is focused

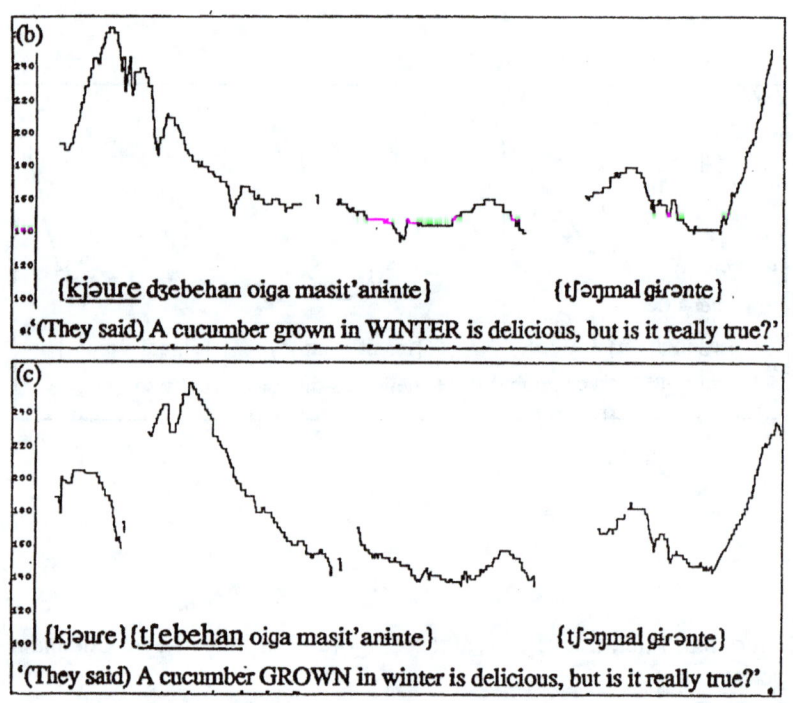

Figure 5.3. (continued)

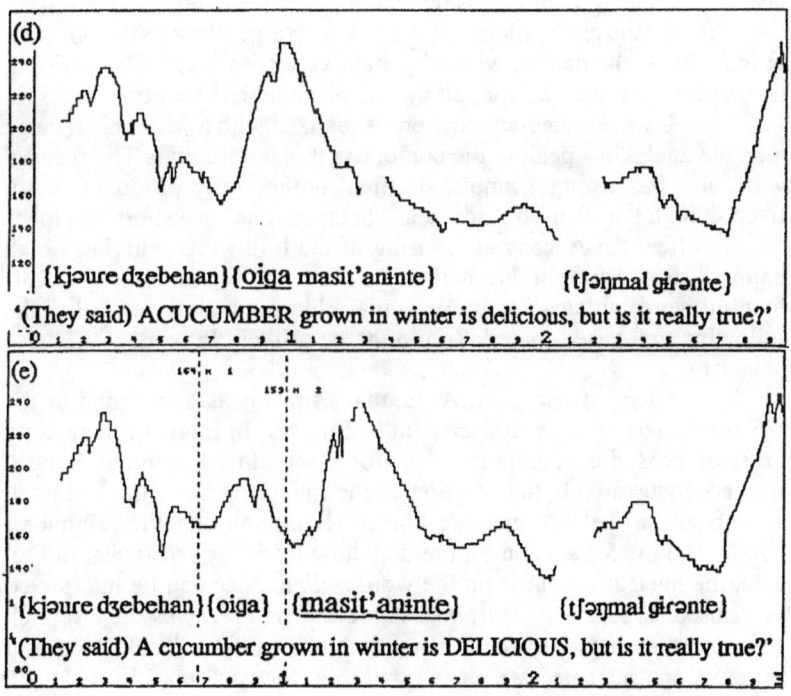

Figure 5.3. (continued)

A similar effect of focus on the phrasing but in the opposite direction is found in Bengali (Hayes and Lahiri 1991) and Chichewa (Kanerva 1990), where focused constituents must be followed by]$_p$, the end of the Phonological Phrase boundary, but need not be preceded by [$_p$, the beginning of the Phonological Phrase boundary. Thus, in these languages, the Phonological Phrase is head final. The phrasings in (4b) and (4c) cannot be accounted for by Cho's focus rule which predicts that there will be a Phonological Phrase boundary between the subject NP [oiga], 'a cucumber', and the VP [matit'anɨnte], 'delicious', which is unaffected by the focus one or two words away.

Figure 5.3d, corresponding to the phrasing in (4d) is a case where the subject noun is focused. As seen in the figure, the main verb is dephrased and forms one Accentual Phrase together with the preceding subject noun, which is different from the neutrally produced utterance in Fig. 5.3a. But, again, this focusing has no effect on the following Accentual Phrase which belongs to a different Intonational Phrase. This dephrasing due to focus across the maximal projection boundary is what Cho's focus rule can explain. Figure 5.3e corresponding to the phrasing in (4e) shows the pattern when the main verb is focused. The phrasing is identical to that of the utterance produced in neutral focus in Fig.5.3a. However, the focused word is realized with a wider pitch range than the analogous peak in the contour with neutral focus. The focused word also has stronger amplitude than the neutrally produced word. Even though the focused Accentual Phrase here is very short, the focus doesn't affect the Accentual Phrasing of the following material, which belongs to a different Intonational Phrase. Thus, the rule is clear: focused word initiates a new Accentual Phrase which covers all of the following unfocused material up to the next likely Intonational Phrase boundary.

This effect of focus on Accentual Phrasing is analogous to the effect of focus on accent placement in English. In English, there is no level of prosodic constituency analogous to the Accentual Phrase. Instead, focus affects the position of the nuclear accent, the last pitch accent within the intermediate phrase (Beckman and Pierrehumbert 1986). The pitch tracks in Figure 5.4 show this effect of focus. In Fig. 5.4a, the nuclear accent is on the word *milk* and, so can be interpreted as focused. In Fig.5.4b, *Marianna* is focused and receives the last pitch accent in the phrase, so there is no pitch accent on *milk*. Both (a) and (b) have one intermediate phrase with one focused word in it. In (c), both words are focused and each focused word bears the nuclear pitch accent of its own phrase. Thus, focus changes the tonal pattern of an utterance by deaccenting all the following words within an intermediate phrase just as focus in Korean changes the tonal pattern by dephrasing all following words in the Intonational Phrase. Since the focused word is the last pitch accent within the intermediate phrase in English, the intermediate phrase is head final in a sense similar to the Bengali case.

Another question related to focus is what is the minimal unit which can be focused: a word or something smaller than a word? Usually, when we think of narrow focus, we think of special attention to a lexical item such as noun, verb, adverb or adjective. This feeling is in keeping with the usual minimal Accentual Phrase when there is no special narrow focus: usually a clitic or a postposition does not form an Accentual Phrase by itself, but rather attaches to the preceding host to form one Accentual Phrase with it. However, it is apparently possible sometimes to focus narrowly on only the postposition or clitic with the expected resulting accentual phrasing as shown in Fig. 5.5. The figure gives pitch tracks of the sentence /ətʃe moimesə maŋatʃik'atʃito pwassninte/, meaning 'At a meeting yesterday, I even saw a colt.' (ədʒe 'yesterday' + moim-esə 'meeting-LOC' + maŋadʒi-k'adʒido 'a colt-even' + pwan-ninde '(I) saw-decl.'), produced by a Chonnam speaker in two versions: (a) when it is uttered with neutral focus and (b) when the clitic, k'adʒido 'even', is narrowly focused. This figure is from Venditti, Jun, and Beckman (1996).

When produced in neutral focus as in Fig.5.5 (a), the clitic forms one Accentual Phrase together with the preceding host noun, maŋadʒi, but when the clitic, k'adʒido, is narrowly focused as in Fig. 5.5 (b), it initiates a new Accentual Phrase and groups together with the following verb, pwanninde, separate from the preceding head noun. This shows clearly that the accentual phrasing is not isomorphic to the syntactic structure. In Chonnam, we can get such a phrasing even when a case marker is narrowly focused. However, my Seoul consultants had difficulty producing this kind of phrasing, especially when they were asked to focus only the case marker. Since the syntactic structure (and even the relevant morphemes) are identical between the two dialects, this difference in what constitutes felicitous prosodic phrasing for focus shows clearly that the prosodic phrasing is more than just a phonological realization of the syntactic organization of an utterance.

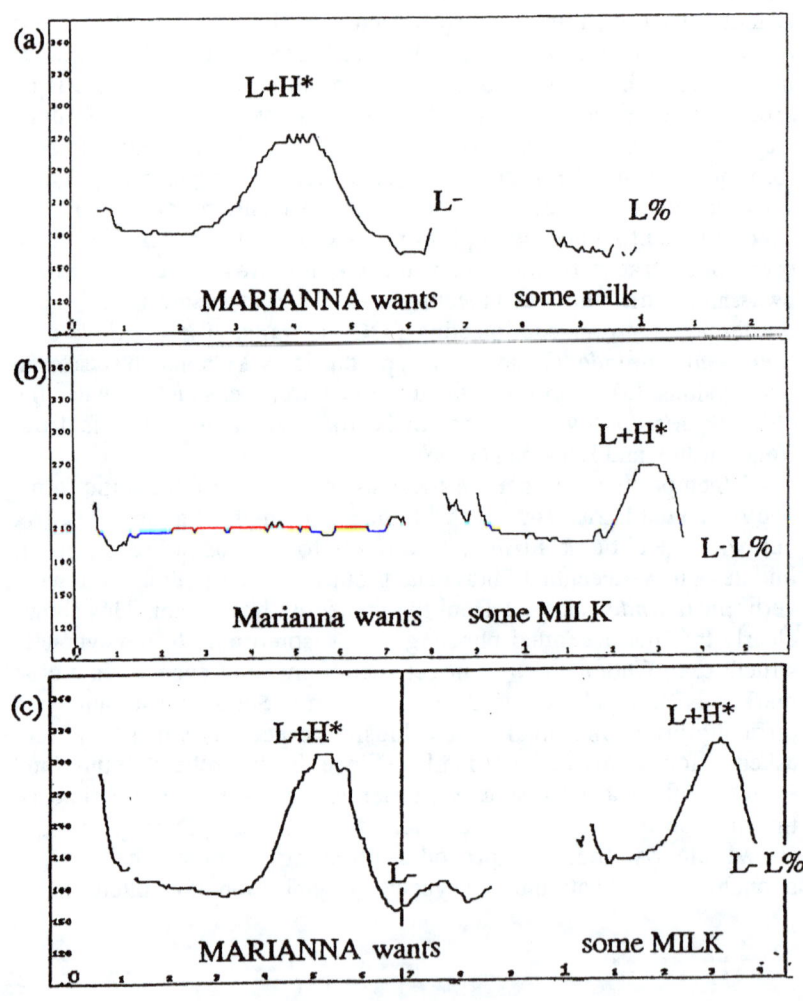

Figure 5.4. Pitch tracks of 'Marianna wants some milk' with focus on (a) *milk*, (b) *Marianna* and (c) both.

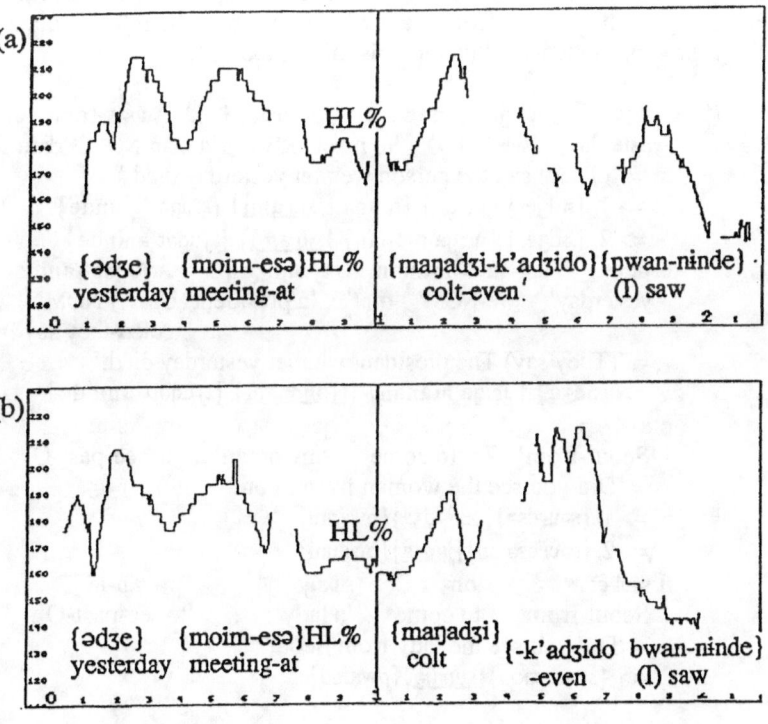

Figure 5.5. Pitch tracks of an utterance produced (a) with neutral focus : {ədʒe} {moimesə}HL% {maɲadʒik'adʒido}{pwan-nɨnde} and (b) when the clitic, -k'adʒido, is narrowly focused: {ədʒe}{moimesə}HL% {maɲadʒi} {-k'adʒido bwan-nɨnde}. In each case, the cursors indicates a medial Intonational Phrase boundary, marked by a HL% boundary tone. (Figure from Venditti, Jun and Beckman forthcoming)

5.4 SEMANTIC WEIGHT FACTOR

In addition to focus, other semantic factors can influence the accentual phrasing in Korean. For example, the semantic complexity of a lexical item seems to be relevant in phrasing, too. That is, when the head noun of a relative clause has a generic meaning such as 'person', 'place', or 'thing', and is thus semantically light (or 'empty' — cf. Bolinger 1972), it tends not to form an Accentual Phrase by itself unless it is focused. On the other hand, if the head noun has many compositional meaning features (e.g., 'a president' or 'a killer' as opposed to any 'person') and is thus semantically richer, it tends to form an Accentual Phrase by itself separate from the preceding verb of the relative clause. The following sentences illustrate this difference.

(5) a. ədʒe   uɾi-ga   mana-n   saɾam-i   tʃugəs-taninde.
    'yesterday' 'we-NOM' 'to meet--REL' 'a man-NOM' 'died'
    = '(They) say the person we met yesterday died.'
    => 1. {ədʒe } {uɾiga} {manan <u>saɾami</u>} {tʃugət'aninde}
    => 2. {ədʒe } {uɾiga manan} {<u>saɾami</u>} {tʃugət'aninde}
  b. ədʒe   uɾi-ga   manan   tʃoŋdʒaŋ-i   tʃugəs-taninde.
    'yesterday' 'we-NOM' 'met'   'a president (Univ.)-NOM'
                                                  'died-they say'
    = '(They say) The president we met yesterday died.'
    => {ədʒe} {uɾiga manan} {<u>tʃoŋdʒaŋi</u>} {tʃugətt'aninde }
  c. səul-esə   on   jətʃa   pw-as-ni
    'Seoul-from'   'to come'   'a woman'   'to see-past-Q'
    = 'Did you see the woman from Seoul?'
    => 1. {səuɾesə}{on <u>jədʒa</u>}{pwanni}
    => 2. {səuɾesə on}{<u>jədʒa</u>}{pwanni}
  d. səul-esə   on   suknjə   pw-an-ni
    'Seoul-from'   'to come'   'a lady'   'to see-past-Q'
    = 'Did you see the lady from Seoul?'
    => {səuɾesəon}{<u>suŋnjə</u>}{pwanni}

The head nouns in (5a) and (5b) have the same phonological weight as well as the same syntactic context and the same relationships hold between the head nouns of (5c) and (5d). Therefore, any difference in accentual phrasing must be related to the difference in semantic weight. In (5a), *saram-i* 'a person-NOM' tends not to form an Accentual Phrase by itself but instead is phrased together with the preceding verb of the relative clause, while in (5b) *tʃoŋdʒaŋ-i* 'a president of a university-

NOM' does tend to form an Accentual Phrase by itself leaving the verb to form an Accentual Phrase together with the preceding subject noun. The same difference holds between (5c) and (5d): The meaning of *jədʒa* 'the woman' is not rich enough for the noun to form its own Accentual Phrase while that of *suŋnjə* 'the lady' is. Four out of nineteen speakers (myself and the eighteen other native speakers) produced 'a man' and 'a woman' in a separate accentual phrasing (as in the 2nd phrasings) different from those in the 1st phrasings of (5a) and (5c) while all nineteen speakers produced phrasings in (5b) and (5d). Notice that the preceding verb of the relative clause, as a monosyllabic and non-focused word, belongs to an Accentual Phrase at either side depending on the following head noun's semantic richness or ability to form an Accentual Phrase. The same pattern can be seen in the examples in (2) above.

Examples from English of a similar relationship between semantic emptiness and pitch accent are given in (6) (from Bolinger 1972: 636).

(6) a. Those are crawling things.
    b. Those are crawling insects.
    c. He was arrested because he killed a man
    d. He was arrested because he killed a policeman.

The sentence in (6a) tends to have its nuclear pitch accent on 'crawling' whereas (6b) tends to accent 'insects'. In the same way, (6c) tends to have the nuclear pitch accent on 'killed' but (6d) has it on 'a policeman'. That is, 'insects' is semantically richer than 'things' and 'a policeman' is semantically richer than 'a man'.

Related to this factor of "inherent semantic weight" is the relative informativeness or predictability of the meaning of the word in the context of the sentence. When a verb is closely related to an argument in meaning and so is predictable, the two tend to form one Accentual Phrase, but when the meaning of a verb is not predictable from that of an argument, they tend to form separate Accentual Phrases. An example is shown in (7). All nineteen speakers agreed on the accentual phrasings in (7).

(7) a. na   pap   mək-illejo   'I want to eat rice'
       'I'   'rice' 'to eat-want' => {na}{pam məgillejo}
    b. na   pap   pəri-lejo   'I want to throw out rice'
       'I'   'rice' 'to throw out-want' => {na}{pap}{pərillejo}
    c. na   tol   mək-illeo   'I want to eat stone'
       'I'   'stone' 'to eat-want' => {na}{tol məgillejo}

In (7a) the verb, 'to eat' does not initiate the Accentual Phrase but belong to the preceding Accentual Phrase initiated by the object noun, 'rice' (/pap/ becomes [pam] due to Obstruent Nasalization). On the other hand, in (7b), the verb 'to throw out' initiates a new Accentual Phrase separate from the preceding object noun, 'rice'. This separation is due to the unpredictability of the meaning of the verb relative to the object noun: We often 'eat' rice but rarely 'throw out' rice. Thus, from 'rice', 'to eat' is highly predictable but 'to throw out' is not. In other words, adding the verb, 'to eat', to the object noun ('rice') is less informative than adding the verb 'to throw out' to the noun.

On the other hand, when speakers were asked to produce a sentence where the meaning of the object was not expected from the meaning of the verb 'to eat' such as [ton] 'money' or [tol] 'stone' as in (7c), most speakers produced an Accentual Phrase including both the unexpected object and the verb, which seems to be contrary to the informativeness or predictability criterion. But, the pitch range of this Accentual Phrase indicated that the dephrasing of the verb was not due to its predictability from the object but because the object was emphasized or focused due to its own unexpectedness in the context of the verb. That is, as shown in Figure 5.6, the peak of the focused Accentual Phrase (c){tol məgillejo} was higher than that of (a){pam məgillejo}. Thus, it seems that there is a hierarchy among semantic factors affecting the accentual phrasing; the focus factor seems to be stronger than the informativeness or predictability in terms of phrasing.

This informativeness, on the other hand, can be expanded to the discourse level. When a word is newly introduced to the discourse, 'new' information, it is focused and thus starts its own Accentual Phrase, but when it is 'old' information, it becomes dephrased. The following dialogue shows this point.

(8) A: satʃʰun-ənni   irim-i   mwəni
    'cousin-old sister'   'name-NOM'   'what-Q'
    = 'What is sister-cousin's name?'
    => {satʃʰunənni}{irimi}{mwəni}?
B: satʃʰun-ənni   irimi   suni-dʒi
    'cousin-old sister'   'name-NOM'   'Suni-decl.'
    = 'Sister-cousin's name is Suni'
    => {satʃʰunənni irimi}{sunidʒi}

In A's question in (8), every word is newly introduced and forms its own Accentual Phrase. In B's answer, however, *irim* 'name' is dephrased since it is old information.

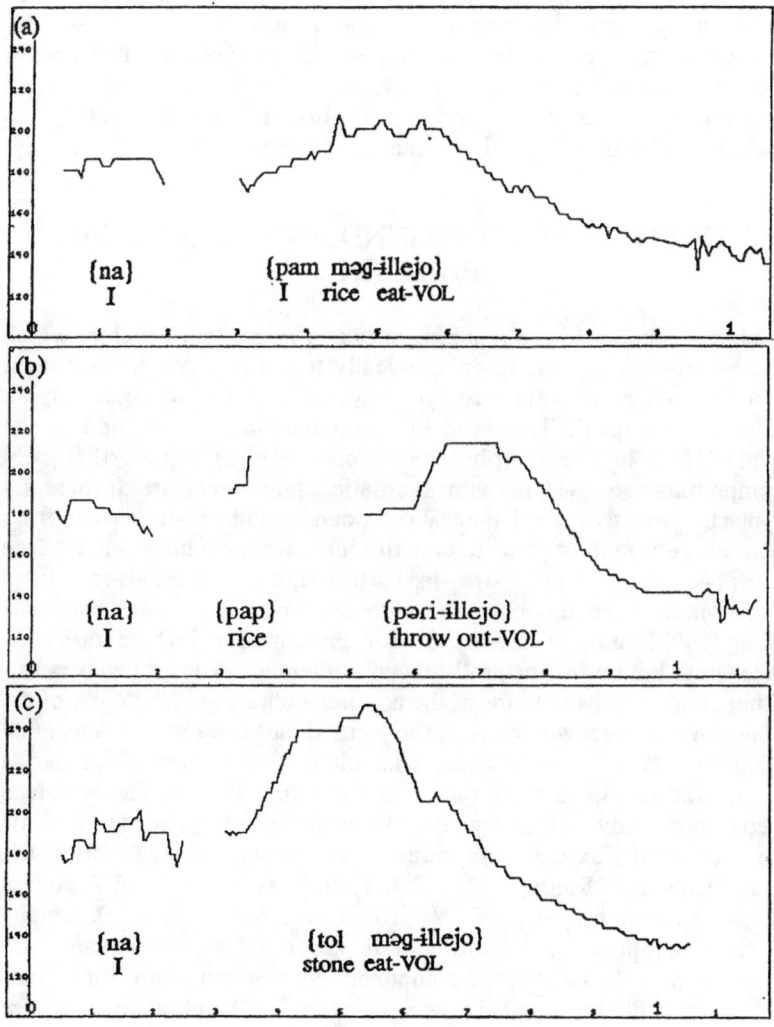

Figure 5.6. Pitch tracks of (7a) {na}{pam məgillejo} (7b) {na}{pap}{pəri-illejo}, and (7c) {na}{tol məgillejo}.

So far, I have shown non-syntactic and non-linguistic factors affecting Accentual Phrase. All these factors have been shown to affect the accentual phrasing to the extent that they determine whether a prosodic word initiates an Accentual Phrase or belongs to the Accentual Phrase including the preceding word. Thus the resulting accentual phrasing is not predictable if we expect to predict the phrasing based only on syntactic information as the Prosodic Phonologists do. However, this is not to deny the importance of syntactic structure. In the next section, I will turn to syntactic influences on Accentual Phrasing by discussing the phrasing of phrasal compounds relative to their internal morphological or syntactic structure.

5.5 PHRASAL COMPOUND AND ACCENTUAL PHRASING

A phrasal compound is a grouping of two or more stems, each of which can be prosodically and morphologically free: that is, each constituent can be used as a syntactic phrase by itself and produceable as an utterance by itself. This kind of compound may be formed in the syntax, not in the morphology. Lieber (1988) argues that root compounds (stem+stem) and synthetic compounds are formed by syntactic processes. Thus, phrasal compounds can be distinguished from lexical compounds whose constituents are not necessarily free morphemes or which are lexically fixed combinations in a subcompound, cocompound or synthetic compound relationship (see Kang (1992) for more detail). A lexical compound as a whole forms one Accentual Phrase in a neutrally focused utterance. Thus it behaves like other lexical words in terms of the accentual phrasing. When part of the constituent is narrowly focused, the focused part can form an Accentual Phrase by itself however. Thus, when the second element is focused, a compound can have more than one Accentual Phrase. The interface between prosody and the lexicon will be discussed in Chapter 6. Some examples of lexical compounds are shown in (9) using the classifications in Kang (1992, 122-131). In these examples, AV=Action Verb (or a verb proper), and SV=Stative Verb (or "adjective"). Among lexical compounds, subcompounds are compounds whose right constituent is the head of the compound; cocompounds are compounds whose constituents are of the same category; synthetic compounds are compounds whose constituents include a noun derived from a verb. As the example shows, all three subtypes of lexical compound behave similarly, forming single Accentual Phrase in isolation or in contexts where the second element is not focused[1].

(9) A. Subcompounds (modifier+head)
  a. N+N=N : $_N[_N[talk]_N[s'aum]]$ -> {taks'aum} 'cock fight'
  b. SV+N=N : $_N[_V[kəm]_N[pəsət]]$ -> {kəmbəsət}
     'black mushroom'
  c. AV+N=N : $_N[_V[s'əl]_N[mul]]$ -> {s'əlmul} 'egg tide'
  d. Adv+N=N : $_N[_{Adv}[pusil]_N[pi]]$ -> {pusilbi} 'drizzle'
  e. AV+AV=AV : $_V[_V[tol]_V[po-]]$ -> {tolbo-}
     'look after (<=turn+look)'

B. Cocompound (head+head)
  a. N+N=N : $_N[_N[pi]_N[paɾam]]$ -> {pibaɾam} 'rain with wind'
  b. AV+AV=AV : $_{AV}[_{AV}[o-]_{AV}[ka-]]$ -> {oga-}
     'come and go'
  c. Adv+Adv=Adv : $_{Adv}[_{Adv}[ili]_{Adv}[tʃəli]]$ -> {iɾidʒəɾi}
     'here and there'

C. Synthetic compound (predicate+argument)
  a. $N[_N[pjəŋ]_N[_V[mag]ke]]]$ -> $_N[_V[_N[pjə_N]_V[mak]]ke]$
     -> {pjə_Nmage}
     'bottle' 'to block'-Nom -> 'Cork of the bottle'
  b. $_N[_N[tʃe]_N[_V[t'əl]i]]]$ -> $_N[_V[_N[tʃe]_V[t'əl]]i]$ -> {tʃet'əɾi}
     'ash' 'to take off'-NOM -> 'ash tray'

The prosodically more interesting kind of compound is the phrasal compound. A phrasal compound consists of more than one lexical word but functions as one syntactic word since only the whole phrase, but not part of it, can be moved or substituted. When the phrasal compound has only two constituent lexical words, the two lexical words generally group together in one Accentual Phrase if neither constituent word is heavy and if the compound is produced with neutral focus. When the phrasal compound has more than two constituent lexical words, the compound generally forms more than one Accentual Phrase, with the position of the phrasal boundary depending partly on the phonological weight of each constituent and partly on the internal structure of the compound. (This phrasing is also sensitive to speech rate as in the case of sentence level phrasing discussed in the section 5.1 above. Thus, even three-word compound may form one Accentual Phrase at fast rates.)

Example (10) shows the effect of weight and internal syntactic structure on the Accentual Phrasing of phrasal compounds at normal rate with neutral focus. A two-word compound can break into two Accentual Phrases if the compound is heavy, as in (10a), with three syllables, versus (10b), with five. Since three-word compounds are almost necessarily heavy, they generally form two Accentual Phrases. Generally, three-word compounds with different internal structure have different accentual phrasings, as shown in (10c) versus (10d), with structures diagrammed in (10f) versus (10g): (10c) has the structure ((AB)C) whereas (10d) has the structure (A(BC)) and these structures correspond to their accentual phrasing. However, the phrasing is not entirely predictable; (10e) has the same ((AB)C) internal structure as (10c) but does not have the same accentual phrasing. Such mismatches between prosodic structure and morphological (or syntactic) structure have also been noted in Nespor and Vogel (1986) and Inkelas (1989) among others.

(10) a. [kwa] [tepʰjo] => {kwa depʰjo}
  'department + representative'
b. [nomutʃa] [tepʰjo] => {nomudʒa}{tepʰjo}
  'Worker + representative'
c. [kukʰwe] [ɨwən] [sənkə]
  'parliament'+'member'+'election'
  => {kukʰwe ɨwən}{səngə} (but *{kukʰwe}{ɨwən səngə})
d. [tʃuŋhakk'jo] [kjotʃaŋ] [sənseŋnim]
  'a middle school'+'principal'+'teacher'
  (=the middle school principal)
  => {tʃuŋhak'jo} {kjodʒaŋ sənseŋnim}
  (but *{tʃuŋhak'jo gjodʒaŋ}{sənseŋnim})
e. [tʃatoŋtʃʰa] [tʃəŋpi] [koŋtʃaŋ]
  'a car'+ 'tuning or fixing'+'factory' (=car fixing factory)
  => {tʃadoŋtʃʰa} {tʃəŋbi goŋdʒaŋ}
  (but *{tʃadoŋtʃʰa tʃəŋbi }{goŋdʒaŋ})

f. the internal structure of 'c' and 'e' vs.
                     the internal structure of 'd'

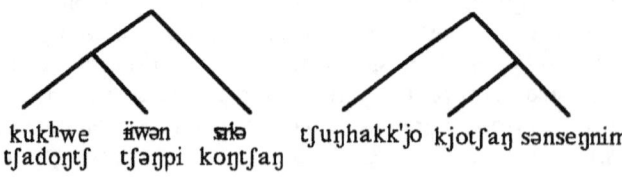

kukhwe   ɨwən   sənkə   tʃuŋhakk'jo kjotʃaŋ sənseŋnim
tʃadoŋtʃ tʃəŋpi   koŋtʃaŋ

Factors Affecting Prosodic Phrasing 179

However, the existence of mismatches does not mean there are no regularities in the Accentual Phrasing of compounds. Interestingly, I found many examples of accentual phrasing that did not conform to the compound's internal syntactic structure when the structure is left-branching, as in (10f), but always, in every example I have examined, the Accentual Phrasing conformed to the internal syntactic structure when it is right-branching, as in (10g). That is, when a three-word compound has the structure in (10f), left-branching, the resulting Accentual Phrase is either {AB}{C} (conforming the internal structure) or {A}{BC} (not conforming the structure). Whereas in right branching structures, the {A}{BC} pattern is overwhelmingly preferred. Examples belonging to each of the two types of accentual phrasing for the left-branching structure are shown in (11A) and (11B). Examples of right branching structures are shown in (11C). In these examples, I have noted the judgements of my nineteen speakers. Examples which have an alternative phrasing with the remark 'very rarely' were cases where two or three of the 19 native speakers phrased the compound in the alternative way. The examples which have alternative phrasings marked with '?' are cases in which all of the subjects did not like the alternative phrasing but a few said they might say or hear it. The examples where the alternative phrasings are marked with a star (*) are cases where all nineteen subjects said they would never expect to say or hear the compound phrased that way.

(11) A. {AB}{C} accentual phrasing for ((AB)C) structure

    a. paksa   nonmun   tʃemok
       'doctor'   'diss.'   'a title' = 'title of Doctoral dissertation'
       => {paks'a nonmun}{tʃemok} or
              very rarely {paks'a}{nonmun dʒemok}
    b. mika   insaŋ   pante
       'rice price' 'raise'   'objection'
       = 'Objection of rice price raise'
       => {mik'a insaŋ}{pande} or (?{mik'a}{insaŋ bande})
    c. pulkkot   noli   kukjəŋ
       'fire'   'play'   'sightseeing' = 'sightseeing of firework'
       => {pulkkon noɾi}{kugjəŋ}   (*{pulkkon}{noɾi gugjəŋ})
    d. seŋsən   kake   tʃuin
       'fish'   'market' 'an owner' = 'Owner of fish market'
       => {seŋsən k'age}{tʃuin}   (*{seŋsən}{k'age dʒuin})

B. {A}{BC} accentual phrasing for ((AB)C) structure

   a. naktʰe   pante   undoŋ
     'abortion' 'objection' 'demo'
    = 'anti-abortion demonstration'
    => {nakt ʰe}{pante undoŋ } (*{nakt ʰe bante}{undoŋ })
   b. ərini   poho   tʃijək
     'child'   'care'   'place' = 'child care place'
    => {ərini}{poho dʒijək} or (?{ərini boho}{dʒijək})
   c. tehakwjən   iphak   sihəm
     'graduate school' 'entrance' 'exam'
    = 'Graduate shool entrance exam'
    => {tehagwjən}{iphak ʃihəm} or
       (?{tehagwjən iphak}{ʃihəm})
   d. kəmpʰjutə   pʰanme   sæp
     'computer' 'sale'   'business'
    = 'computer sale business'
    => {kəmpʰjutʰə}{pʰanme saəp} or
      (?{kəmpʰjutʰə pʰanme}{saəp})
   e. sate   jəŋəkwa   kjosu
     'Coll. of Edu.' 'Dept. of Eng.' 'a professor'
    = 'a professor of Dept. of English, College of Education'
    => {sade}{jəŋək'wa gjosu} or
     (very rarely {sade jəŋək'wa}{kjosu})

C. {A}{BC} accentual phrasing for (A(BC)) structure

   a. MBC   kimjo   tirama
     'Munhwa Broadcasting Co.' 'Friday' 'a drama'
    = 'MBC Friday drama'
     => {embisi}{kimjo dirama} (* {embisi gimjo}{tirama})
   b. səulheŋ   kipheŋ   jəltʃʰa
     'Seoul bound' 'express' 'train'
    = 'Express train for Seoul'
    =>{səurheŋ}{kipheŋ jəltʃʰa} (* {səurheŋ gipheŋ}{jəltʃʰa})
   c. kwaŋtʃu   muhwa   paŋsoŋkuk
     Kwangju city Munhwa Broadcasting Co.
    = Kwangju MBC
    => {kwaŋdʒu}{muhwabaŋsoŋguk}
      (* {kwaŋdʒu muhwa}{paŋsoŋguk})
   d. səulte   heŋtʃəŋ   tehakwən
     Seoul Nat'l Univ. administration graduate school

= Graduate School of Administration of Seoul National Univ.
=>{səulde}{heŋdʒəŋdehagwən}
(*{səulde heŋdʒəŋ}{tehagwən})

An interesting thing to note about the "exceptional" preferred phrasings in B is that the second and third nouns in all these examples are often used as phrasal compounds by themselves. That is, for example, {iphak ʃihəm} in example B(c) is often used alone to mean 'an entrance exam in any level'. So, one could argue that the preferred phrasings in the B types may be possible because the second and the third noun of the phrase are semantically closer to each other and more lexicalized compared to the relation between the first and second noun of the phrase. However, B(e) and A(a) suggest this should not be the reason because the first two nouns in B(e) are also used as a compound and, in A(a), both combinations (the first and the second or the second and the third noun) are equally possible compounds alone, yet the two examples show vastly different preferences for Accentual Phrasing. Alternatively, since most structures in (11) have {A}{BC} phrasing, one could argue that there is a prosodic preference for this phrasing, which is violated only with reluctance to conform to the ((AB)C) structure in the examples in (11A). However, this leaves unexplained why there is a preference for {A}{BC} phrasing overall.

Whatever possible explanations there may be, it is clear that there is a set of examples of phrasing either conforming or not conforming the syntactic structure when the structure is left branching, but there is no example or it is at least hard to find an example of Accentual Phrasing violating the syntactic structure when the structure is right branching. Thus, it seems that within the phrasal compound there is a syntactic constraint on the accentual phrasing for the right-branching structure but not for the left-branching structure. Very interestingly, the same kind of syntactic constraint on the accentual phrasing is found at the sentence level and this will be discussed in the following section.

5.6 THE SYNTACTIC CONSTRAINT ON THE ACCENTUAL PHRASE

Syntax has been assumed to provide the information that is relevant for phrasal phonology either directly or indirectly. Thus, proponents of Prosodic Phonology define the Phonological Phrase based on the syntactic structure. As we have seen before, there were cases where the phrasings prescribed by these theories match the accentual phrasings, suggesting that the Accentual Phrase is also sensitive to the syntactic structure. But there were other cases where the predicted grouping into Phonological Phrases does not match the accentual phrasing, suggesting that there must be nonsyntactic factors affecting the Accentual Phrase.

In general, when the accentual phrasing matches the syntactically predicted phonological phrasing, it is often the case that the Accentual Phrase boundary coincides with the edge of a maximal projection for a higher level syntactic constituent, i.e., boundaries of the first branching maximal projections of a root sentence. Places where an Accentual Phrase boundary is most likely to match the maximal projection boundary are shown in (12).

(12) a. subject NP vs. predicate VP
  b. Topic XP vs. IP (the rest of the sentence)
  c. XP (Extracted or moved) vs. IP
  d. Sentential adverb vs. the rest of the sentence
  e. Main clause vs. subordinate clause
  f. Coordinate clause boundary

Words belonging to different maximal projections at a higher level tend to not to form an Accentual Phrase together. In fact, the boundary between the maximal projections in each of the sequences in (12) is often the boundary of an Intonational Phrase. Thus, a clause boundary or a boundary after an XP that has been fronted, either by topicalization or by movement, can be regarded as a strong boundary in terms of prosodic separation. When a part of a sentence is moved out of its original position, the moved constituent generally forms a separate Intonational (hence Accentual) Phrase by itself and this seems to reflect the change in the syntactic structure.

For the boundaries within the maximal projection, the accentual phrasing is not fixed but varies more than the boundary between the maximal projections. However, the variability of the accentual phrasing does not seem to be completely random relative to the syntactic structure. Selkirk (1986) and Hale and Selkirk (1987) argued that two parameters function as syntactic constraints on the prosodic structure. The first is the designated category parameter. This principle incorporates the hypothesis that for each level P_i of the prosodic hierarchy there is a single designated category DC_i of syntactic structure, (e.g. maximal projection for Phonological Phrase or lexical word for Prosodic Word), with respect to which phonological representation at level P_i is defined. The second is the end parameter,

Factors Affecting Prosodic Phrasing

and embodies the hypothesis that only one end (Right or Left) of the designated category DC_i is relevant in the assignment of a prosodic constituent P_i: the R/L end of each DC_i in syntactic structure coincide with the edges of successive P_i in prosodic structure.

Based on experimental data, however, we know that these syntactic constraints are not descriptively and explanatorily adequate in defining the domain of segmental or suprasegmental phonological rules. The designated category constraint predicts either too many or too few domains, especially for structure at lower levels of the hierarchy: The actual phrasings or the actual domains of the phonological rules are more variable than we can predict based on these syntactic constraints alone. On the other hand, however variable the phrasing is, there must be some rules or constraints that allow children to acquire the phrasing in order to understand and produce well-formed utterances in their native language. The rules or constraints could be syntactic, semantic, or pragmatic, or even nonlinguistic, in nature.

In order to explore possible syntactic constraints on Accentual Phrasing, I examined all possible accentual phrasings of several complex sentences. Two of these sets of possible phrasings are shown in (13) and (14). In these examples, each curly brace refers to an Accentual Phrase boundary and dots indicate that either the existence or absence of a phrase boundary is possible. As the following examples show, the range of choices for the phrasing is fairly large. However, there are places where speakers normally are very reluctant to put an Accentual Phrase boundary, and there are also places speakers are normally reluctant to phrase a sequence of words together.

The sentence in (13), [suniɑ tʃʰekk'wa jənpʰiɾɨl sɑtt'a] 'Suni bought a book and a pencil.', has the structure shown by the tree diagram. This sentence can be phrased in at least four possible ways, each with a somewhat different pragmatic effect or different focusing. The first pattern, (13a), shows that each prosodic word can form its own Accentual Phrase. This pattern is possible when each word is focused or newly introduced in the discourse context. The second pattern, (13b), is the phrasing predicted by the prosodic phonologists. This pattern is what is produced with neutral focus in isolation. The other patterns are still all possible phrasings, except for the last one, (13e), where we are very reluctant to group the subject noun together with the left constituent of the following compound noun while excluding the right hand constituent of the compound. The phrasing in (13c) suggests narrow focus on the first object NP and the verb, while the phrasing in (13d) suggests narrow focus only on the first object NP.

(13) suni-ga   tʃʰek-k'wa   ənpʰil-il   sass-ta.
    'Suni-NOM'   'a book-and' 'a pencil-ACC' 'bought'
    =>'Suni bought a book and a pencil'

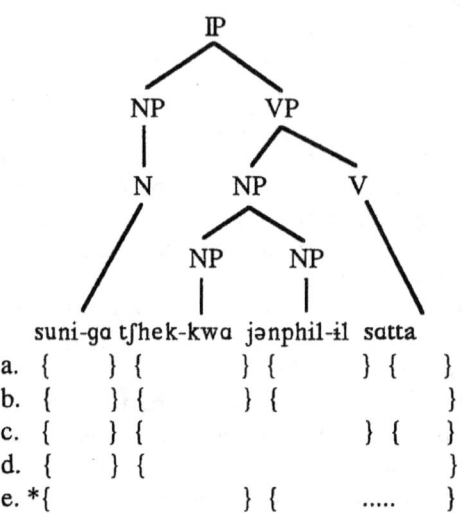

```
suni-ga tʃhek-kwa jənphil-il satta
a. {       } {       } {       } {       }
b. {       } {       } {       }         }
c. {       } {       }         } {       }
d. {       } {       }                   }
e. *{           } {          .....       }
```

Another example with a different syntactic structure is shown in (14), [jəɲinɛ kaŋadʒiga ədʒɛ tʃadoŋtʃʰaɛ tʃʰijətt'a] 'Youngi's puppy was run over by a car yesterday'. This sentence can also be phrased in many ways — in at least seven patterns, a - g. However, the starred five patterns, h - l, sound bad. That is, the subject noun phrase, either as a whole or in part, is very unlikely to group together with the following time adverb, ətʃe, excluding the rest of the sentence as in (14h,i). Also a time adverb is not likely to be grouped with the following PP excluding the final verb as in (14j). Patterns in (14k,l) are not likely to occur because these patterns also have the adverb and PP in the same Accentual Phrase excluding the verb, and this shows that including the preceding word to the problematic sequence of words (the adverb and PP) does not affect the judgement as much as including the following word. That is, for (14 j,k, and l), when the rest of the sentence *following* the time adverb is included, these become fine as in (14e, f and g). Note that among the seven possible phrasing patterns, only the fourth, (14d), where the left edges of the subject NP, AdvP and VP correspond to the left boundary of each phrase, is what is expected by the prosodic phonologists. However, the phrasing pattern which is produced most often by eighteen other native speakers was (14a) and not

(14d). I think this is due to the pragmatically salient elements of the sentence: Puppy's death by being run over is a surprise, thus the word *kaŋadʒi-ga* 'puppy' and *tʃʰijətta* 'was run over' tend to be focused.

(14) jəɲi-nɛ   kaŋadʒi-ga   ədʒɛ   dʒadoŋtʃʰa-ɛ tʃʰijətta.
'Youngi-GEN' 'a puppy-NOM' 'yesterday' 'a car-by' 'was run over'

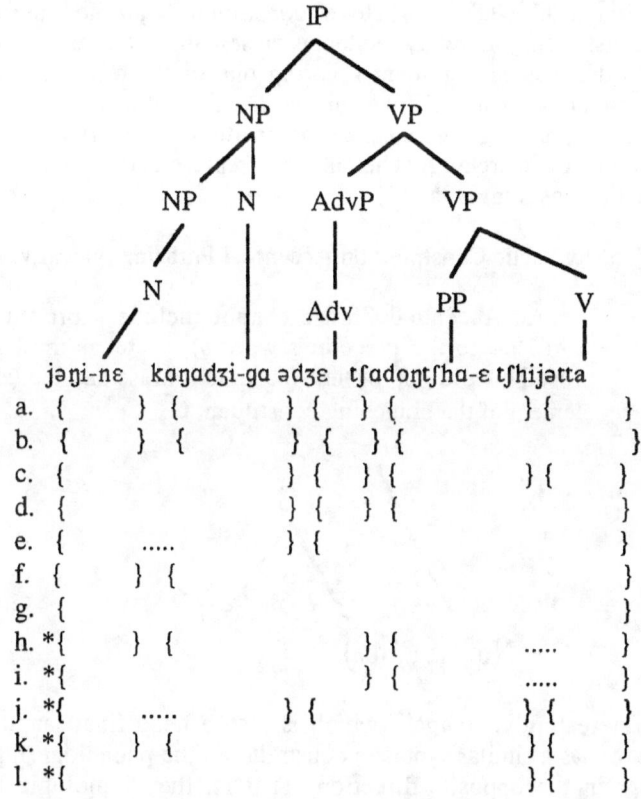

In summary, even though there are several possible ways to phrase an utterance depending on factors described in previous sections, not every combination is possible and these starred phrasings have something in common in terms of the syntactic structure. (14h and i) are bad because the time adverb is the rightmost element of the Accentual Phrase but is the left element of its branching syntactic constituent, the higher VP . Similarly, (14j,k,l) are all bad since the PP is the rightmost element of the Accentual Phrase but is the left element of its branching syntactic constituent, the lower VP. The syntactic position of the other prosodic word does not matter. Based on these data, I propose a negative syntactic constraint on the accentual phrasing as follows: At least in Korean, an Accentual Phrase cannot include a prosodic word 'ω' to the preceding word(s), if 'ω' is the last prosodic word of the Accentual Phrase and the *left* element of the *branching constituent* 'C' ('C' for whatever constituent; I am not sure whether this constituency is really syntactic or semantic, but at this moment, due to the lack of argument favoring one or the other, I will call it syntactic constituent.). As we can see from (14h) and (14i), branching affects the phrasing regardless of the position of the branching node in the syntactic hierarchy. A schematic tree representation for this negative syntactic constraint is in (15).

(15) Syntactic Constraint on Accentual Phrasing (Negative)

An Accentual Phrase cannot include a prosodic word 'ω' to the preceding word(s), if 'ω' is the last prosodic word, $ω_n$ of the Accentual Phrase and the left element of the branching constituent C

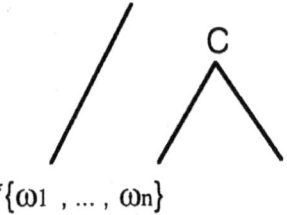

Interestingly, Bengali, which is also a head final language like Korean, has a similar syntactic constraint on the phonological phrasing except in the opposite direction. That is, the Phonological Phrase cannot include a prosodic word if the word is the first word of the Phonological Phrase and syntactically is the rightmost element of the branching constituent. Hayes and Lahiri (1991) presented this constraint in terms of the c-command relation : Two consecutive prosodic words, XY, can be grouped into a single Phonological Phrase (P-phrase) only if X c-commands Y. (X *c-commands* Y iff the minimal branching node dominating X dominates Y.) However, to explain a P-phrase whose syntactic structure has a branching constituent which also contains a branching constituent, e.g. $_{PP}[_{NP}[A\ N]\ P]$, they proposed a recursive application of c-command: ".. in a string of heads, each of which c-commands a maximal projection on its left, the whole string may form a single P-phrase. Thus, in this example, first, a P-phrase is formed corresponding to the branching NP and second P-phrase is formed corresponding to the branching PP, because 'P' c-commands 'NP'.."

Korean data could be accounted for by this c-command relation requiring the opposite direction of c-command. But, since the accentual phrasing is not sensitive to the sentence internal structure in detail, but only to the branchingness or constituency of prosodic words, which may reflect an information unit or semantic unit, I prefer the negative syntactic constraint on the accentual phrasing instead of the recursive application of c-command.

This syntactic constraint lets us predict all the possible accentual phrasings and all the impossible phrasings of an utterance, but it cannot help us to predict the actual phrasing. The actual phrasing is determined by weighing all the factors affecting the utterance discussed earlier. Non-syntactic factors, namely speech rate and the phonological weight of the resulting phrase, do affect the accentual phrasing but not obligatorily. The effect of these factors is realized as a tendency, and not as a fixed result. However, as discussed before, narrow focus on the phrasing has a fixed effect on the phrasing. Any narrowly focused prosodic word initiates an Accentual Phrase and includes all the following words if they are not focused and belong to the same Intonational Phrase. Thus, based on the focus factor and the syntactic constraint, we can define formal rules for Accentual Phrase construction as follows.

(16) The Accentual Phrasing rules
    a. Every prosodic word may be an Accentual Phrase.
    b. A focused word must be the left-most word in an Accentual Phrase.
    c. An Accentual Phrase can include any number of prosodic words as long as:
       i. the last prosodic word is not the left element of a branching constituent
       ii. all the prosodic words are not focused.

It has shown that rate and weight effect the accentual phrasing: fast rate tends to put more prosodic words, while slow rate tends to put fewer prosodic words within an Accentual Phrase. A heavier prosodic word tends to form an Accentual Phrase on its own whereas a lighter prosodic word tends to group together with an adjacent prosodic word. But these effects are overridden by focus and by the syntactic constraint in forming the Accentual Phrase. There seems to be a hierarchy among factors affecting the prosodic phrasing and this is compatible with a general alignment account proposed by McCarthy and Prince (in press) and Pierrehumbert (1993). These non-syntactic or non-linguistic factors influence the accentual phrasing only in so far as they do not violate the Accentual Phrasing Rules (16) and the Syntactic Constraint (15).

Diagrams (17-21) show possible Accentual Phrases for all the possible syntactic structures containing four prosodic words, assuming there is no rate and weight effect. Each square, long or short, refers to an Accentual Phrase. Due to the syntactic constraint, the right branching structure, (17), has fewer possible accentual phrasings, 4 out of 8. The left branching structure (18) can have all the eight phrasings since every terminal element is the right end of the branching constituent structure except for the first terminal element. The mixed structure (19) can have 6 out of 8 phrasings. The nested right branching (20) has 5 out of 8 phrasings and the nested left branching (21) has 6 out of 8 possible phrasings. Stars indicate the awkward phrasings in (19), (20) and (21). Example sentences corresponding to each structure are given below the phrasing. Each of these sentences were confirmed by 9 Chonnam native speakers and 10 Seoul speakers.

For the structure in (17), all the example sentences had either the first or the second type of phrasing when the sentence was uttered with neutral focus. For sentences in (18), the majority of the native speakers produced the neutrally focused phrasing as the second type for (a), the fourth type for (b) and the first type for (c). Sentences in (19) showed more variability in terms of phrasing with neutral focus: (a) was uttered in either the first, the third or the fifth type of phrasing, (b) was uttered in either the second or the third type of phrasing, (c) was uttered in either the third or the fifth type of phrasing and (d) was uttered in either the first or the third type of phrasing. For the structure in (20) and (21), all the speakers produced the example sentences as the third type with neutral focus except (20e); i.e. speakers tend to form the nested constituent as one Accentual Phrase. (20e) was neutrally produced in the second phrasing by most of the speakers.

(17) right branching structure and possible accentual phrasings

Ex. a. toŋseŋ-i kaŋatʃi-lɨl meu tʃoah-e
    'brother-NOM' 'a puppy-ACC' 'very' 'to like-decl.'
    -> '(My) Brother likes a puppy very much'
b. jəŋhi-ga tosəkwan-esə sosəltʃek-ɨl pilj-əs-te
    'Younghi-NOM' 'a library-LOC' 'a novel-ACC' 'borrowed-decl.'
    -> 'Younghi, from the library, borrowed the novel.'
c. jəŋhi-ga sosəltʃek-ɨl tosəkwan-esə pilj-əs-te
    'Younghi-NOM' 'a novel-ACC' 'a library-LOC' 'borrowed-decl.'
    -> 'Younghi borrowed the novel from the library.'
d. jəŋhi-ka jəŋsu-hantʰe tʃaŋnankam-ɨl tʃu-əs-te
    'Younghi-NOM' 'Youngsu-DAT' 'a toy-ACC' 'gave-decl.'
    -> 'Younghi, to Youngsu, gave a toy.'
e. jəŋhi-ka tʃaŋnankam-ɨl jəŋsu-hantʰe tʃu-əs-te
    'Younghi-NOM' 'a toy-ACC' 'Youngsu-NOM' 'gave-decl.'
    -> 'Younghi gave a toy to Youngsu.'
f. jəŋsu-hantʰe jəŋhi-ka tʃaŋnankam-ɨl tʃu-əs-te
    'Youngsu-DAT' 'Younghi-NOM' 'a toy-ACC' 'gave-decl.'
    -> 'To Youngsu, Younghi gave a toy.'

(18) left branching structure and possible accentual phrasings

Ex. a. kaɲatʃi-lɨl tteɾi-n toŋseŋ-i miwə-jo
    'a puppy-ACC' 'to hit-REL' '(my) brother-ACC' 'to hate-decl.'
    -> 'I hate (my) brother who hit the puppy.'
  b. atʃu tʃakɨn kiɾim-ɨl po-ass-ni
    'very' 'small' 'a picture-ACC' 'to see-past-Q'
    -> '(Did you) see a very small picture?'
  c. tʃokɨmah-ko jepɨn kutu-lɨl sa-ssta
    'small-and' 'pretty' 'a shoe-ACC' 'to buy-past'
    -> '(I) bought a small and pretty shoes.'

Factors Affecting Prosodic Phrasing

(19) mixed branching structure and possible accentual phrasings

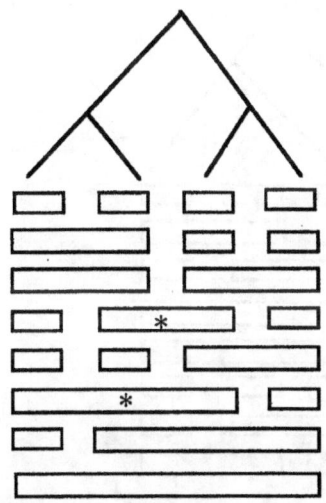

Ex. a. jəŋi-ne toŋseŋ-i mantukuk-il mək-əss-te
   'Younghi-GEN' 'brother-NOM' 'the wonton-ACC' 'ate-decl.'
   -> 'Younghi's brother ate the wonton soup.'
b. us-nin əlkul-i nəmu kwijəpta
   'to smile-REL' 'a face-NOM' 'too' 'pretty'
   -> 'smiling face is too pretty.'
c. ton-il tʃətʃʰuk-hamjən itʃa-ka puth-tʃi
   'money-ACC' 'to save-if' 'an interest-NOM' 'add-ASSERT'
   -> 'If save money, an interest grows'
d. inseŋ-in kil-ko jesul-in tʃ'alpta
   'life-TOP' 'long-and' 'art-TOP' 'short'
   -> 'Life is short and art is long.'

(20) nested right branching structure & possible accentual phrasings

Ex. a. tʃʰamse-nɨn tʃagɨn namu-ɾɨl tʃoaha-nda
   'a sparrow-TOP' 'small' 'a tree-ACC' 'to like-decl.'
   -> 'A sparrow likes a small tree.'
b. jəŋhi-nɨn iɾəbəɾi-n kudu-ɾɨl tʃʰadʒ-at'a
   'Younghi-TOP' 'lost-REL' 'a shoe-ACC' 'to find-past'
   -> 'Younghi found the lost shoes.'
c. əmma-ga p'aɾi-n upʰjən-ɨɾo pone-sj-ət'a
   'Mom-NOM' 'fast' 'mail-INST' 'to send-HON-PAST-DEC'
   -> 'Mom sent (it) via fast mail.'
d. jəŋsu-ɨn səuɾ-einnɨn hak'jo-esə kaɾitʃʰi-nta
   'Youngsu-TOP' 'Seoul-in' 'a school-LOC' 'to teach-DEC.'
   -> 'Youngsu teaches at a school in Seoul.'
e. sezan-e adʒu jumjəŋhan kɨɾim-ija
   'Cezanne-GEN' 'very' 'famous' 'a picture-DEC.'
   -> 'Cezanne's very famous picture.'

(21) nested left branching structure and possible accentual phrasings

Ex. a. irəbəri-n pamsek kabaŋ-il siŋoh-et-t'a
'lsot-REL' 'brown' 'a bag-ACC' 'to report-past-DEC'
-> '(I) reported the brown bag (I) lost.'
b. sigol-einnɨn oɾedwe-n tʃip-tɨl-ɨn siŋgiha-ta
'a village-LOC' 'old-REL' 'a house-PL.-TOP' 'is mysterious'
-> 'The old houses in a village are mysterious.'
c. t'ərədʒi-n tʃagɨn kudu-ɾɨl pəɾjə-t'a
'torn-REL' 'small' 'a shoe-ACC' 'to throw out-PAST DEC'
-> '(I) throw out the torn small shoes.'

Diagram (17) shows all possible accentual phrasings for a purely right-branching syntactic structure. Scrambling makes no difference, as is shown by (17b-c) and (17d-f); the pattern is the same if the original and the scrambled sentence have the same constituent structure. Since the moved or extracted word is the leftmost constituent in the structure, we can predict that any extracted or moved word always forms an Accentual Phrase by itself except when there is only one word following or when the whole sentence forms one Accentual Phrase by focusing the moved constituent. This is the reason why the Intonational Phrase boundary is more likely to come between a topic word and the rest of the sentence: This is the place where there is an Accentual Phrase break most of the time. A similar tendency can be found in (19). The boundary between two clauses, main vs. subordinate or main vs.

main, is often the place where the Intonational Phrase boundary falls. As we can see from the tree, the beginning of the second clause is the left element of the branching constituent, thus the second clause always initiates an Accentual Phrase unless all the words in the second clause belong to the preceding Accentual Phrase. In other words, the boundary between two clauses is the place where the Accentual Phrase boundary occurs most of the time, and so is felt as a strong prosodic boundary which is likely to attract the Intonational Phrase boundary.

As mentioned earlier, Selkirk (1984) notes considerable variability for the intonational phrasing and tries to explain the variability using semantic conditions on intonational phrasing. She says that a single syntactic constituent can have a host of intonational phrasings (IP) and some of them contain IPs that are not isomorphic to any syntactic constituent. An example is '(This is the cat)(that chased the rat)(that ate the cheese). As the semantic approach, she proposed the Sense Unit Condition on intonational phrasing: Any constituent satisfying the head-modifier or argument-head relation can be a well-formed IP. The definition of a sense unit is given as follows (Selkirk 1984:291).

(5.130) Two constituents, C_i, C_j, form a sense unit if (a) or (b) is true of the semantic interpretation of the sentence.
(a) C_i modifies C_j (a head)
(b) C_i is an argument of C_j (a head)

The following example is from Selkirk (1984) showing all possible intonational phrasings for the sentence, 'Jane gave the book to Mary', with two ill-formed phrasings.

(22) a. (Jane gave the book to Mary)
  b. (Jane)(gave)(the book)(to Mary)
  c. (Jane)(gave the book to Mary)
  d. (Jane gave the book)(to Mary)
  e. (Jane gave)(the book)(to Mary)
  f. *(Jane)(gave)(the book to Mary)
  g. *(Jane gave)(the book to Mary)
  h. (Jane)(gave the book)(to Mary)

(22d) is a well-formed intonational phrasing since 'John' and 'the book' are arguments of the verb 'gave' and so can form a single constituent with it, while 'to Mary' forms a sense unit on its own. (22f,g) are not good because 'the book to Mary' do not form a sense unit. For (22h), though the immediate constituent of 2nd IP, V and NP ('gave the book'), do not form a syntactic constituent together, they do form a sense unit. Thus vocatives, certain types of parentheticals, tag questions, and other sorts of nonargument, non modifier expressions should be fated to constitute IPs on their own. The sense unit also suggests that a preposed phrase is not obligatorily an IP on its own if it bears a modifier or argument relation to another constituent with which it could be grouped in an IP. However, the preposed material is often, as she puts - even quite often - set off as a separate IP. Furthermore, nonrestrictive modifiers such as nonrestrictive relative clauses are always separate IPs, not included in the same IP with the constituent they modify. Thus, these are not explained by the Sense Unit Condition. For these, she suspects that it is probably to be explained in terms of the discourse function or "meaning" of preposing and the "meaning" or discourse function of intonational phrasing. Since this intonational phrasing can not be predicted from the syntax alone, Selkirk (1986) even excludes the Intonational Phrase from her algorithm for building the prosodic hierarchy, i.e. end-based prosodic hierarchy.

Nespor and Vogel (1986 p.219) explain the variability of the intonational phrasing by a restructuring rule. However, the restructuring of the Intonational Phrase may even change the structure of φ, by putting an Intonational Phrase boundary in the middle of φ. To preserve the Strict Layer Hypothesis, Nespor and Vogel devise a restructuring rule for φ as well. For example, they posit a restructuring rule for a sentence with a list and with multiple genitives, saying every list or genitive forms its own Intonational Phrase. However, since all the adjectives or the genitives to the left of the head of the NP will be joined into a single φ with the head noun by the basic φ construction rule, they suggest a restructuring rule for φ-phrasing: Restructuring will have to take place to assign φ status to the adjectives in sentences such as that in (23a and b).

(23) a. [$_I$[My friend's]$_I$[neighbor's]$_I$[aunt's]$_I$[mother]$_I$[knows]$_I$[a famous writer]$_I$]$_I$
=> [$_I$[My friend's]$_\phi$[neighbor's]$_\phi$[aunt's]$_\phi$[mother]$_\phi$[knows]$_\phi$ [a famous writer]$_\phi$]$_I$

b. [$_I$The big]$_I$ [$_I$ fat]$_I$ [$_I$ugly]$_I$ [$_I$ nasty beast]$_I$ [$_I$ scared away the children]$_I$
=> [$_I$The big]$_\phi$[fat]$_\phi$[ugly]$_\phi$[nasty beast]$_\phi$[scared away the children]$_\phi$]$_I$

This suggests that the phonological phrasing may be reformed after the intonational phrasing. (This is similar to Cho's Focus Rules, which restructure the Phonological Phrase already formed.) Thus, the Intonational Phrase is the source of major exceptions to the general idea that the prosodic hierarchy is built bottom up by grouping smaller units into larger ones on the basis of their grammatical relations. (For this idea, see Nespor and Vogel's definitions of each prosodic unit formation as well as such statements as "now that the Phonological Phrase has been constructed, we can construct the next unit in the prosodic hierarchy, the Intonational Phrase (I)" (Nespor and Vogel, 1986:187).

The necessity for restructuring φ after the application of I-restructuring suggests also that the syntactic information delivered by the Phonological Phrase may be lost and overridden by the semantic or pragmatic information delivered by the Intonational Phrasing. This contrasts with my prosodic model, in which both the Intonational Phrase and the Phonological Phrase are formed based on the tonal pattern and influenced by the same factors (see Chapter 5). That is, there is no Accentual or Intonational Phrase building rules, rather these phrases are defines after a sentence is uttered influenced by all possible factors affecting the phrasing. Since the intonational contour for the Intonational Phrase includes the tonal patterns of the Accentual Phrase, the boundary of an Intonational Phrase matches the boundary of an Accentual Phrase.

5.7. CONCLUSION

I have shown that the Accentual Phrasing is influenced by nonsyntactic and nonlinguistic factors such as speech rate, phonological weight, focus and semantic weight. Thus, the actual Accentual Phrasing of utterances is a lot more varied than we can predict based on their syntactic structure, directly or indirectly. This variability of phrasing, especially for the Intonational Phrase, has been noticed by other prosodic phonologists who have tried to reconcile this with syntactic determinism by proposing *ad hoc* restructuring rules.

However, as shown in my Korean data, the variability of Accentual Phrasing is not totally free in terms of the syntactic (or semantic) structure. I proposed that there is a syntactic constraint on the Accentual Phrasing that the left element of a branching constituent does not form an Accentual Phrase together with the preceding prosodic word(s) if it is the last prosodic word of the Accentual Phrase. This constraint explains all the variability of accentual phrasing and predicts all possible well-formed and ill-formed accentual phrasings. Finally, I discussed some other approaches to the variability of accentual and intonational phrasing, and showed that they are unsatisfactory.

NOTES

1. When part of the constituent is narrowly focused, the focused part can form an Accentual Phrase by itself however. Thus, when the second element is focused, a compound can have more than one Accentual Phrase. The interface between prosody and the lexicon will be discussed in Chapter 6.

VI

Interface Between the Prosody and the Lexicon

6.1 THE PROSODIC WORD

I have been describing that the Accentual Phrase as a constituent that is higher than the Prosodic Word (ω) level in the prosodic hierarchy; one Accentual Phrase can be the same as the Prosodic Word but can have more than one Prosodic Word. Since, in this model, the prosodic constituents are defined in terms of the intonation pattern, and the Accentual Phrase is the lowest prosodic level which can be defined based on the tonal pattern, the Prosodic Word is somewhat problematic. I will begin by defining the Prosodic Word indirectly based on the assumptions of the Strict Layer Hypothesis. That is, following the Strict Layer Hypothesis, the smallest Accentual Phrase must be the same as the Prosodic Word, or, the Prosodic Word is defined as the minimal sequence of segments which can be produced as one Accentual Phrase, thus maybe a better term would be an (Accentual) Prosodic Word. In general, the minimal sequence of segments produceable as an Accentual Phrase is a stem and its affixes (prefixes, inflectional or derivational suffixes, postpositions and clitics). This definition, however, does not answer the crucial question: is there really a constituent ω in the prosodic hierarchy?

Proponents of Prosodic Phonologists claim that there is the Prosodic Word below the Phonological Phrase and higher than the syllable or the foot. Hayes (1989) claim the domain of this constituent is equal to the grammatical word and Nespor and Vogel (1986) claim it can be equal to or smaller or larger than the grammatical word (= 'Q' in their terminology) . But still both of them agree that the Prosodic Word is larger than the foot and smaller than the Phonological Phrase, conforming to the Strict Layer Hypothesis.

However, when we consider the Accentual Phrasing of a compound word (see Chapter 5) or the minimal Accentual Phrase formed by narrow focus in Korean (see Section 5.5), we can find the domain of the (Accentual) Prosodic Word being smaller than a lexical item and even as small as the syllable within a lexical word, thus smaller than the Phonological Word or Prosodic Word proposed by Korean phonologists: Cho (1987) proposes the Phonological Word is a lexical item and all following postpositions or case markers; Kang (1992) proposes the Prosodic Word is a prefix and a stem with the following suffixes. According to Cho (1987) and Kang (1992), the Prosodic Word they defined serves as a domain of lexical phonological rules in Korean such as Coda Neutralization and /t/-palatalization. This suggests that the Prosodic Word, e.g. a stem plus following suffixes, must form a level of Prosodic Hierarchy larger than a level of syllable. This indicates that there is mismatch between their Prosodic Word and my (Accentual) Prosodic Word: My (Accentual) Prosodic Word can be smaller than their Prosodic Word. But more interestingly, since my (Accentual) Prosodic Word is still an Accentual Phrase having the tonal pattern and being the domain of Lenis Stop Voicing, this means that Accentual Phrase, which behaves like their Phonological Phrase in terms of serving as domain of several postlexical phonological rules, can be smaller than their Phonological Word, which is against the Strict Layer Hypothesis.

A possible solution would be to consider their Phonological Word as a property of lexicon and my (Accentual) Prosodic Word might be a property of postlexical level. Or, we may need a devise of promotion under focus.

In the next section, I report the results of the experiment showing that there is a prosodic level which is the domain of phonetic feature reduction effect and which is smaller than the Accentual Phrase level. This may support that there is the Prosodic Word level which is lower than the Accentual Phrase. Since the corpus in the experiment is a single noun, either one lexical item or lexical compound, we cannot test if there is a phonetic feature reduction domain smaller than a lexical item, e.g. a noun.

6. 2 EXPERIMENT 4: VOT LENITION

6.2.1 Introduction

Phonetic studies show that the pronunciation of segments depends on word and phrase level prosody (e.g., Lehiste, 1960). Many of these effects can be subsumed under the notion "lenition". For example, Pierrehumbert and Talkin (1989) found that the 'gestural magnitude' of

/h/ is less in 'weak' positions such as word medially or in deaccented words; (overall amplitude is smaller, energy is more concentrated in the first harmonic).

Keating et al.(1983) survey phonetic studies to show that many languages have different allophones of voiced or voiceless stops depending on position within a word or a phrase and on degree of stress. A cross linguistic tendency seen in these phonetic studies is that voicing-related phonetic gestures, such as the glottal opening gestures for voicelessness or aspiration, become lenited or weakened depending on position at some prosodic level. Thus, in languages with voiceless stops only, voiceless unaspirated stops tend to be voiced word medially (e.g., Mandarin, Choctaw, Cuna, Korean, Tamil, cited in Keating et al.). In addition, in languages whose initial stop contrasts involve short lag with long lag VOT values, there is a common pattern showing the word initial voiceless aspirated stops are deaspirated word medially (e.g., Lisker & Abramson 1964 for English).

A question that arises in looking at these studies is what is the domain of the lenition effects. Clearly it is not always the word. In Polish, word final stops which can only be voiceless phonologically become voiced before a vowel-initial word and, in Burmese, word-initial voiceless stops becomes voiced in phrases, especially after a "weakened" (toneless and reduced) syllable. That is, the domain of these lenition effects can be larger than a word.

Korean is believed to show a similar lenition phenomenon word medially as shown in Keating et al.'s survey. That is, traditionally it is believed that the slightly aspirated voiceless stops (or lenis stops) become voiced intervocalically within a word. But as we have seen in Chapter 3, the domain of lenition for the slightly aspirated voiceless stop in Korean is the Accentual Phrase, a level larger than the word. The next question is then whether there is any other phonetic feature of voicing whose lenition effect is bounded by a word level.

Since it is cross-linguistically common for word-initial voiceless aspirated stops to become deaspirated word-medially, and since Korean has voiceless aspirated stops word initially and medially, Korean could show a similar lenition phenomenon. To the extent that VOT duration would decrease due to this lenition, VOT duration would be expected to depend on position in a word or a phrase. To see whether there is any regular VOT lenition, and if there is, whether the domain of lenition is the Accentual Phrase or something else, the following experiment was designed.

6.2.2 Predictions of VOT domain

In this experiment, the VOT duration of /p^h/ was measured in different positions in a word and a phrase (word initial and medial and phrase initial and medial) to see whether there is any prosodic effect at all, whether or not it is a lenition (i.e., a decrease of VOT in the Prosodic Word or the Accentual Phrase-medial position), and finally, what is the domain of the possible prosodic effect is. Three outcomes are possible, with different interpretations:

Outcome 1 : If there is no prosodic effect on aspiration, there will be no significant difference in VOT duration depending on the prosodic position.

Outcome 2 : If there is a prosodic effect on aspiration, and if its domain is the Accentual Phrase, then there will be two significant groupings of the VOT duration; one group in Accentual Phrase initial and the other group in medial.

Outcome 3 : If the domain is some unit smaller than the Accentual Phrase only (such as the prosodic word), there would be two groupings of VOT duration; one group in Prosodic Word initial and the other group in medial.

Outcome 4: If both the Prosodic Word and the Accentual Phrase are the domain, there would be three groupings of VOT duration; one group in the Accentual Phrase initial, the other two groups in the Accentual Phrase medial position: Prosodic Word initial and Prosodic Word medial.

6.2.3 Methods

Subjects

Four native Chonnam speakers, three males and one female, participated in this experiment. Speakers 1 and 2 were in their late twenties and had lived in the United States for 3 years. Speaker 3 was in his early thirties and had lived in the United States for 2 months. Speaker 4 was in his early twenties and has never been in the United States.

Materials

1, 2, or 3 syllable words where /p^h/ was either a word (here, same as a stem) initial or a word medial syllable onset were put in the frame sentence.:

(1) igəs-ɨn ____ hago ____ gɨman
    'This-TOP ____ and ____ be.' (= These are _ and _.)

Twenty-eight words were put in either position of the frame sentence which was read in either of the following accentual phrasings.

(2) 1. {igəsɨn} { ____ hago} { ____ gɨman}
    2. {igəsɨn} { ____ hago ____ gɨman}

There were total 64 sentences (32 frame sentences for each phrasing above). The first accentual phrasing above, where each of the two noun phrases forms its own Accentual Phrase, is often found in neutrally focused readings. The second accentual phrasing, where the two noun phrases are merged into one Accentual Phrase, is found when the first conjunct noun phrase is narrowly focused. To get this phrasing, each subject was told to emphasize (or to put a focus on) the first conjunct item by giving an example before recording. Figure 6.1 is an example pitch track illustrating different phrasings of the carrier sentence depending on the focus. The words, noun phrase, used in the this figure are not from the corpus example but have the same structure. Words containing sonorant sounds were chosen to have good pitch tracks. Table 6.1 shows the target words with initial and medial /p^h/.

Procedures

For speakers 1, 2, and 3, the recording was made in a sound-attenuated booth in the phonetics Lab, Linguistics dept. of OSU. For speaker 4, the recording was made in a sound-attenuated booth in the Language Research Center, the Chonnam National University, Kwangju, Korea. Subjects read each sentence five times at a normal rate. The sound was digitized at 10 kHz sampling rate and the sound waveforms were displayed using SPED, a waveform editing program developed by Keith Johnson and Philip Enny. The duration of VOT was measured using SPED from the beginning of the stop burst to the beginning of the complex sinusoidal waveform for the following vowel. Depending on the position of /p^h/ within the word and within the Accentual Phrase, eight types were defined as shown in Table 6.2. These types are grouped into three groups depending on their prosodic condition.

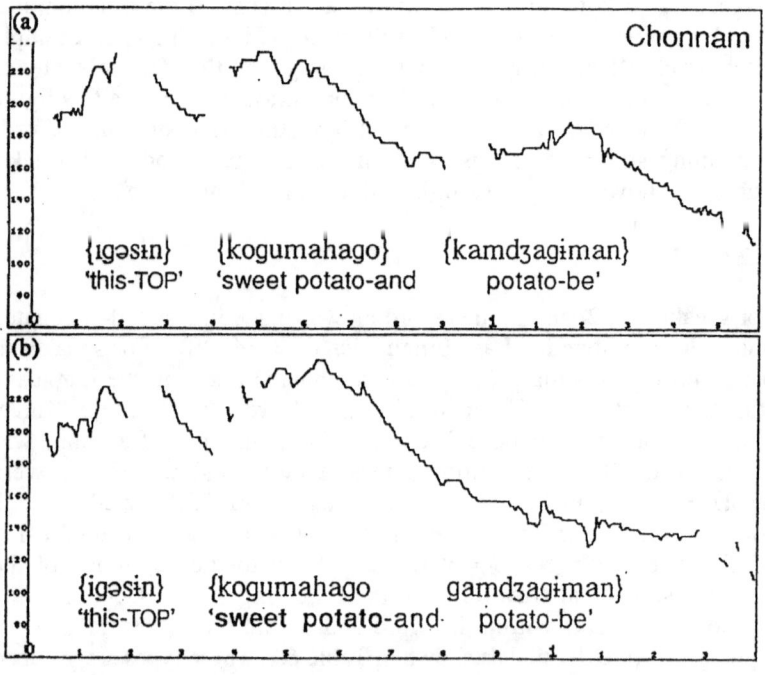

Figure 6.1. Pitch tracks of [igəsɨn kogumahago kamdʒagɨman]. 'These are a sweet potato and a potato', showing different phrasings by (a) neutral focus (b) focusing the first conjunct.

The Prosody and the Lexicon

Table 6.1. Target Words with Initial /pʰ/ (top)
and with Medial /pʰ/ (bottom)

< 11 Words with initial /pʰ/ >			
pʰa	'green onions'	pʰado	'surge'
pʰaɾe	'sea lettuce'	pʰadʒaŋ	'wave length'
pʰaɾi	'a fly'	pʰadzən	'a grilled food with onions'
pʰaɾaŋse	'a blue bird'	pʰatʃʰuls'o	'a police station'
pʰadʒama	'pajamas'	pʰatʃʰulbu	'a maid'
pʰagimtʃʰi	'pickled green onions'		
< 17 Words with medial /pʰ/ >			
jaŋpʰa	'onions'	tanpʰa	'a short wave'
inpʰa	'silvery waves'	tʃaŋpʰa	'a long wave'
jəpʰa	'aftershock'	kjəkpʰa	'destruction'
sopʰa	'ripples'	jaŋpʰak'aŋ	'onion snack'
tʃupʰasu	'frequency'	hwipʰaɾam	'a whistle'
mapʰaɾam	'the south wind'	kodʒupʰa	'a high frequency'
tʃʰodanpʰa	'ultra-sonic'	tʃaɲɹipʰa	'defender of justice'
pʰumpʰaɾi	'street vender'	insaŋpʰa	'impressionist art'
naŋmanpʰa	'romantic art'		

Table 6.2. Eight Types Depending on Prosodic Position of /pʰ/.

Type 1: { } {pʰ ___} {   } ⎫
Type 2: { } {   } {pʰ ___} ⎬ Word initial and Accentual phrase initial
Type 3: { } {pʰ _____}   ⎭

Type 4: { } { ____ pʰ ___ } —— Word initial and Accentual phrase medial

Type 5: { } {_pʰ_} {   }   ⎫
Type 6: { } {   } {_ pʰ ___} ⎬ Word medial and Accentual phrase medial
Type 7: { } {_pʰ_____}   ⎪
Type 8: { } {_____ pʰ ___} ⎭

6.2.4 Results and Discussion

Although precise relationships among all 8 types are not the same across subjects, every subject shows that the duration of VOT is generally longer phrase initially (group 1-3) than phrase medially (group 4-8). At the same time, VOT is longer word initially, (in group 4), than word medially (groups 5 to 8). Figure 6.2 shows the mean duration (in ms) of each group for each subject.

A one-way ANOVA was run on the VOT durations for the 8 types and showed a significant main effect of types ($p < .01$). A Tukey test was performed between types at alpha = 0.05 level. Each speaker shows somewhat different relationships among types within each group but all speakers show a significant difference between three prosodic groupings: i.e. a significant difference between the word initial and the word medial groups as well as between the Accentual Phrase initial and medial groups. There was no significant difference among types within these three groupings.

Therefore, there were three significant groupings depending on the position within a word or a phrase: 1. word-initial and phrase-initial, 2. word-initial but phrase-medial, 3. word-medial (and of course phrase-medial). This suggests that there is a prosodic word effect in medial weakening. It also suggests that there is a strengthening effect at the Accentual Phrase boundary. This is not due to the focus effect since the VOT duration of type 3, the focused Accentual Phrase initial position, is not always the longest one compared to the other non-focused Accentual Phrase initial VOT duration. Only 2 out of 4, speaker 1 and 3, show the lengthened VOT due to the focus. These results together suggest that the prosodic word and the Accentual Phrase serve as the domain of a phonetic feature reduction and furthermore suggest there is a hierarchy of strength of prosodic position. That is, the prosodic word is the smaller domain of VOT duration reduction than the Accentual Phrase.

Since there is a boundary effect (longer VOT at left edge) of each prosodic level with different strength, the realization of the feature [+spread glottis] would be different depending on the prosodic position. The feature would be stronger at the boundary of the Accentual Phrase than the boundary of the prosodic word. The strength of the prosodic position would be realized by a phonological feature in a phonetic representation. That is, the laryngeal feature of [+spread glottis] in a strong prosodic position would have a longer VOT duration than that in a prosodically weak position. Thus, the strength of each feature can be represented in terms of its connection to the prosodic level as shown in (3) below.

(3) Phonetic realization of [+spread glottis] depending on the prosodic position

$$\alpha\{\omega(\text{ [+spr. glo.] ... [+spr. glo.]... })\ \omega(\text{[+spr. glo.] ... })\ ...\ \}\alpha$$
$$\quad\quad\quad\ |\quad\quad\quad\quad\ |\quad\quad\quad\quad\quad\ |$$
$$\quad\quad\quad\text{VOT}_1\quad\quad\text{VOT}_2\quad\quad\quad\text{VOT}_3$$
$$\Rightarrow \text{VOT}_1 > \text{VOT}_3 > \text{VOT}_2$$

The feature [+spread glottis] in P-word initial boundary would be realized as a longer VOT duration, (VOT_1 and VOT_3) than that within the P-word (VOT_2) and this word-initial [+spread glottis] would be realized as a further longer VOT if it occurs at the Accentual Phrase initial boundary (VOT_1) than at the Accentual Phrase medial position (VOT_3). However, this does not mean that this VOT reduction is a categorical change. This shows that the phonetic interpretation of strength of the phonological feature is gradual bounded by the prosodic level.

Summary

This investigation of phonetic experiment of Korean suggests that there is a hierarchy of strength of prosodic position. The prosodic word is the smallest domain of the phonetic feature reduction phenomena and the Accentual Phrase is the next higher domain of this phenomena. The duration of aspiration was reduced word medially compared to word initially and it was reduced phrase medially compared to phrase initially.

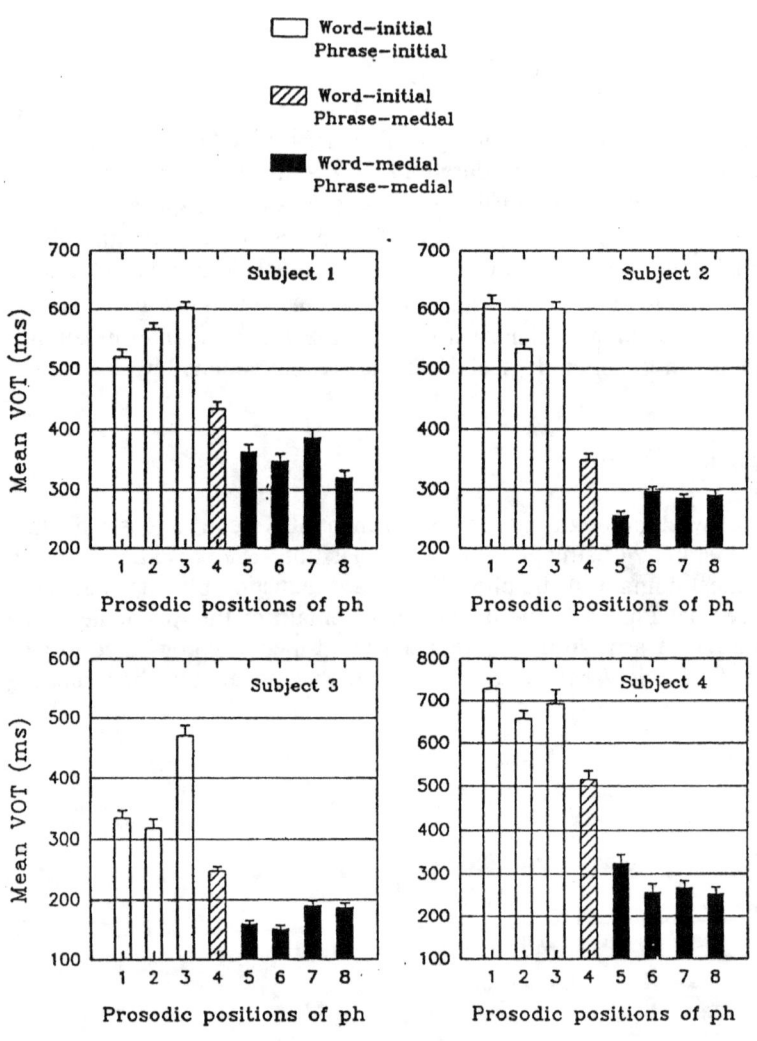

Figure 6.2. Bar graphs showing 3 different groupings of the mean duration of VOT in ms.

6.3 THE PROSODIC WORD AND THE ACCENTUAL PHRASE

So far, I have shown that there is some constituent (call it Prosodic Word) at a level lower than the Accentual Phrase which provides another domain for phonetic feature reduction phenomenon. The next question is how small a string can be produceable as an Accentual Phrase. A stem cannot be produced in more than one Accentual Phrase even with narrow focusing and a stem and a derivational suffix cannot form two Accentual Phrases. But a prefix and a stem, a stem and delimiters, or between constituents within a compound can be produced with more than one Accentual Phrase. Examples are shown in (4). Here, { } means the edges of each Accentual Phrase. In these examples, the first answer of each question shows the case when a part of a grammatical word is produced with more than one Accentual Phrase. Since the stem is the answer to the interrogative question word, it is focused and so forms its own Accentual Phrase. Since the lenis stop is at the beginning of the Accentual Phrase in the first answer of (a) and (d), it is voiceless.

(4) a. [prefix+stem] i.e. nal+kjeran 'a raw egg (not cooked)'
   Q: nal - mwərago? 'new -what?'
   A: {nal}{kjeran} 'a raw EGG' or
       {nal gjeran} 'a raw egg' or
       {kjeran} 'an EGG'
b. [stem + delimiter] i.e. maɲadʒi-k'adʒido 'even a colt'
   Q: maɲadʒi - mwərago? 'colt -what?'
   A: {maɲadʒi}{k'adʒido} 'colt -EVEN' (= even a colt) or
       {maɲadʒi k'adʒido} 'EVEN a cold' or
       ?{k'adʒido} 'EVEN'
c. [stem] i.e. tʃaɲnankam 'a toy'
   Q: tʃaɲ - mwərago? 'tʃaɲ - what?'
   A: *{nankam} - no meaning (but, {tʃaɲnankam} 'a toy')
d. [stem + stem] (=compound) i.e. pi+param 'rain with wind'
   Q: pi - mwərago? 'rain-what ?'
   A: {pi}{param} 'rain with WIND' or
       {pi baram} 'rain with wind' or
       {param} 'WIND'

(4a) shows a case when a prefix can form a separate Accentual Phrase (and hence separate Prosodic Word) from the following stem. (4b) shows when a stem and a delimiter each forms a separate Accentual

Phrase. (4c) shows that a stem cannot be broken into two smaller Accentual Phrases suggesting that it cannot be two Prosodic Words. These examples show that, in these contexts, a prefix or a delimiter or a bare noun stem can form one Accentual Phrase by itself with its own meaning, but a part of a stem cannot. This semantic analyzability and phonological independence of prefixes and delimiters show that they are in a level separate from the stem internal level.

The fact that a stem and a prefix is the smallest chunk of segments which can be produced as one Accentual Phrase suggests that these are minimal Prosodic Words or (Accentual) Prosodic Words. This idea is supported by the claim that the stem and the prefix are the domain of lexical phonological rules such as /t/-palatalization and Coda Neutralization (O. Kang 1992 and Y. Kang 1992). Since the domain of these rules is a unit smaller than the traditional Prosodic Word (i.e., a grammatical word), Kang (1992) extends Selkirk's end based theory to posit the left edge ($_{lex}°$) of a lexical category (N, A, V, Adv...) as a lexical Prosodic Word. Her lexical Prosodic Word formation Rule is repeated in (5) (Kang, 1992:135).

(5) Korean Prosodic Word formation Rule (lexical) (=KPWR)
 $lex°[$ --> $\omega($ (lex is a lexical category)

Before these lexical categories (N,V,A, Adv.) map into ω's in the lexicon, the preceding prefix meets the condition of $_{lex}°[$ by Feature Percolation Convention (Lieber 1980): the feature marked on the head of the word determines the lexical category (i.e., morphological category) of the word. Then, the left edge of N is marked as ω. An example is given in (6).

(6) a. Prefixation   [təs $_N$[os]]
                            'outer' 'cloth'
    b. Percolation $_N$[təs $_N$[os]]
    c. KPWR   ω(təs)ω(os)

Since lexical categories map into ω's in the lexicon, Kang proposes another rule 'Stray Adjunction/Incorporation' by which prosodically dependent elements such as suffixes or clitics are incorporated into the preceding ω in two steps; the derivational suffix is added lexically and the lexically created ω is then also present postlexically where the clitics or functional suffixes such as Case marker or Tense marker are available in the syntax and they are incorporated postlexically to the preceding ω. Thus Kang claims that ω is visible both in and out of the lexicon[1] (see also Booij and Rubach 1987, Inkelas 1989, Zec and Inkelas 1990).

Interestingly, a prefix such as *seŋ* - 'raw', *nitʃ*- 'late', *tʃʰo* - 'early' can, even though very rarely, also form one Accentual Phrase if it is in a context that puts narrow focus on it. Example sentences are shown in (7). For both (a) and (b), B's answer is not the only possible phrasing, but the whole word, a prefix and a stem, can form one Accentual Phrase with higher pitch.

(7) a. A: {kɨ}{talgjal}{məg-ille}? 'Do you want to eat that egg?'
    'that' an egg' 'to eat-Q'
    B: (wondering if the egg is raw or cooked)
    {igə}{seŋ}{talgjal-ija}? 'Is this a RAW egg?'
    'this' 'raw' 'egg-be-Q'
  b. A: {x-ɾil} {tʃigɨm}{po-l-s'u-is'-ilk'a} 'Can I see X now?
    'X-ACC' 'now' 'to see-REL-a way-be able to-Q'
    B: {x-nɨn} {tʃʰo} {jəɾim-e-na-itʃ'i}
    'X-ACC' 'early' 'summer-in-only-exist'
    'X is only in EARLY summer.'

Thus, it seems that the Prosodic Word in my model matches the lexical Prosodic word proposed by O. Kang (1992). However, as mentioned above, the fact that clitics can also form one Prosodic Word in my model does not match Kang's Prosodic Word since the suffixes or clitics (Topic marker, Conjunction marker and delimiter) are within ω by her Prosodic Word rule. In actual conversation, however, emphatic delimiters such as -*tʃʰigonin* or -*putʰə* can easily form one Accentual Phrase as shown in (8). These delimiters have an inherent emphatic meaning and are not narrowly focused so that the following words are not included in the same Accentual phrasing.

(8) a. A: {i} {kadʒuk kabaŋ} {pis'a-dʒi} {an-ni}
    this leather bag expensive not-Q
    'Isn't this bag expensive?'

   B: {kadʒuk kabaŋ}{-tʃʰigonin}{an-bis'adʒi}
    a leather bag - as for not-expensive
    'It is cheap AS a leather bag.'

  b. A: {kɨ}{saŋtʃəm} {maŋhe-t'e}
    that store is bankcrupt-they say
    'They say that store is bankrupt.'

B: {kaps-i}　{neɾi-n-gət}　{-putʰə-ga}　{isaŋha-diɾa}
'price-NOM'　'to cut down-REL-the fact'　'starting from-NOM'　'strange-DEC'
'it was strange starting from the fact that the price was cut down.
=> I wonder why the price was cut down.'

However, since there is no lexical phonological rule applying only within clitics, the possibility of forming one Accentual Phrase may be a too strong condition for the Prosodic Word formation, or we may need to allow for promotion of the clitics into a Prosodic Word, as in the promotion of English clitics under focus. Alternatively, since the smallest Accentual Phrase in a neutrally focused context does not in general separate prefixes or clitics from their stem, we may limit the Prosodic Word as the smallest sequence of segments produceable in one Accentual Phrase in neutral focus. Then, the domain of the Prosodic Word will be the same as a stem plus affixes. Also, we may need an experiment to see if the Prosodic Word smaller than the grammatical word, i.e. a stem, is the domain of phonetic feature reduction phenomena.

6.4 CONCLUSION

Unlike the Accentual Phrase, the Prosodic Word does not have any distinctive tonal specification of its own. Therefore, I have defined the Prosodic Word as the minimal sequence of segments forming one Accentual Phrase in an neutral-focused utterance. However, the domain of minimal Accentual Phrase formed under narrow focus is in conflict with the Strict Layer Hierarchy since the minimal Accentual Phrase is the same size as the Accentual Phrase, thus the Phonological Phrase, but is also possible to be smaller than the Phonological Word. It was suggested that we may need to treat these as a separate property between a lexical and a postlexical level or we may need to devise promotion under focus.

Using a single noun in different prosodic positions within the Accentual Phrase, I showed that the Prosodic Word as well as the Accentual Phrase is the domains of phonetic feature lenition effect and that this Prosodic Word domain is smaller than the Accentual Phrase domain. It was suggested that we may need a further experiment to find out whether the stem is a prosodic unit which can be the domain of phonetic feature lenition effect.

NOTES

1. In addition to the two stage application of Stray Adjunction rule, Kang posits two stage application of the KPWR: lexical application and postlexical application. Thus, a stem and a prefix form a ω by the lexical application of the KPWR and all non-lexical categories such as determiners or modifiers form a ω by the postlexical application of the rule. The categories which can form the lexical prosodic word can be language specific.

VII

Conclusion

In this book, I proposed an account of prosodic structure above the word level in Korean, a structure that is based on the intonational pattern of an utterance. I argued that this tonally defined prosodic structure can better predict and account for the domain of segmental phonological rules and explain the variability of the domain due to non-syntactic factors. In Chapter 2, the intonational structure of two dialects, Seoul and Chonnam, was described and two prosodic constituents were defined based on the tonal pattern: the Intonational Phrase and the Accentual Phrase. In Chapter 3, based on instrumental data, I showed that these tonally defined prosodic constituents also serve as the domain of several postlexical phonological rules in Korean. Furthermore, I showed that the Accentual Phrase can better account for the domain of Lenis Stop Voicing rule in Korean than the Phonological Phrase proposed by Cho (1987), Silva (1989) and Kang (1992) based on the syntactic structure of a sentence, whether the algorithm adopts Selkirk's end based or Nespor and Vogel's relation based theory

In Chapter 4, I showed that the Intonational phrase also serves as the domain of the segmental phonological rules of Obstruent Nasalization, Spirantization and /s/-palatalization. In Chapter 5, I discussed many non-syntactic and non-linguistic factors affecting the Accentual phrasings, factors such as focus and speech rate. I also proposed a syntactic constraint on the phrasing. In Chapter 6, I tentatively defined the Prosodic Word level in the prosodic hierarchy in this model and compared it with the lexical Prosodic Word proposed by O. Kang (1992). An experiment was reported to show that there is a prosodic unit smaller than the Accentual Phrase in terms of the domain of VOT reduction. Further research was suggested to see if the Prosodic Word defined by the potential for Accentual Phrasing is the domain of phonetic feature lenition.

Since the phonological rule domain is cued by the phrasal tonal pattern of an utterance, it would be interesting to see if the intonationally similar languages also shows similar phenomena. For example, is the domain of French liaison the same as the tonally defined rhythm group (cf. Fletcher 1991). Furthermore, the relation between the segmental realization and the intonational contours would contribute to the field of speech synthesis in the future. Finally, to better understand the mechanism of determining the intonation of an utterance, we need further research related to the discourse and pragmatics.

Appendix A (Chapter 2)

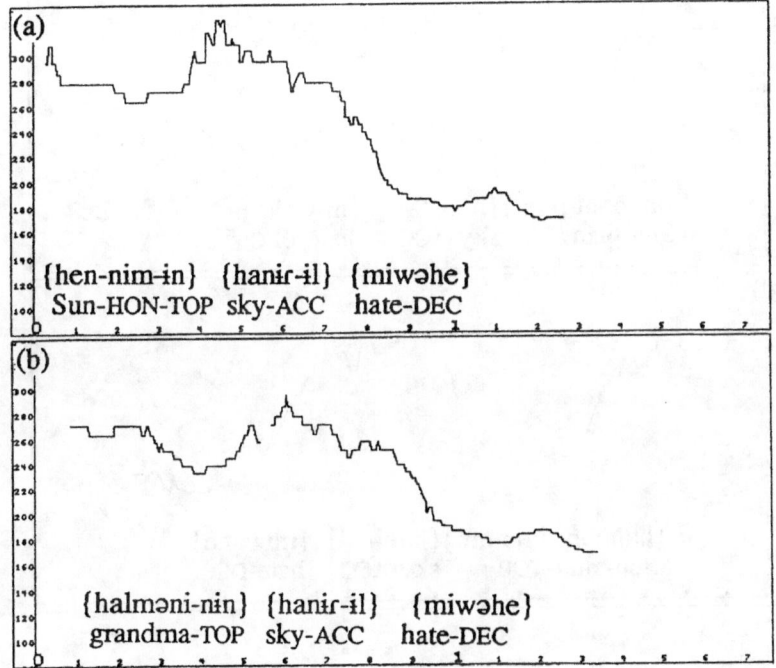

Figure 7.1 Pitch tracks of same sentences as in (4) uttered by the Seoul speaker (S2)
    a. {hennim-in}{hanɨr-il}{miwəhe} => 'Sun (honor.) hates sky'
    b. {halməni-nin}{hanɨr-il}{miwəhe} => 'Grandma hates sky'
    c. {halməni-boda}{hanɨr-il}{miwəhe}
                                     => '(X) hates sky more than grandma'
    d. {halməni+imo-nin}{hanɨr-il}{miwəhe}
                                     => 'Grandma's aunt hates sky'
    e. {halməni+imobu-nin}{hanɨr-il}{miwəhe}
                                     =>'Grandma's uncle hates sky'.

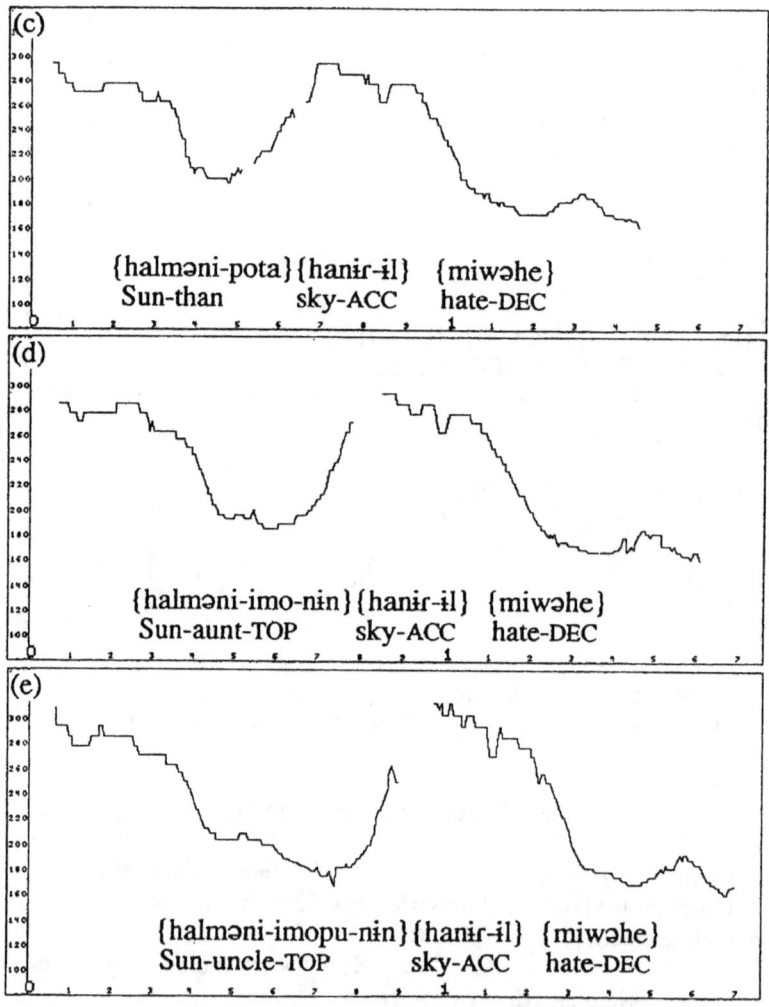

Figure 7.1. (continued)

Appendix B (Chapter 3)

Table 7.1. Frequency of Voicing (Word-initial & Acc. Phr-initial)

Subj	Rate	signal	Clearly voiced	Clearly voiceless	Ambig-uous	total
1	fast	Audio	7	97	5	109
		EGG	8	94	11	113
	normal	Audio	1	124	6	131
		EGG	1	125	11	137
	slow	Audio	0	170	4	174
		EGG	0	173	1	174
2	fast	Audio	4	82	21	107
		EGG	4	96	7	107
	normal	Audio	1	137	2	140
		EGG	0	138	2	140
	slow	Audio	0	169	9	178
		EGG	0	168	10	178
3	fast	Audio	4	131	6	141
		EGG	4	131	6	141
	normal	Audio	2	151	4	157
		EGG	2	149	6	157
	slow	Audio	1	165	0	166
		EGG	1	165	0	166
4	fast	Audio	9	116	4	129
		EGG	11	118	0	129
	normal	Audio	3	136	3	142
		EGG	3	140	1	144
	slow	Audio	2	161	2	165
		EGG	3	160	2	165
5	fast	Audio	9	145	7	161
		EGG	6	147	7	160
	normal	Audio	9	152	5	166
		EGG	8	153	5	166
	slow	Audio	2	177	3	182
		EGG	1	179	2	182

Table 7.2. Frequency of Voicing (Word-initial and Accentual Phrase-medial)

Subj	Rate	signal	Clearly voiced	Clearly voiceless	Ambiguous	total
1	fast	Audio	63	0	3	66
		EGG	62	0	4	66
	normal	Audio	33	0	11	44
		EGG	36	0	8	44
	slow	Audio	18	0	1	19
		EGG	18	0	1	19
2	fast	Audio	77	3	6	86
		EGG	77	1	8	86
	normal	Audio	45	1	3	49
		EGG	45	1	3	49
	slow	Audio	9	1	0	10
		EGG	8	1	1	10
3	fast	Audio	24	1	6	31
		EGG	24	1	6	31
	normal	Audio	11	0	?	13
		EGG	11	0	2	13
	slow	Audio	12	1	0	13
		EGG	12	0	1	13
4	fast	Audio	57	2	7	66
		EGG	54	4	8	66
	normal	Audio	40	3	10	53
		EGG	44	2	5	51
	slow	Audio	26	0	3	29
		EGG	27	0	2	29
5	fast	Audio	32	0	2	34
		EGG	26	0	9	35
	normal	Audio	21	0	2	23
		EGG	20	0	3	23
	slow	Audio	10	0	1	11
		EGG	9	0	2	11

Bibliography

Ahn, Sang-Cheol (1985) *The Interplay of Phonology and Morphology in Korean*, Ph.D. diss., Univ. of Illinois at Urbana-Champaign, Hanshin Publishing Co. Seoul.

Beckman, Mary and Jan Edwards (1990) "Lengthenings and shortenings and the nature of prosodic constituency," in Kingston, John and Mary Beckman (eds.) *Papers in Laboratory Phonology I: Between the Grammar and Physics of Speech.*, 152-178. Cambridge University Press. Cambridge, England.

Beckman, Mary and Jan Edwards (1991) "The articulatory kinematics of final lengthening," *Journal of the Acoustical Society of America* 89 (1):369-382.

Beckman, Mary E. and Janet Pierrehumbert (1986) "Intonational structure in Japanese and English," *Phonology Yearbook* 3:255-309.

Beckman, Mary E., Kenneth DeJong, Sun-Ah Jun and Sookhyang Lee (1992) "The Interaction of Coarticulation and Prosody in Sound Change," *Language and Speech* 35 (1,2):45-58.

Bickmore, Lee (1990) "Branching Nodes and Prosodic Categories," in S. Inkelas and D. Zec (eds.)*The Phonology-Syntax Connection*, 1-18. Chicago: University of Chicago Press.

Bing, J. (1979) *Aspects of English Prosody*. Ph.D. dissertation, University of Massachusetts at Amherst.

Bolinger, Dwight (1951) "Intonation: Levels versus configuration," *Word* 7(1):199-210.

Bolinger, Dwight (1958) "A theory of pitch accent in English," *Word* 14:109-149.

Bolinger, Dwight (1961) "Contrastive accent and constrastive stress," *Language* 37: 83-96.

Bolinger, Dwight (1972) "Accent is Predictable (If You're a Mind Reader)," *Language* 48:633-644.

Bolinger, Dwight (1982) "Intonation and its parts," *Language* 58:505-533.

Browman, Catherine P. and Louis Goldstein (1986) "Towards an articulatory phonology," *Phonology Yearbook* 3:219-252.

Browman, Catherine P. and Louis Goldstein (1990) "Tiers in articulatory phonology, with some implications for casual speech," in Kingston, John and Mary Beckman (eds.) *Papers in Laboratory Phonology I: Between the Grammar and Physics of Speech.*, 152-178. Cambridge University Press. Cambridge, England.

Brown, Gillian (1983) "Prosodic Structure and the Given/New Distinction," in A. Cutler and D.R. Ladd, (eds.), *Prosody: Models and Measurements.* 67-77. Springer-Verlag, Berlin.

Chen, Matthew (1987) The syntax of Xiamen tone sandhi," *Phonology Yearbook* 4:109-149.

Chen, Matthew (1990) "What must Phonology Know about Synax," in S. Inkelas and D. Zec (eds.)*The Phonology-Syntax Connection*, 19-46. Chicago: University of Chicago Press.

Cho, S.B. (1967) *A Phonological Study of Korean with a Historical Analysis.* Uppsala: Universitetet.

Cho, Young-mee Yu (1987a) "Phrasal Phonology of Korean," in S. Kuno et al. (eds.) *Harvard Studies in Korean Linguistics* II, Cambridge, MA: Harvard Univ. Press.

Cho, Young-mee Yu (1987b) "The Domain of Korean Sandhi Rules," Paper presented at the 62nd LSA meeting.

Cho, Young-mee Yu (1990) "Syntax and Phrasing in Korean," in S. Inkelas and D. Zec (eds.)*The Phonology-Syntax Connection*, 47-62. Chicago: University of Chicago Press.

Clark, Robert, Arthur Coladarci and John Caffrey (1965) *Statistical Reasoning and Procedures*, Charles E. Merrill Books, Inc., Columbus, OH.

Cohn, Abigail (1989) "Stress in Indonesian and Bracketing paradoxes", *Natural Language and Linguistic Theory* 7:167-216.

Cohn, Abigail (1990) *Phonetic and Phonological Rules of Nasalization*, Ph.D. diss. UCLA Working Papers in Phonetics, 76.

Cooper, W. and J. Sorensen (1977) "Fundamental frequency contours at syntactic boundaries," *Journal of the Acoustical Society of America* 62:683-692.

Cowper, Elizabeth A. and Keren D. Rice (1986) "Are phonosyntactic rules necessary?," *Phonology Yearbook* 4:185-194.

Dart, Sarah N. (1986) "An aerodynamic Study of Korean Stop Consonants: Measurements and Modeling," *Journal of the Acoustical Society of America* 81 (1):138-147.

deJong, Kenneth (1989) "Initial Tones and Prominence in Seoul Korean", paper presented at the 117th meeting of the Acoustical Society of America. Syracuse, N.Y. Appeared in *Working Papers in Linguistics*, 43:1-14. Ohio State University (1994).

Fery, Caroline (1992) *Focus, Topic and Intonation in German*. A draft version.

Fletcher, Janet (1991) "Rhythm and final lengthening in French," *Journal of Phonetics* 19:193-212.

Fougeron, Cécile (1996) "Variation de débit nasal en fonction de la position prosodique de [n] et [ã] en Français", in *the Proceedings of XXIth Journée d'Etudes sur la Parole*.

Fougeron, Cécile and Patricia Keating (1995) "Demarcating prosodic groups with articulation", a paper presented at the 129th meeting of the Acoustical Society of America. Washington, DC.

Fougeron, Cécile and Patricia Keating (1996) "The Influence of Prosodic Position on Velic and Lingual Articulation in French:

Evidence from EPG and Airflow data", in *the Proceedings of Autrans Conference on Speech Production and Modeling.*

Gee, T.P. and F. Grosjean (1983) "Performance structures: A Psycholinguistic and Linguistic Appraisal," *Cognitive Psychology* 15:411-58.

Geers, A. (1978) "Intonation Contour and Syntactic Structure as predictors of apparent segmentation," *Journal of Experimental Psychology: Human Perception and Performance* 4 (2):273-283.

Goldsmith, John (1976) *Autosegmental Phonology*. Ph.D. diss. Massachusetts Institute of Technology. Available from the Indiana University Linguistics Club, Bloomington.

Goldsmith, John (1992) *Autosegmental and Metrical Phonology*, Blackwell, Oxford.

Gordon, Matthew (1996) "Nasal duration and amplitude as a function of stress and prosodic phrasing in Estonian" a paper presented at the 131st meeting of the Acoustical Society of America, Indianapolis, Indiana.

Hale, K. and E. Selkirk (1987) Government and tonal phrasing in Papago," *Phonology Yearbook* 4:151-183.

Han, M.S. and R.S. Weitzman (1970) "Acoustic Features of Korean /P,T,K/, /p,t,k/ and /p^h,t^h,k^h/", *Phonetica.* 22:112-128.

Hayes, Bruce (1984) "The Phonology of Rhythm in English," *Linguistic Inquiry* 15:33-74.

Hayes, Bruce (1989) "The Prosodic Hierarchy in Meter", in Kiparsky, Paul and Gilbert Youmans (eds.) *Perspectives on Meter*, 203-260, New York: Academic Press.

Hayes, Bruce (1990) "Precompiled Phrasal Phonology," in S. Inkelas and D. Zec (eds.)*The Phonology-Syntax Connection*, 85-108 Chicago: University of Chicago Press.

Hayes, Bruce and Aditi Lahiri (1991) "Bengali Intonational Phonology," *Natural Language and Linguistic Theory* 9:47-96.

Hirshberg, Julia (1993) Lecture notes. LSA Summer Institute. The Ohio State Univ.

Hombert, J.M. (1978) "Consonant Types, Vowel Quality, and Tone", in Victoria Fromkin (ed.) *Tone: A Linguistic Survey,* 77-112, Academic Press.

Hsu, Chai-Shune & Sun-Ah Jun (1996) "Is Tone Sandhi Group part of the Prosodic Hierarchy in Taiwanese?", papper presented at the 3rd joint meeting of ASA and ASJ. Honolulu, Hawaii.

Hyman, Larry M. (1987) "Prosodic Domain in Kukuya," *Natural Language and Linguistic Theory,* 5(3):311-333

Hyman, Larry M., Francis Katamba and Livingstone Walusimbi (1987) "Luganda and the strict layer hypothesis," *Phonology Yearbook* 4:87-108.

Inkelas, Sharon (1989) *Prosodic Constituency in Prosodic Phonology,* Ph.D. dissertation, Stanford University.

Inkelas, Sharon and Draga Zec, eds. (1990) *The Phonology-Syntax Connection.* The University of Chicago Press, Chicago & London.

Ito, Junko (1991) "Prosodic Minimality in Japanese," Papers from the Parasession on the Syllable in Phonetics and Phonology, *CLS* 26-II, Chicago.

Ito, Junko and Mester, R.Armin (1992) "Weak Layering and Word Binarity," Linguistics Research Center, Cowell College, UCSC

Jackendoff, R. S. (1977) *X' Syntax: A Study of Phrase Structure.* Cambridge, Mass.: MIT Press.

Jun, Jongho. (1992) "Metrical Weight Consistency in Korean Partial Reduplication", ms. UCLA.

Jun, Sun-Ah (1989) "The Accentual Pattern and Prosody of the Chonnam Dialect of Korean," in S. Kuno et al. (eds.) *Harvard Studies in Korean Linguistics III.*:89-100, Harvard Univ., Cambridge, Mass.

Jun, Sun-Ah (1990a) "The Domains of Laryngeal Feature Lenition Effects in Chonnam Korean," presented at the 119 meeting of the Acoustical Society of America, State College, Pennsylvania. Appeared in *Working Papers in Linguistics*, 43:15-29. (1994) Ohio State University.

Jun, Sun-Ah (1990b) "The Prosodic Structure of Korean - in terms of voicing," in E-J. Baek (ed.) *Proceedings of the Seventh International Conference on Korean Linguistics*, Vol. 7:87-104., Univ. of Toronto Press.

Jun, Sun-Ah (1992) "The Domain of Nasalization and the Prosodic Structure in Korean" in Ho-Min Sohn (ed.) *Korean Linguistics* 7:11-29. Hanshin Publishing Co., Seoul, Korea.

Jun, Sun-Ah (1993) "Asymmetry of prosodic effects on the glottal gesture in Korean" paper presented at *LabPhon* 4, Oxford University, England. Published as "Asymmetrical prosodic effects on the laryngeal gesture in Korean" in B. Connell and A. Arvaniti (eds.) *Phonology and phonetic evidence: Papers in Laboratory Phonology* IV:235-253 (1995), Cambridge Univ. Press.

Jun, Sun-Ah (1994) "The Status of Lenis Stop Voicing Rule in Korean," in Dikran Karaguezian (ed.) *Theoretical Issues in Korean Linguistics*, 101-114, CSLI, Stanford University Press.

Jun, Sun-Ah (1995) "A Phonetic Study of Stress in Korean." a paper presented at the 130th meeting of the Acoustical Society of America, St. Louis, MO.

Jun, Sun-Ah (1996) "Influence of microprosody on macroprosody: a case of phrase initial strengthening," a poster presented at the Laboratory Phonology Conference V, Evanston, IL. July 1996. Appeared in *UCLA Working Papers in Phonetics* 92:97-116.

Jun, Sun-Ah (in preparation) "The Accentual Phrase in the Korean Prosodic Hierarchy", ms. UCLA. Los Angeles.

Jun, Sun-Ah and Mary E. Beckman (1993) "A gestural-overlap analysis of vowel devoicing in Japanese and Korean," Paper presented at the 67th Annual Meeting of the Linguistic Society of America, Los Angeles, California.

Jun, Sun-Ah and Mary E. Beckman (1994) "Distribution of Devoiced High Vowels in Korean," *Proceedings of the International Conference on Spoken Language Processing*, Volume 2:479-482.

Jun, Sun-Ah and Cécile Fougeron (1995) "The Accentual Phrase and the Prosodic Structure in French" in *the Proceedings of XIIIth International Congress of Phonetic Sciences*. Vol. 2:722-725 Stockholm, Sweden.

Jun, Sun-Ah and Mira Oh (1992) "The Domain of Spirantization and /s/-palatalization in Korean," in the *Proceedings of the 1992 Seoul International Conference on Linguistics*, 186-198, The Linguistic Society of Korea, Seoul. Also appeared in Ik-hwan Lee et al. (eds.)*Linguistics in the Morning Calm* 3:315-325, Seoul.

Jun, Sun-Ah and Mira Oh (1996) "A Prosodic Ananlysis of Three Types of Wh-phrases in Korean" *Lanuage and Speech* 39, No. 1

Kaisse, Ellen M. (1985) *Connected Speech: The Interaction of Syntax and Phonology*, New York, NY: Academic Press.

Kaisse, Ellen M. (1990) "Toward a Typology of Postlexical Hierarchy," in S. Inkelas and D. Zec (eds.)*The Phonology-Syntax Connection*, 127-144 Chicago: University of Chicago Press.

Kaisse, Ellen M. and Patricia A. Shaw (1985) "On the theory of Lexical Phonology," *Phonology Yearbook* 2:1-30.

Kaisse, Ellen M. and Arnold M. Zwicky (1987) "Introduction: syntactic influences on phonological rules," *Phonology Yearbook* 4: 3-11.

Kagaya, Yoshioka. (1974) "A Fiberscopic and Acoustic Study of the Korean Stops, Affricates, and Fricatives," *Journal of Phonetics* 2: 161-180.

Kanerva, Jonni (1990) "Focusing on Phonological Phrases in Chichewa," in S. Inkelas and D. Zec (eds.)*The Phonology-Syntax Connection*, 145-161, Chicago: University of Chicago Press.

Kang, Hyeon-Seok (1995) "Acoustic and Intonational Correlates of Informational Status of Referring Expressions in Standard Korean" *Ohio State University Working Papers in Linguistics* 45:98-130

Kang, Ongmi (1990) "A Prosodic Hierarchy Analysis of Aspiration and Consonant Mutation in Korean," in E-J. Baek (ed.) *Proceedings of the Seventh International Conference on Korean Linguistics*, Vol. 7:105-120., Univ. of Toronto Press.

Kang, Ongmi (1992) *Korean Prosodic Phonology*. Ph.D. dissertation. University of Washington.

Kang, Yongsoon (1992) "Prosodic Structure of Korean." in the *Proceedings of the 1992 Seoul International Conference on Linguistics*, 199-208, The Linguistic Society of Korea, printed by Hanguk Munhwasa, Seoul.

Keating, Patricia A. (1985) "Universal Phonetics and the Organization of Grammars," *Phonetic Lingusitics*, 115-132. Academic Press.

Keating, Patricia A. (1990) "Phonetic Representations in a Generative Grammar," *Journal of Phonetics*, 18:321-334.

Keating, Patricia, Wendy Linker, and Mari Huffman (1983) "Patterns in allophone distribution for voiced and voiceless stops", *Journal of Phonetics* 11:277-290.

Kim, Chin-Woo (1970) "A Theory of Aspiration," *Phonetica* 21:107-116.

Kim, Chin-Woo (1972) "Two Phonological Notes: A-Sharp and B-Flat," in M. Brames, (ed.), *Contributions to Generative Phonology*, 155-170, University of Texas Press.

Kim, Gyung-Ran (1992) "(Non)Branchingness in Prosodic Phonology," in the *Proceedings of the 1992 Seoul International Conference on Linguistics*, 741-750, The Linguistic Society of Korea, printed by Hanguk Munhwasa, Seoul, Korea.

Kim, Hyung Yup (1990) *Voicing and Tensification in Korean: A Multi-Face Approach*. Ph.D. diss., Univ. of Illinois at U.-C.

Kim, Kee-Ho (1987) *The Phonological Representation of Distinctive Features: Korean Consonantal Phonology*, Ph.D. dissertation, University of Iowa.

Kim, Soo-Gon (1976) *Palatalization in Korean*. Ph.D. dissertation. The University of Texas at Austin.

Kim-Renaud, Young-Key (1974) *Korean Consonantal Phonology*. Ph.D. dissertation, University of Hawaii.

Kiparsky, Paul (1982) "Lexical Phonology and Morphology," in I.S. Yang (ed.) *Linguistics in the Morning Calm* I:3-92, Linguistic Society of Korea, Seoul: Hanshin Publishing Co.

Kiparsky, Paul (1985) "Some Consequences of Lexical Phonology," *Phonology Yearbook* 2:85-138.

Koo, Hee San (1986) *An Experimental Acoustic Study of the Phonetics of Intonation in Standard Korean*, Ph. D. diss., Univ. of Texas at Austin. Hanshin Publishing Co. Seoul.

Kubozono, Haruo (1989) "Syntactic and rhythmic effects on downstep in Japanese," *Phonology* 6:39-67.

Ladd, D. Robert (1978) "Stylized intonation," *Language* 54: 517-540.

Ladd, D. Robert (1979) "Light and Shadow: A study of the Syntax and Semantics of Sentence Accent in English," in L. Waugh and F. van Coetsem (eds.) *Contributions to Grammatical Analysis: Semantics and Syntax*. Baltimore: University Park Press.

Ladd, D. Robert (1980) *The Structure of Intonational Meaning*, Indiana University Press, Bloomington and London.

Ladd, D. Robert (1983) "Phonological features of Intonational Peaks," *Language* 59:721-759.

Ladd, D. Robert (1986) "Intonational phrasing: the case of recursive prosodic structure," *Phonology Yearbook* 3:311-340.

Ladd, D. Robert (1988) "Declination 'reset' and the hierarchical organization of utterances," *Journal of the Acoustical Society of America*, 84:530-544.

Ladd, D. Robert (1992) "Compound Prosodic Domains," ms. University of Edinburgh.

Lee, Ho-Young (1990) *The Structure of Korean Prosody*. Ph.D. dissertation. University College London

Lee, Hyon-Bok (1964) *A Study of Korean (Seoul) Intonation*. M.A. thesis. University of London.

Lee, Hyon-Bok (1976) "Intonation in Korean," *Language Research* (Seoul National University), 1:131-43.

Lee, Sang Do (1987) *A Study of Tone in Korean Dialects*. Georgetown University, Ph.D. dissertation.

Lee, Sook-hyang (1989) "Intonational Domains of the Seoul Dialect of Korean," a paper presented at 117th meeting of the Acoustical Society of America. Syracuse, N.Y.

Lehiste, Ilse (1973a) "Phonetic disambiguation of syntactic ambiguity," *Glossa* 7:107-121.

Lehiste, Ilse (1973b) "Rhythmic units and syntactic units in production and perception," *Journal of the Acoustical Society of America* 54.

Lehiste, I., J.P Olive and L.A. Streeter (1976) "Role of duration in disambiguating syntactically ambiguous sentences," *Journal of the Acoustical Society of America* 60:1199-1202.

Liberman, Mark (1975) *The Intonational System of English*, MIT dissertation. [Reproduced 1978 by the Indiana University Linguistics Club, Bloomington.]

Liberman, Mark and Janet Pierrehumbert (1984) "Intonational Invariants under changes in pitch range and length", in M. Aronoff and R. Oehrle (eds.) *Language Sound Structure*, 157-233, Cambridge, MA: MIT Press.

Liberman, Mark and Alan S. Prince (1977) "On Stress and Syllabification," *Linguistic Inquiry* 8:249-336.

Lieber, Rochelle (1988) "Phrasal Compounds in English and the morphology-syntax interface," *Papers from the Parasession on Agreement in Grammatical Theory, CLS* 24:202-222.

Martin, Samuel E. (1954) *Korean Morphophonemics*. William Dwight Whitney Linguistic Series. Linguistic Society of America.

Martin, Samuel R. (1975) *Accent and Morphology*. Yale University, Ph.D. diss.

McCarthy, John and Alan S. Prince (1990) "Foot and Word in Prosodic Morphology: The Arabic Broken Plural," *Natural Language and Linguistic Theory* 8:209-283.

McCarthy, John and Alan S. Prince (in press) "Generalized Alignment," in *Yearbook of Morphology*.

McCawley, J. (1968) *The Phonological Component of a Grammar of Japanese*. The Hague: Mouton.

McHugh, Brian (1990) "The Phrasal Cycle in Kivunjo Chaga Tonology," in S. Inkelas and D. Zec (eds.)*The Phonology-Syntax Connection*, 217-242. Chicago: University of Chicago Press.

Mohanan, K.P. (1986) *The Theory of Lexical Phonology*. Dordrecht: D. Reidel.

Nespor, Marina and Irene Vogel (1986) *Prosodic Phonology*. Foris, Dordrecht.

Odden, David (1990a) "Syntax, Lexical Rules and Postlexical Rules in Kimatuumbi," in S. Inkelas and D. Zec (eds.)*The Phonology-Syntax Connection*, 259-278 Chicago: University of Chicago Press.

Odden, David (1990b) "C-command or edges in Makonde," *Phonology* 7:163-170.

Oh, Mira (1992) "Prosodic Analysis of Korean Palatalization", ms. Ewha Woman's University.

Pierrehumbert, Janet (1980) *The Phonetics and Phonology of English Intonation*, MIT dissertation. [Reproduced 1987 by the Indiana University Linguistics Club, Bloomington.]

Pierrehumbert, Janet (1990) "Phonological and Phonetic Representation," *Journal of Phonetics* 18:375-394.

Pierrehumbert, Janet (1993) "Alignment and Prosodic Heads," in *ESCOL* 10:287-298, The Ohio State University.

Pierrehumbert, Janet and Mary Beckman (1988) *Japanese Tone Structure*, MIT Press, Cambridge, MA.

Pierrehumbert, Janet and Julia Hirshberg (1990) "The meaning of intonational contoursin the interpretation of discourse," in P. Cohen, J. Morgan, and M. Pollack, (eds.), *Intentions in Communication*, 271-311, MIT Press, Cambridge, MA.

Pierrehumbert, Janet and David Talkin (1992) "Lenition of /h/ and Glottal Stop," in G. Docherty & D.R. Ladd (eds.) *Papers in Laboratory Phonology II: Gestures, Segment, Prosody*, 90-116, Cambridge University Press. 1992.

Poser William J. (1984) *The Phonetics and Phonology of Tone and Intonation in Japanese*. Cambridge, MA: MIT dissertation

Price, P., M. Ostendorf, S. Shattuck-Hufnagel, and C. Fong (1991) "The Use of Prosody in Syntactic Disambiguation," *Journal of the Acoustical Society of America*, 90(6):2956-2970.

Rice, Keren (1992) "On Defining the Intonational Phrase: Evidence from Slave," *Phonology* 4:37-60.

Scott, D. (1982) "Duration as a cue to the perception of a phrase boundary," *Journal of the Acoustical Society of America*, 71:996-1007.

Selkirk, Elisabeth O. (1978) "On Prosodic Structure and Its Relation to Syntactic Structure," in T. Fretheim, (ed.) (1981) *Nordic Prosody II.*, 111-140, Trondheim: Tapir.

Selkirk, Elisabeth O. (1980) "Prosodic Domains in Phonology: Sanskrit Revisited," in . Aronoff and M.-L. Kean (eds.) *Juncture*, 107-129, Saratoga: Anma Libri.

Selkirk, Elisabeth O. (1984) *Phonology and Syntax: The Relation between Sound and Structure*, MIT Press, Cambridge, MA, and London, England.

Selkirk, Elisabeth O. (1986) "On Derived Domains in Sentence Phonology," *Phonology Yearbook* 3:371-405.

Selkirk, Elisabeth O. (1990) "On the nature of prosodic constituency," in Kingston, John and Mary E. Beckman (eds.) *Papers in Laboratory Phonology I : Between the Grammar and Physics of Speech, 179-200.* Cambridge Univ. Press, Cambridge:England

Selkirk, Elisabeth and K. Tateishi (1988) "Constraints on Minor Phrase Formation in Japanese," *CLS* 24:316-336.

Selkirk, Elisabeth and Tong Shen (1990) "Prosodic Domains in Shanghai Chinese," in S. Inkelas and D. Zec (eds.)*The Phonology-Syntax Connection*, 313-338 Chicago: Univ. of Chicago Press.

Silva, David James (1989) "Determining the Domain for Intervocalic Stop Voicing in Korean", in S. Kuno et al. (eds.) *Harvard Studies in Korean Linguistics III.*:177-188, Harvard Univ. Cambridge, MA.

Silva, David James (1991) "Lenis Stop Voicing in Korean: Assimilation or Weakening?," in S. Kuno et al. (eds.) *Harvard Studies in Korean Linguistics IV.* Cambridge, MA: Harvard Univ.

Silva, David James (1992) *The Phonetics and Phonology of Stop Lenition in Korean*, Ph.D. dissertation. Cornell University

Silverman, Kim (1993) "Assessing the Contribution of Prosody to Speech Synthesis in the Contexts of an Application," Paper to be presented at the ESCA Workshop on Prosody. 27-29 Sept. 1993. Lund, Sweden.

Sproat, Richard (1986) "Malayalam Compounding: A Non-Stratum Ordered Account," in *The Proceedings of WCCFL* 5, 268-288, CSLI, Stanford University.

Steedman, Mark (1991) "Structure and Intonation," *Language* 67, No.2:260-296.

Steriade, Donca (1982) *Greek Prosodies and the Nature of Syllabification*, Ph.D. dissertation, MIT, Cambridge, MA.

Terken, Jacques and Julia Hirshberg (in preparation) "Deaccentuation and Persistence of Grammatical Function and Surface Position," draft, AT&T Bell Laboratories.

The Chonnam Province Hall (1992) (ed.) *Thongkje Yeonpo (An Annual Report of Statistics.*), Kwangju, Korea.

Venditti, Jennifer, Sun-Ah. Jun and Mary Beckman (1996) "Prosodic cues to syntactic and other linguistic structures in Japanese, Korean, and English" in J. Morgan and K. Demuth (eds.) *Signal to Syntax.*, pp287-311. Lawrence Erlbaum Assoc., Inc.

Vogel, Irene and Istvan Kenesei (1990) "Syntax and Semantics in Phonology," in S. Inkelas and D. Zec (eds.)*The Phonology-Syntax Connection*, 339-364 Chicago: University of Chicago Press.

Whitney, W.D. (1889) *Sanskrit Grammar*. 2nd edition. Cambridge, Mass.: Harvard University Press.

Zec, Draga and Sharon Inkelas (1990) "Prosodically Constrained Syntax," in S. Inkelas and D. Zec (eds.)*The Phonology-Syntax Connection*, 365-378 Chicago: University of Chicago Press.

Zec, Draga and Sharon Inkelas (1992) "The Place of Clitics in the Prosodic Hierarchy," in the *Proceedings of WCCFL* 10:505-519, CSLI, Stanford University.

Zwicky, Arnold (1985) "Clitics and Particles," *Language* 61:283-305.

Zwicky, Arnold and Ellen Kaisse (1987) "Syntactic Conditions on Phonological Rules," *Phonology Yearbook* 4:1-263.

Index

Accent Placement
    in English, 168
Accentual Phrase, 4, 29
    Formal Rules for
        Construction, 187
    Formalization of tone
        pattern, 53
    Phrase Final Rising
        Pattern, 34
    The Number of Accentual
        Phrases, 88
    Variability of the Phrasing,
        182
Actual Phrasing, 24
Aspirated Stops, 201
Bengali, 186
Branching
    Constituent, 186
    Left-Branching, 179
    Nested Left Branching,
        188
    Nested Right Branching,
        188
    Right-Branching, 179
C-command Relation, 186
Categoricality, 92, 115, 207
    Obstruent Nasalization,
        104
Chonnam Dialect, 33, 42
    Tonal Pattern of, 43
Citation form, 64
Clitic Group, 9
Coda Neutralization,
    133, 200
Compositional Meaning,
    172
Compound
    Cocompounds, 176
    Internal Structure, 177
    Lexical Compounds, 176
    Phrasal Compound, 176
    Root Compounds, 176
    Subcompounds, 176
    Synthetic Compounds,
        176
Contrastive Docus, 106,
    162
Dephrasing, 164
Derived Geminate Fricative,
    152
Direct Syntax Approach, 6
Electroglottograph (EGG),
    75. *See also*
    Laryngograph
End Based Theory, 9
Feature Percolation
    Convention, 210
Final Rising, 51
Focal Phrase, 162
Focus
    Contrastive, 42
    Effect of , 163
    Focus Factor, 162
    Minimal Unit of, 169
    Neutral Focus,
        168, 169
    Promotion Under
        Focus, 200
Geminate Fricative, 140

Gesture
- Blending of, 93
- Gestural Score, 92
- Invariant Gestures, 92
- Magnitude of, 200
- Overlapping Invariant Underlying, 93
- Reduction of Gestural Magnitude, 93

Glottal Gesture of /s/, 53
Gradation, Graduality, 92, 104, 207
- Phonetic Phenomenon, 93

Head Final, 168
Head Initial, 164
Hierarchy
- Among Semantic Factors, 174
- Strength of Prosodic Position, 206

Indirect Syntax Approach, 6
Information,
- Old and New 174

Information Unit or Semantic Unit, 187
Inherent Emphatic Meaning, 211
Inherent Semantic Weight, 173
Initial Rising, 51
Intermediate Phrase, 28, 168
Interpolation, 30
Interrogative Pronouns, 163
Intersonorant /h/-Deletion, 65
Intervocalic Obstruent Voicing, 67 *See also* Lenis Stop Voicing
Intonational Framework, 28
Intonational Phonology, 3

Intonational Phrase, 4, 28, 101
- Pause, 124
- Boundary Tone, 28, 34, 101
- Lengthening of the Last Vowel, 124
- Non-isomorphic to Syntax, 102
- Variability of the Phrasing, 101, 194

Korean Obstruents, 52
Laryngeal Feature, 43
Laryngograph, 75
Lenition Effects
- Domain Of, 201
- Vowel Length Contrast, 56

Lenis Stop Voicing, 27
- The Frequency of Voicing, 88
- Phrase Initial, 79
- Phrase Medial, 79

Lenition, 200
Lowest Prosodic Level, 199
Major Phrasing, 16
Maximal Projection, 10
Meaning, Informativeness or Predictability, 173
Minor Phrase, 15, 35
Murmured or Breathy [h]., 76
Negative Syntactic Constraint, 186
Isomorphic to Syntax, 155, 194
Nuclear Accent, 168
Obstruent Nasalization, 103
- The Degree and Timing, 112
- Across the Phonological Phrases or The Accentual Phrases, 116

Perception Of Voicing, 92
Reduction, Phonetic Feature, 206
Phonological Independence, 210

Index

Phonological Phrase, 11
  Formation rule, 12
Phonological Weight, 159, 177
Phonological Word, 11
Phrase Tone, English, 28
Pitch Accent, 28
Post Obstruent Tensing, 52, 94
Postlexical Phonological Rule, 68
Prosodic Constituents, 5
Prosodic Hierarchy, 6, 33
  Bottom Up, 196
Prosodic Phonology, 3, 5
Prosodic Structure Wellformedness Constraint, 6
Prosodic Word, 60, 199, 209
Relation-Based Theory, 12
Restructuring Rule, 65, 102, 195
Scrambling, 193
Semantic Analyzability, 210
Semantic Complexity of a Lexical Item, 172
Sense Unit Condition, 102, 194
Seoul Dialect, 33
Shared Phrase, 17
Speech Rate Effect, 87, 157
Spirantization and /s/-Palatalization
  Domain of, 131
Split Phrase, 17
Strict Layer Hypothesis, 6, 58, 195, 199
Syntactic Constraint, 181
Syntax Based Phrasing, 19
Syntax-Phonology Mapping, 10
/t/-Palatalization, 200
Target Position, 93
Tense Fricative, 152
Tokyo (Standard) Japanese, 29
Tone Melody, 55
Tone Underspecification, 30
Undershoot, Phonetic, 31, 40
Universal Association Convention, 55
Utterance, 58
VOT Values, 201
Vowel Devoicing, 92
Vowel Shortening, 98

For Product Safety Concerns and Information please contact our EU representative GPSR@taylorandfrancis.com
Taylor & Francis Verlag GmbH, Kaufingerstraße 24, 80331 München, Germany

www.ingramcontent.com/pod-product-compliance
Lightning Source LLC
Chambersburg PA
CBHW071823300426
44116CB00009B/1411